CIVIL WAR SPOKEN HERE
A DICTIONARY OF MISPRONOUNCED PEOPLE, PLACES AND THINGS OF THE 1860'S

by
ROBERT D. QUIGLEY

Collingswood
C.W. HISTORICALS
1993

ISBN 0-9637745-0-6 softcover

Printed in the United States of America

First Edition

C.W. Historicals
P.O. Box 113
Collingswood, N.J. 08108

Cover: "Good-bye comrade. God be with you!"
The 50th Anniversary of Gettysburg, 1913.
Pennsylvania State Archives
Pennsylvania Historical & Museum Commission
Box 1026, Harrisburg, PA 17108-1026

Illustrations: ***Battles and Leaders of the Civil War.*** eds., Robert U. Johnson and Clarence C. Buel. 4 vols. New York, 1884-1888.
The Soldier in our Civil War. Abridged Edition, New York, 1894.

Dedication:

To my wife, Susan, who gave up a perfectly good, easily pronounced last name when she married me.

FORWARD

Robert David Quigley, known as Bob to his friends, associates, and those who listen to his local radio talk show aired on WTAR (1320 AM, Waterbury, Connecticut), is well informed on a number of subjects, quick-witted, and a joy to know. I met Bob and his attractive wife Susan in the mid-1980s on a field trip to the Shenandoah battlefields that I was leading for the New York Civil War Roundtable. The New Yorkers, a congenial group, annually in mid-May spend three or four days in a bus visiting Civil War battlefields. On this, as well as on subsequent visits to other battlefields, at Gettysburg College's Civil War Institute, and at the South Central Connecticut Civil War Round Table, of which he is vice president, I got to know Bob and to appreciate his knowledge, dedication, and repartee. When I spoke at the South Central Connecticut Civil War Round Table in June 1992, Bob's introduction was entertaining and appreciated.

At that time Bob spoke to me about his interest in the correct pronunciation of the names of persons, places, and things associated with the Civil War. This piqued my curiosity, because as a public speaker long involved with the Civil War, I know how embarrassing it is when you are told by a member of the audience or tour group that you have just committed the cardinal sin of mispronouncing the name of a local hero or heroine or a geographic feature. On a personal note, I have long known the difficulty that most people have in pronouncing my surname correctly.

Other examples spring to mind. Soon after enlisting in the Marine Corps I learned that most out-of-staters, in referring to the capital of my native state, said HEL-ena not HEL-na, and unless they were from Montana, likewise butchered the name of the light cruiser that honored the city's name. This was particularly disturbing because *Helena,* until sunk on July 5, 1943, in the battle of Kula Gulf, had been in the forefront of the Pacific War against Japan. Another vivid World War II memory is that "Slim" Arnold, a Louisianian and a brother member of Lt. M. "Stormy" Sexton's 3rd Platoon, Company C, 3rd Marine Raider Battalion, habitually pronounced Gua-dal-canal GUAD-ANAR-CANAL.

In 1947 my parents moved from Montana to Indiana, taking up residence in Peru. I soon learned that unless you were an outlander, you said PE-rue.

In September 1955, I joined the National Park Service and reported for duty at the Vicksburg National Military Park. At Vicksburg, Superintendent James R. McConaghie's first priority was public service--a lecture and battlefield tour to any groups visiting the park. Most school groups were from Mississippi and Louisiana, and consisted of fifth graders, junior high students, or high school seniors. Children and teenagers tend to be uninhibited. They took pleasure in interrupting the "Yankee" historian to inform him that BO-vina, the village eight miles east of Vicksburg, where Lt. Gen. John C. Pemberton had his headquarters before the battle of Champion Hill, was pronounced BO-VI-na, and that Yokena, the village ten miles south of Vicksburg on the road to Hankinson's Ferry and Port Gibson, was YOCH-na. Louisiana youngsters snickered when I mentioned Bayou MA-con, a water course that Maj. Gen. James McPherson proposed to exploit in reaching the Red River by way of Lake Providence, rather than saying BY-YOU MAY-SON.

At the same time, an opinionated friend steeped in Civil War lore, along with many other subjects, exposed a chink in his armor by continuously referring to the best-known leader of the Army of the Potomac's Irish Brigade as Thomas Francis MEA-GHER . Alas, I knew better. In Montana, one of our 56 counties is named for the general, who in 1867 was pushed overboard from a steamboat and drowned in the Missouri River while serving as Territorial Secretary. There is also an equestrian statue of the general in front of the state capitol. Like all Montana school children, I had been taught that the country's name was pronounced MARR.

Because of our nation's diversity and the fashion in which it was peopled, we, as long as we travel about, will have to learn from the locals and the families how to pronounce the names of places and persons close to them. It took a long time after moving from Mississippi to Virginia and many patient words from friends to say TOT-O-POT-UH-mee rather than TOW-TOW-PO-TO-MOY, and MAT-ta-po-NI not MAT-ta PO-ny.

I only wish that Bob Quigley's *Civil War Spoken Here* had been available when I first became seriously interested in the War, because even the best presentation is compromised when a pronunciation is botched. In January 1988, the guest speaker at the Capitol Hill Civil War Round Table was William Safire, who justifiably prides himself on his writing and public speaking skills. His historical novel titled *Freedom* had been published only a month before. There was a standing room audience as Safire shared with us his thoughts about Lincoln, the Emancipation Proclamation, and associated events. On two occasions during his presentation and the ensuing question and answer period Safire, speaking of the great battle that took place on April 6-7, 1862, call it SHA-lo. I remember this miscue but little else of Bill Safire's talk.

On reading the Quigley draft, I noted that even after more years spent in the study of the Civil War than I care to recall, there were names, places, and ships, as well as French military terms, that I habitually mispronounce. Since then I have been careful to say Maj. Gen. Darius (duh-RIE-us) Couch (KOWCH) and Patrick R. Cleburne (KLAY-burn), Nueces (noo-AY-sis) and Combahee (KUM-bee), USS *Quinsigamond* (kwin-SIG-uh-mund) and USS *Unadilla* (yoo-nuh-DILLA), and *point d'appui* (pwan-da-PWEE) and *vivandiére* (vee-vahn-DYAIR).

But, *Civil War Spoken Here* is much more than a pronunciation dictionary. Each entry is followed by one or more paragraphs providing, as warranted, thumbnail biographies, geographic and historical place data, ship's histories, or a discussion of military terms and their derivation. These paragraphs, written in graceful style, have more reader appeal than found in other late 20th-century Civil War dictionaries. The last paragraph under each entry provides information on the derivation of the name or term and a guide on how its pronunciation evolved. The Quigley publication is more than a reference work, it is entertaining. But for people, like myself and the author who are in the education and communication fields, the spoken word is vital and mispronounced names compromise your credibility with your audience. This became painfully apparent to the several thousand in attendance at the formal opening of the visitor center at Pea Ridge National Military Park on the Memorial Day weekend in 1963. The then-director of the National Park Service in his remarks mispronounced on several occasions the name of one of the Confederate leaders, saying Col. Louis HER-BERT rather than Colonel ay-BAIR.

Edwin C. Bearss
Washington, D.C.

PREFACE

Over the years, I had read countless books and magazine articles about the American Civil War. I reached a point where I considered myself one of the better informed buffs around. At conferences, battlefield tours, and monthly round table meetings I would dazzle them all with feats of instant recall that even amazed me. But deep down, I knew that I was living a lie. Hidden beneath the facade of "expert level" knowledge was a dark little secret. How could I possibly tell my Civil War friends that for me, all too often, the printed word could never become the spoken word? How could I shame myself in front of these good people by confessing that sometimes I avoided talking about things because I was unsure of the words I spoke? It was as though I had become a closet illiterate, a person who calls an 800 number in the middle of the night to secure the anonymous delivery, in a plain brown wrapper, of Hooked On Phonics!! Yet, there they were, those names and words, the ones I kept running across in my Civil War reading, the ones I hadn't the faintest idea how to pronounce, the ones I dared not give voice to.

They say the average American male, no matter how hopelessly lost, will never stop the car to ask for directions. This is true, but there is a corollary to that bit of conventional wisdom: he will also never ask how to pronounce something. It is possible there are women similarly afflicted, though I doubt it. Women always ask things; being omnificent isn't that important to them.

And so, the years passed, and I did my best to avoid saying the unpronounceable names that popped up in my reading with annoying regularity. From time to time, I would hear speakers at meetings, or conferences, use one of the taboo words, and I would make a point of remembering how they said it. Bravely, I would adopt that pronunciation, only to make the horrifying discovery it might be wrong. A month later another speaker, using the same word, would say it completely differently. Who was right? Maybe, neither one was; maybe they were both wrong! It was a terrible dilemma, and at times I convinced myself that my obsessive fear of saying something incorrectly was stupid. I was foolishly agonizing over something trivial, I told myself. After all, who would be picayune enough to worry about some general's name being mispronounced? Then, it happened.

At a Civil War conference in Fredericksburg, Virginia I was talking with Robert K. Krick, Chief Historian of the Fredericksburg and Spotsylvania National Military Park and author of several books, and I mentioned the name of a certain Colonel John Brockenbrough, whose role at the Battle of Gettysburg I was much interested in. I said the late colonel's last name any number times, pronouncing it with the swaggering confidence born of absolute certainty, "BROCK-n-bro," I said. That's when Mr. Krick interrupted, "No, it's pronounced BRO-uhn-bro." I was mortified. How could I dispute the word of Robert K. Krick?

Robert K. Krick, the dual reincarnation of Douglas Southall Freeman and Bell I. Wiley. Robert K. Krick, who though suffering the decided disadvantage of having been born in New Jersey, had, through pluck and hard work, raised himself up in this world to become a Virginian, while I, poor wretch, retained traces of my native Long Island accent, and still had a strong tendency to add the letter 'R' to the end of the word "idea." Of course, Bob Krick was, as always, the perfect gentleman in making the correction. Charitably, he told me that he himself had made the same mistake many times. I knew better. Bob Krick doesn't make mistakes. Bob Krick knows everything...and Ed Bearss knows the rest. I knew then that I either had to beat this thing, or never utter a word with confidence again.

As it turned out, I discovered other people who had the same obsession with mispronounced words that I do. It was nice to find out that the problem I had with the pronunciation of certain words and proper names in Civil War history was one that I shared with many other serious buffs, and even a few professional historians. Not being alone made it a little easier to deal with. However, a solution to the problem was not going to be easy to come up with. The war had taken place nearly a hundred and thirty years ago. All the participants were long dead, and history books don't talk.

One of the big problems with Civil War history is a matter of technology. Unlike more recent historic events of equal or nearly equal importance, like World War II, for example, we have no soundtrack of the American Civil War. Reenactors can get together in large groups and raise enough hell with blank cartridges, the agonized cries of feigned woundings, bugle calls, and cannon explosions to give some idea of what a battle might have sounded like. But, for little details, like how a man pronounced his last name, we must depend on the written record. Tiny dots on the map whose names exploded into the national consciousness for a brief moment in time, because men fought an engagement there, have gone back to being tiny dots on the map. Only the locals living there now know how the name of the place is pronounced. The family names of generals that once blazed in the columns of *The New York Herald*, and were uttered over morning coffee at countless breakfast tables have now faded into the anonymity of some local phone directory. Forgotten news, forgotten words. Words like Antietam, Gettysburg, and Spotslyvania, where the butcher bill was high, and the battlefield is kept alive by the Park Service and the tourists, are still familiar to us. We know the proper pronunciation, the words have never left the public consciousness. But other places and other people have.

I always thought it would be neat if there was some type of pronouncing dictionary that could give the searching pilgrim the answer he sought. If such a dictionary existed it might inspire a reader who was, let's say, the great, great grandson of some nearly forgotten Civil War notable, to share the secret of just how his family pronounces their inscrutable last name. Thus, with each revision of this wonderful book, we would be learning how to decode more and more words that defy even the most advanced knowledge of phonetics.

But, alas, the book never appeared. So, after years of complaining, I decided to do it myself. Putting together a list of proper names of places, people and things that have given me pause over the years, and combining that with suggestions from fellow buffs, historians and other interested parties, I have made a beginning attempt at a Civil War pronouncing dictionary.

The format of the book is relatively simple. After the word in question I have put a **pronouncer**, followed by a brief definition. The **pronouncer** is the type used in foreign phrase dictionaries written for tourists and business travelers who have no foreign language skills. After years of looking up a word's pronunciation in the dictionary, only to be totally confused by a string of hieroglyphics, I decided that the simple format of the traveler's phrase book was best. The definition following the pronouncer serves the dual purpose of informing and entertaining. It also tells, where the information is relevant or interesting and how I went about getting the proper pronunciation. Sometimes, the problems encountered in finding how a name is said turns out to be a pretty good yarn. Also, in the definition, is the occasional remark that was just too good to pass up. We may as well enjoy ourselves in the pursuit of verbal excellence.

As to the issue of pronunciation and local accents, I have made the following determination: more than a century has passed since the Civil War and in that time there has been a homogenization, of sorts, of the various regional dialects in this country. Mass communication, standardized education and the media have had a big effect on the way people talk. To the untrained ear, a person from Richmond, Virginia these days doesn't sound a whole lot different from someone who lives in Hartford, Connecticut. Aside from the fact that Americans move frequently, either because of job transfers, or college attendance, or whatever, one big reason for a certain sameness developing in our speech patterns and pronunciations has to be television and radio.

You may have noticed that no matter where you go in America, radio and television announcers all seem to sound alike. With the exception of broadcast stations in very remote rural area towns, the guy or gal who spins the records, or gives the local news sounds just like the one you listen to back home. With this in mind, I have selected as my standard of pronunciation what I like to call the Neutral American Broadcast Accent. Of course, certain names, especially place names, are best and properly pronounced in the local accent of the region they are located in. My selection of the Neutral Broadcast Accent does not affect or change important regional pronunciation differences where they are relevant. My reason for choosing it is to prevent the **pronouncers** used in the dictionary from being biased in favor of a New York, or Boston accent, for example. New Yorkers and Bostonians sometimes do things with o's and a's that render American English a foreign tongue.

One final thought before embarking on this journey into the realm of amateur lexicography. As I said earlier on, we have no soundtrack of the American Civil War. We will never know, for instance, what Robert E. Lee's voice really sounded like, or how Abraham Lincoln sounded that day in November 1863 when he delivered the Gettysburg Address. When you consider how much a person's voice, and the way they intone their words, affects our judgment of them, it's unfortunate that most of history is forever silent to us. But, then, perhaps it is a good thing. Imagine the agony of traveling back in time, and finding out that Stonewall Jackson, The Mighty Stonewall, in real life sounded like actor Don Knotts playing Barney Fife on the Andy Griffith Show? *Sic transit gloria mundi.*

Bob Quigley,
Waterbury, Connecticut
22 November 1992

ACKNOWLEDGEMENTS

This is the part of the book where you thank everyone who has in some way contributed to the completion of the work. Writing a book, even a small book is a considerable undertaking for the average person. The sense of relief and satisfaction one experiences when the task is completed, and the manuscript is finally on the way to the printers, is immense. One finds oneself slipping out of the role of "the lonely writer toiling away at his computer" and assuming the new role of "the published author whose generous praise for others knows no bounds." I have just undergone this transformation myself, and it feels good. So, with this happy frame of mind firmly in place let me proceed to give some well deserved thanks to a fine group of people.

First of all, there is Blake Magner, my editor. Blake was the first person to read the manuscript one snowy weekend when a bunch of us Civil War buffs were trapped by a blizzard at West Point. His enthusiastic response to it, and his decision to publish it made it one the best weekends I've had in about a decade. Blake walked me through the process of preparing the manuscript, told me what's done, and what's not done. Obviously, without his efforts, you wouldn't be reading this book right now.

Much of the research for this book was done by telephone. This was not to save time or trips to the library. In order to get some idea of the proper pronunciation of a word you have to hear it. I had initially sent out letters to various people inquiring about the pronunciation of different words, only to find that I had to call them anyway to verify, or clarify what they had written back. So, my thanks to Robert K. Krick, Chief Historian at the Fredericksburg-Spotsylvania National Military Park for his help and advice. Thanks also for the telephonic advice from Don Pfanz and Frank O'Reilly, also at Fredericksburg; Ted Alexander, Historian at Antietam National Battlefield; Dennis Frye, Historian at Harpers Ferry; Jim Blankenship at Petersburg and City Point; the folks down at the Gettysburg National Military Park, and Ed Bearss, Chief Historian of the National Park Service, who, incredibly, answers his own phone!! The National Park Service is the only branch of our government that makes paying taxes seem worthwhile.

There were lots of other phone calls to people who don't work for the NPS: my thanks to Orville Fitts of Kansas City, Marion Brown Hagerstand of Oklahoma, Guy Swanson of the Museum of the Confederacy, and author-historian, Dr. Richard McMurry, who was trapped at West Point with us in the blizzard and had to listen to all my worst jokes while he gave me some great pronouncers.

Special thanks to David Ward of Hotchkiss School in Lakeville, Connecticut who suggested to me that I might think about writing a book on the Civil War's most unpronounceable names. It was a very fruitful thought, David. My friend Jerry Russell also needs some thanks: Jerry, who is President of the Conference of Civil War Round Tables and a crusader for battlefield preservation, gave me encouragement, names, and phone numbers, the three ingredients I needed to get this book done. Thanks to Todd Brodeur and in addition, before I forget about a really important person without whose encouragement and support this book would not have been possible...thank you, Susan.

Finally, I want to thank the late Bruce Catton. I realize that this famous author often takes it in the neck from history snobs who point out that he was a journalist, not a historian. Fine. He was also the man who brought the Civil War to a whole generation of Americans. I picked up my first Civil War book when I was thirteen years old, after I read it I was hooked for life. It was a book called *A Stillness at Appomattox* by Bruce Catton. Every once in while I pick it up and reread it. It's like a favorite old song, it gets better with the passing years.

SOME WORDS ON PRONUNCIATION

The "pronouncers" I use in this book are phonetic and based on the "re-spelling" method. I have avoided using any diacritical marks, any letters from the International Phonetic Alphabet, and any symbols that represent sounds. All pronouncers are given in letters of the English alphabet.

Stressed, or emphasized syllables are done in capital letters. In the case of words where two syllables are stressed, but one is given primary stress, I have used two different sizes of capital letters. For example, the word Powhatan is rendered POW-uh-TAN. This indicates that the first syllable gets less stress than the last syllable. In words of only one syllable, where stress is not a factor, lower case letters are used in the pronouncer.

Rather than confuse and discourage you with a lengthier explanation of pronunciation methods used in this book, I think you will fare much better using the book, and becoming familiar with the re-spelling method. Believe me when I tell you that I have adopted this type of pronouncer because it is practically idiot proof. By the way, I'm the idiot it was designed for.

Abatis -(AH-buh-tee)

An obstacle. An arrangement of felled trees with the branches facing toward the enemy from a defensive position. One of the oldest forms of fortification. It is one of those French words that crept into military terminology during the Napoleonic era. West Pointers loved using these French terms, but you get the feeling that the enlisted men probably called the abatis, "a bunch of felled trees." The natural tendency with the word "abatis" is to say, **uh-BAY-tis**, and quite frankly, that pronunciation sounds more like what it is supposed to be describing. To further complicate things, some dictionaries list **uh-BAT-is** and **uh-BAT-ee** as alternate, correct pronunciations. If you look in a British English dictionary it is likely you will find **uh-BAY-tis** listed as a proper pronunciation. Bear in mind, British English and American English have some very definite differences: The British, for example, say the word "filet," as in filet of Sole, **FIL-et**, whereas Americans tend to go with the French pronunciation. This difference is true in any number of cases involving words of French derivation.

The spelling of French military terminology, like the rest of that wonderfully fluid language, seems to be heavily freighted with extra letters that are never pronounced. Asked to comment on this phenomenon, the French will almost always dismiss the English speaking questioner with strident tones of Gallic contempt.

Adelbert -(uh-DEL-burt)

as in Adelbert Ames, Major General U.S.V.

Not too many parents are naming their little boys Adelbert anymore. Today, the very idea of giving a kid a name like Adelbert would probably be considered by some a form of child abuse. In the case of Adelbert Ames, born in Rockland, Maine on Halloween 1835, an unusual first name, at least to 20th century ears, did not seem to have an adverse effect on his future. Aside from a distinguished military career, which included being awarded the Medal of Honor, General Ames was also to outlive all his contemporaries. At the time of his death in 1933, he was the last surviving full rank general officer from either side in the Civil War.[1]

As a boy, Ames became a sailor and was a mate on a clipper ship. He entered West Point in 1856 and graduated fifth in the class of 1861. Since the Civil War had already broken out, he went right into action and began a military career characterized by a rapid rise in the ranks. By 1863 he was a brigadier general in the Army of the Potomac. Ames fought in every major campaign with that army until Petersburg, when he transferred to North Carolina and participated in the capture of Fort Fisher. By this time he was a major general of volunteers.

In the postwar years Ames meteoric rise sputtered out when he became involved in Reconstruction politics in Mississippi. After 1876 he faded into relative obscurity and lived the remaining fifty-seven years of his life pursuing various jobs, both public and private. His business ventures made him a wealthy man. Ames served as a brigadier general during the Spanish-American War. His wife, incidentally, was the daughter of Benjamin "Beast" Butler, politician and political Civil War general.[2] Fortunately, Butler's daughter was far more physically attractive than her cross-eyed, misshapen father.

Using standard references (dictionaries, biographical encyclopedias, etc.) I found there are several different ways of pronouncing the name Adelbert. Finding out which one General Ames used turned into a long and often fruitless search. I eventually settled on **uh-DEL-bert** (as opposed to **AD-ul-burt** and **AY-dul-burt**) after discovering that his nickname was "Del," at least while he was at West Point. Additional support for the second syllable emphasis came from sources in Maine and a Civil War historian who knew Ames family members.[3]

Albemarle -(AL-buh-MARL)

as in Albemarle County and CSS *Albemarle*.

The CSS *Albemarle* was commissioned into Confederate service in April 1864. The 152-foot long ironclad, commanded by Cdr. James Cooke, was armed with two 6.4-inch Brooke guns. The *Albemarle* was designed to operate in the shoal waters off the coast of North Carolina.[4] The ship saw her first action two days after she was launched when she participated in a successful Confederate attack on Plymouth, North Carolina and sank the Union gunboat, the USS *Southfield*. A month later the *Albemarle* engaged a squadron of Federal gunboats at the mouth of the Roanoke River and was damaged. Six months later, the *Albemarle* was blown up during a daring Union raid on Plymouth, thus ending a short, but illustrious career.

The *Albemarle's* name is difficult to pronounce for those of us who aren't accustomed to saying it frequently. I suspect that residents of Albemarle County, Virginia, who have frequent cause to use their county's name, have no trouble at all with this word; nor do those who live in the vicinity of Albemarle Sound on the North Carolina coast. Many of the rest of us, however, do. Albemarle is one those words that reminds me of an oversized sandwich, the kind that is so large your front teeth can barely gain purchase.

As you bite down on it, the whole thing begins to come apart, with tomato slices, gobs of mayonnaise, and sections of pickle flying off in different directions, not to mention large sections of lettuce moving sideways out of the sandwich with each bite. I have no wish to explore the Freudian implications of this analogy, I just think it conveys a palpable sense of how I feel when I attempt to say **Albemarle**. For those of you who have a similar problem with this name, my advice is to say it carefully, say it slowly and watch out for flying mayonnaise!

Alcibiades -(al-suh-BIE-ah-deez)

as in Alcibiades DeBlanc, Lieutenant Colonel, 8th Louisiana.

Colonel DeBlanc was a lawyer from St. Martinsville, Louisiana prior to the Civil War. He helped raise the Attakapas Guards when the war came. DeBlanc's regiment was part of Harry Hays' Brigade in Early's Division at the Battle of Gettysburg. He was shot in the face during the fighting on Cemetery Hill on July 2, 1863, putting him out of action for the rest of the war. During the postwar years DeBlanc became a judge on the Louisiana Supreme Court.[5]

Alcibiades is certainly one of more exotic first names you are likely to come across in your Civil War studies. It is a name taken from the history of Ancient Greece. Alcibiades was an Athenian politician and general, the son of Cleinias and Deinomache. He was a pupil and a pal of Socrates[6] (Imagine! "Hey, honey. Better set an extra place for dinner. Socrates will be dropping over around six. Make sure we've got plenty of coffee; you know how he loves to sit around and talk for hours and hours."). Anyway, Alcibiades was celebrated for his great beauty and talents. He finally got into deep political trouble and was put to death in 404 B.C. The name Alcibiades was also used by Alfred Tennyson as a pseudonym when he wrote in *Punch* magazine.

Correct pronunciation of this classically derived name is a case of knowing which syllable gets stressed. I found pronouncers readily available in several good dictionaries.

Alpheus-(al-FEE-iss)

as in Alpheus Williams, Brigadier General U.S.V.

Connecticut born Alpheus Starkey Williams was one of the abler non-professional soldiers to reach the rank of general during the Civil War. Williams, who graduated from Yale in 1831, practiced law before the war. In the late 1830s he moved to Detroit, Michigan where he became a newspaper owner and a probate judge. When the Mexican War came he acted as lieutenant colonel of a regiment of Michigan volunteers.[7]

Williams' association with the state militia in Michigan led to his being commissioned brigadier general when the Civil War broke out.

General Williams saw service in the Shenandoah Valley in 1862 under the inept, but well meaning, Nathaniel Banks and was a division commander under the same general at the Battle of Cedar Mountain in August 1862. After John Pope's short lived Army of Virginia was defeated at Second Manassas, Banks Second Corps became the Twelfth Corps of the Army of the Potomac; command of which was given to Joseph K. F. Mansfield. Williams remained a division commander, and after Mansfield was killed at Antietam took command of the corps until superseded by Henry Slocum. Williams resumed divisional command and fought well at Chancellorsville and Gettysburg. He was transferred west in late 1863. When the Eleventh and Twelfth Corps were consolidated to form the Twentieth Corps, Army of the Cumberland, Williams was again given a divisional command. From then on Williams fought as part of Sherman's army, and though never commissioned a major general, his command and responsibilities were of that rank.

After the war, he was appointed minister to the Republic of Salvador. In 1874 he was elected to Congress and died in Washington during his second term in 1878. Williams has left us with a very good collection of wartime letters. For insight and depth of feeling they are unique and reflect, quite poignantly, the complexity and intellect of this high ranking civilian soldier.

Alpheus is a name not often heard these days. We live in a time with an inexhaustible supply of Chris', Jasons, Erics, Kevins and Michaels with the occasional Cody thrown in. Alpheus and Cadmus and Abiel and Cyrus are names from another age. Thus, we encounter a pronunciation problem common to names not often heard: which syllable gets the emphasis? My own tendency with the name Alpheus was to say it as, **ALF-ee-us**. Pronunciation of the name was found with relative ease in many standard reference works. There is no evidence that Alpheus Williams used any unusual phonetic variations with his first name.

Alpheus, like Alcibiades, is derived from Greek mythology. Alpheus was a river god who fell in love with the nymph of Arethusa, changing himself into a river so he could mingle with her when she turned herself into a fountain to escape him.[8] Given the moral constraints of nineteenth century America I seriously doubt if General Williams ever attempted to emulate his mythological namesake.

Ammen -(AM-en)

as in Jacob Ammen, Brigadier General U.S.V.

Jacob Ammen was one of the older professional soldiers to participate in the Civil War. He was born in Virginia in 1806 and raised in Ohio. Graduated from West Point in 1831, he resigned from the army in 1837 to teach mathematics at private colleges. Ammen reentered Federal service after Fort Sumter as a captain of the 12th Ohio. He fought at the Battle of Shiloh and the Siege of Corinth. He later served in various staff positions and on courts martial until his resignation in 1865. In the postwar years he worked as a surveyor and engineer. He was also appointed to the Isthmus of Panama Commission to examine routes for the proposed canal. Ammen died in 1894.

Jacob Ammen is important to the student of the Civil War because of his diary entries describing the Battle of Shiloh. Ammen led the 10th Brigade of Nelson's Division which arrived late in the day on April 6, 1862. His description of the shattered condition of Grant's troops at the conclusion of fighting on that day is often cited in histories of the battle.

Pronunciation of Ammen's last name could be difficult for those not familiar with the name. The possibility exists that some buffs might pronounce it, **AY-men**, or **ay-MEN**, as though they were concluding a prayer.

Apalachicola -(AP-uh-LACH-uh-KOH-luh)

as in Apalachicola, Florida.

Apalachicola is a city on the northwest Florida coast (part of the Florida panhandle) on Apalachicola Bay, at the mouth of the Apalachicola River. On January 6, 1861 the Federal Arsenal in the town was seized by state forces in anticipation of secession, which occurred four days later. A Federal blockade of Apalachicola Bay went into effect on June 7, 1861. By the following spring Federal presence in the Gulf of Mexico had become overwhelming, and on April 3, 1862 Apalachicola surrendered to the U. S. Navy.

Apalachicola is one those long names that comes under the "divide and conquer" rule of pronunciation. It is actually a fairly simple name to pronounce, possessing no silent letters, or hidden sounds of letters that aren't there. Pronouncers are readily available in standard reference works. When divided into six syllables it becomes comprehensible. In fact, a good way to remember which of those syllables gets emphasis is to think of it as a beverage: "Apalachi Cola hits the spot, twelve full ounces...etc."

Aquia -(uh-KWI-uh)

as in Aquia Creek, Virginia

Aquia Creek was never the scene of any famous battle or engagement during the Civil War. However, this tributary of the Potomac River, which originates at the west bank of the river and travels in a generally northwesterly direction, is important because of its strategic location. The mouth of the creek is large and during the war a major landing place and rail head was sited there. Supplies and troops could easily be brought down the Potomac from Washington and deposited at Aquia Landing, which was only a few miles north of Fredericksburg. Most of the major battlefields of Northern Virginia were never far from Aquia Creek. The grim business of transporting the wounded to hospitals in Washington was also handled from Aquia.

Aquia is derived from the Algonquian Indian language and probably means "sea gull." The obscurity of the meaning is caused by the fact that, at some time in the past, the original Indian word was changed to a pseudo-Latin form. Due to the influx of non-native Virginians into the area around Fredericksburg in the past twenty years, thanks mostly to the relentless and costly growth of the Federal government in Washington, several alternate pronunciations of Aquia have cropped up. I have heard reports of radio announcers referring to it as **uh-KEE-uh**, to cite just one example.[9]

This reminds me of a situation that has reportedly developed in the vicinity of the town of Litchfield, Connecticut, which is about twenty miles from where I live. There is an old road just outside of town that is named "Cathole Road," and has been pronounced **KAT-HOLE**, two words, for as long as anyone can remember. In recent years a goodly number of people from New York and other foreign locales have moved into the Bantam-Litchfield area, and some of these people, it is alleged, have taken to pronouncing the name of the old road as **kuh-TOL-ee**. So, an old road with an unusual name, a name that has an interesting story attached to it, is now pronounced so it sounds like a dessert item on the menu of an Italian restaurant![10]

Armistead -(ARM-sted)

as in Lewis Addison Armistead, Brigadier General C.S.A.

Lewis Armistead was a brigade commander in Lee's Army of Northern Virginia, and his big moment in the Civil War was also his last. He led the only Confederates to break the Union line during Pickett-Pettigrew Charge on the third day of the Battle of Gettysburg. Leaping over the stone wall at the Angle on Cemetery Ridge, leading about 150 men, sword in hand, Armistead made it as far as Cushing's Battery. He was mortally wounded and became one of the six Confederate generals killed at Gettysburg. Prior to the war he had been a good friend of Winfield Scott Hancock, Major General, Army of the Potomac. It was Hancock's men who shot Armistead down. The dying Armistead asked to see Hancock, who unfortunately was down with his own wound at the time. We include Armistead's name in our dictionary because many people pronounce the **'i'** in the middle of it. Alas, it is silent, just as poor Lewis has been these many years.

Bennett Wood Green in his turn of the century study of Virginia speech patterns, *Word-Book of Virginia Folk-Speech*, lists the name Armistead as being pronounced **UM-sted**. I suspect that Green may have been putting a Virginia accent on the first syllable, a sort of Southern sounding **'A.'** It is also possible that people living in Virginia in 1899 may have had stronger accents than they do now. The correct pronunciation of Lewis Armistead's name, in Virginia and elsewhere, is as I have specified.[11]

Aroostook -(uh-ROOS-tuk)

as in the USS *Aroostook*.

Just a few days after the fall of Fort Sumter, Abraham Lincoln issued a proclamation establishing a blockade of all Southern ports. This blockade was the largest such undertaking attempted up until then, covering more than 3,500 miles of coastline. The North had eight ships in commission in home waters in April 1861. When the British press learned of this they ridiculed the idea of blockading the Southern coast with one ship for every 375 miles.[12] Since the U. S. Navy was totally inadequate for the task, a program of ship building and ship purchasing was implemented immediately. Among the ships built during that first year of war were twenty-three so-called, "ninety-day gunboats." These were light draft wooden gunboats armed with one big gun (an 11-inch Dahlgren) and a pair of howitzers. Each of the ninety-day gunboats displaced 630 tons, was steam driven and double masted. Aside from the *Aroostook*, the other ships were *Cayuga, Chippewa, Chocura, Huron, Itasca, Kanawha, Katahdin, Kennebec, Kineo, Marblehead, Ottawa, Owasco, Pembina, Penobscot, Pinola, Sagamore, Sciota, Seneca, Tahoma, Unadilla, Winona,* and *Wissahickon.*[13]

The *Aroostook* was named for the river in Maine. Pronunciation is often a problem for people who are unfamiliar with the Indian names of northern New England. "Aroostook" is such a peculiar looking word, with the double **'o'** appearing twice, that confusion as to which syllable is emphasized is understandable. It might be added as a note of historical interest that a border dispute in 1839 between Canada and the United States led to the bloodless, Aroostook War.

The border between the Canadian province of New Brunswick and the state of Maine in the Aroostook region became an issue that very nearly led to war between the United States and Great Britain. Fortunately, before hostilities commenced, a truce was arranged, and a boundary commission set up to iron out differences of opinion. The final outcome was the Webster- Ashburton Treaty of 1842.

<u>Asboth</u> -(AS-both)

as in Alexander Sandor <u>Asboth</u>, Brigadier General U.S.V.

Hungarian refugee Sandor Asboth was born in Hungary in 1811, where he worked as a government engineer until the Hungarian Revolt of 1848. When the revolution came Asboth joined the forces of Lajos Kossuth in their fight against Austrian rule. He followed Kossuth into exile, first to Turkey, then to the United States in 1851. Asboth became citizen, and when the war came he received an appointment to the staff of Major General John Frémont in Missouri. He was appointed brigadier general in March 1862 and commanded a division at the Battle of Pea Ridge, where he was wounded. By 1863 Asboth was in command at Columbus, Kentucky, and later the District of West Florida where he was again severely wounded in the face and left arm. After the war, he was appointed U. S. Minister to Argentina and Uruguay. During this period, 1866-1868, he went to Paris to have the bullet removed from his face by a noted surgeon. The operation seemed to make matters worse and the wound never again healed. Asboth died in Buenos Aires in January 1868.

The Hungarian pronunciation of Asboth's name is **OSH-bot,** the **'o'** in both places being pronounced as the **'o'** is in the English word "**not.**"[14] The Americanized version is pretty much as I have indicated above. I have included the name in the dictionary because it is somewhat unusual and having some quideline on pronouncing it might prove helpful to people. Incidentally, Asboth's real first name was Sandor. He was called "Alexander" because it is the English equivalent of Sandor.[15]

<u>Atchafalaya</u> -(uh-CHAF-uh-LIE-uh)

as in <u>Atchafalaya</u> River, Louisiana.

Practically the only time you will come across references to the Atchafalaya River will be when you read about the Red River Campaign. The Atchafalaya branches off the Red River at Simmesport, Louisiana, then runs generally south. No major battle took place on the Atchafalaya, but the name pops up often enough as a ferrying point, a place where small skirmishes took place, and a point of reference to make proper pronunciation important. In fact, knowing how to pronounce this polysyllabic word will be a source of wonderment to your fellow buffs.

The Red River Campaign is not the most widely studied undertaking of the Civil War. Not too many students of the war have a detailed knowledge of it. Thus, the name Atchafalaya is one whose familiarity is pretty much confined to Louisiana and vicinity. By saying it correctly you will, as I said, impress your Civil War friends, and possibly even get some restrained compliments from the odd professional historian.

Atzerodt -(ATZ-uh-rot)

as in George Andrew Atzerodt, Lincoln Assassination conspirator.

Described by Margaret Leech in her classic book, *Reveille in Washington*, as "a droll, disreputable little German-American, who worked at the trade of carriage maker at the Maryland town of Port Tobacco...eager to earn a large fee for a night's work,"[16] little else is known about George Atzerodt. Perhaps this is because there is little to know. The information available portrays him as pretty much a bum who got caught up in something much bigger than he was capable of understanding. At the time he became associated with Booth & Company, he lived near Port Tobacco, Maryland with his mistress and their two-year-old daughter. He suffered from consumption, and was a carriage painter by trade who kept a shop in the town. For a price, Atzerodt would ferry people across the Potomac in the dead of night so they could take care of whatever business they had in the nearby Confederacy. Atzerodt was one of many people in Port Tobacco to earned extra money this way. The town itself was a well known smuggling center.[17] The reason he was selected by Booth & Company was because he had a reputation for charging reasonable rates. Ultimately, this greedy, pathetic man would become entangled first in John Wilkes Booth's Lincoln kidnapping plot, and then in the plot to kill the President. George Atzerodt's life would end on the gallows.

Pronunciation of Atzerodt's name is pretty straightforward. I checked with various sources, both printed and verbal, and found no surprises. It is a German name, but does not have any umlauts or other diacritical marks to complicate matters. The name is said as it is spelled. The only variation is the occasional pronunciation of the **ATZ** at the beginning as **ADZ**, thus it becomes **ADZ-uh-rot**.

Auchmuty -(AWK-MYOO-tee)

as in Richard Tylden Auchmuty, Captain U.S.V.

Auchmuty is one of the more unusual names you will find beginning with the letter 'A.' The name of Captain Auchmuty turns up a couple of times in *Battles and Leaders of the Civil War*, as well as a more recent book, Stephen Sears, *To The Gates of Richmond*. In both cases the good captain is quoted on the subject of the Battle of Gaines's Mill. Auchmuty was on the staff of Brigadier General George Morell, commander of the First Division, Fifth Corps, Army of the Potomac. In 1895 a collection of Auchmuty's letters was privately published.

Captain Auchmuty worked as an architect after the war and became well known as a philantropist. He and his wife founded the New York Trade Schools for the training of young people in manual and scientific skills. He died in July 1892.[18]

Auchmuty is a Scottish name.[19] When pronounced with a proper Scots accent this means the first syllable (Auch) ends with a guttural sound from the middle soft palate and involves vibrating the uvula (YOO-vyuh-luh). I realize this description is somewhat revolting, but think of the even more revolting consequences of attempting such a sound in a public place without any prior practice. It is for this reason I have given the Americanized pronouncer for Auchmuty.

Averell -(AV-rul or AHV-rul)

as in William Woods Averell, Brigadier General U.S.V.

General Averell was a professional soldier prior to the Civil War. He graduated in the lower third of the Class of 1855 at West Point, was assigned to garrison duty at Jefferson Barracks in Missouri, did a tour at the Cavalry School in Carlisle, Pennsylvania and then went to the Southwest to fight Indians. Averell started off the war as a lieutenant in the 3rd U. S. Cavalry, was promoted to captain and then became colonel of the 3rd Pennsylvania Cavalry just after the Battle of Bull Run. By the time of McClellan's Peninsula Campaign he was a brigade commander. Averell fought at Antietam in September of 1862 and later that month was promoted to brigadier general. In February 1863 he was given command of the 2nd Cavalry Division of the Army of the Potomac. It was in this command that he assured his place in Civil War history thanks to the Battle of Kelly's Ford.

The cavalry fight at Kelly's Ford on the Rappahannock River took place on March 17, 1863. Averell had been ordered to attack Confederate cavalry believed to be in the vicinity of Culpeper. Averell's troopers crossed the ford during the late morning of the 17th and were met by Fitzhugh Lee's Brigade of cavalry around noon. The five-hour-battle that followed was a back and forth affair with Lee being heavily outnumbered by the Federals. Though he had gained the tactical advantage by late in the day, Averell decided to withdraw and claim a victory. His reasons for withdrawing included the suspicion that Confederate infantry was arriving on the field to reinforce Lee. Though this was not true, Averell felt justified. Army commander Joe Hooker did not feel the same way and ultimately sacked Averell. Kelly's Ford is often cited by Civil War historians as being a watershed for Federal cavalry, bringing about a "miraculous transformation" that turned it into a formidable fighting force. More realistically, the fight at Kelly's Ford reflected the growth and seasoning of Federal troopers. It was not, however, "a Journey to Demascus."[20]

For the rest of the war W. W. Averell served under various commanders, including Philip H. Sheridan in the Shenandoah Valley. He resigned from the army at the end of the war and did a stint in the diplomatic corps. He was U. S. Consul General to British North America (Canada) from 1866 to 1869. He lived until 1900.

Pronunciation of Averell's name presents some problems. According to historian Ed Bearss, descendants of W. W. Averell use the **'ah'** sound when pronouncing the first letter in the name just as, they claim, their Civil War ancestor did. Many, if not most, Civil War historians I have encountered, however, say the name as **AV-rul**. For this reason I have included both pronouncers and concluded that either one is correct. Just remember, **AY-rul** is not correct.

Ayres -(**airz**)

as in Romeyn Beck Ayres, Major General U.S.V.

It never occurred to me until recently, that there is a whole generation of younger Civil War buffs out there who never heard of old-time motion picture star Lew Ayres. Ayres rose to stardom because of the 1930 film, *All Quiet on the Western Front*. This oversight was brought to my attention when someone asked me how General Romeyn Ayres' last name was pronounced, to which I replied, "Just like the actor, Lew Ayres." "Lew, who?" my questioner shot back. Well, that incident prompted me to include Ayres' name in the dictionary.

When the Civil War broke out Romeyn Ayres was a captain of the 5th U. S. Artillery. Ayres had graduated from West Point in 1847 and was, among other things, an authority on Latin. He served with the Army of the Potomac throughout the war. Up until the Battle of Chancellorsville, Ayres was an artillery commander. He served as Chief of Artillery for General William F. "Baldy" Smith's Division from October 1861 to November 1862, and the same position in the Sixth Corps until April 1863. After that, Ayres was appointed to a brigade command in the Fifth Corps which he led at Chancellorsville and then a division commander at Gettysburg. He remained with the 5th Corps for the rest of the war in both brigade and division command. After 1865 he remained in the army and died in 1888.

Brigadier General Lewis Addison Armistead

B

Badeau -(buh-DOH)

as in Adam Badeau, Colonel U.S.V.

Adam Badeau, a fine fellow in his own right, makes it into the history books because he was one of General U. S. Grant's military secretaries. He was also a leading historiographer of Grant. Badeau was born in New York City in 1831. He was well educated and became an accomplished writer. When the war came he first served as an ADC on the staff of General William T. Sherman with the rank of captain. Wounded at Port Hudson, he later joined Grant's military family in 1864 and participated in the Overland Campaign. At the end of the war he remained in the army with the regular rank of colonel and was ADC to Grant from 1866-69. He served in various consulates and legations during Grant's presidency and accompanied the general on his tour of Europe. Henry Adams was an acquaintance of Badeau's in the postwar years, and he left this description of the former military secretary. Badeau, said Adams, was "exceedingly social, though not in appearance imposing. He was stout; his face was red, and his habits were regularly irregular; but he was very intelligent."[21]

Pronunciation of Badeau's name probably doesn't present a problem for most people. However, I decided to put it in the dictionary because I found myself, over the years, tripping up on the name every time I read it, and hesitating every time I had occasion to say it. This indicated to me that I was not certain of the pronunciation. Undoubtedly, there are others who are similarly afflicted. Aside from reference books, I ran Badeau's name by a few Lincoln historians, like Mark Neely, author of *The Abraham Lincoln Encyclopedia*, and encountered no bizarre pronunciation twists.

bas-relief -(BAH-ri-LEEF)

as in "Above the archway was a bas-relief of the battle scene carved in granite."

Bas-relief is a form of sculpture where the carved figures are raised slightly from the background. You might think of it as a carved picture. Much of the monumental statuary in our nation's battlefield parks employ the use of bas-relief, usually in panels at the base of larger statues.

Mispronunciation of this term is widespread. The most frequently used erroneous pronunciation is **BASE-ri-LEEF**. This is perfectly understandable. Bas-relief is French, which is derived from the Italian, *bassorilievo,* which means, you guessed it, base relief. Now, there are some dictionaries that offer **BAHS-ri-LEEF** as an alternative pronunciation, but you would do well to stick to the standard one. Unfortunately, the French got to be the ones who named this technique of sculpture and so we are stuck with saying it their way. When I first heard bas-relief pronounced properly I envisioned "carvings of sheep" or some sort of Federal program that paid subsidies to the poor creatures for growing wool.

<u>Bearss</u> -(bahrss)

as in Edwin Cole <u>Bearss</u>, Chief Historian, National Park Service.

No Civil War buff can consider his education complete unless he has been on a battlefield tour with Ed Bearss. Bearss is more than a historian, he is a walking, talking database of Civil War information. A native of Montana, a decorated veteran of World War II, author of numerous books and articles on the war, including the definitive three-volume history of the Vicksburg Campaign, Ed Bearss is a leading authority on the American Civil War. He has been with the National Park Service for almost forty years and has had a hand in setting up many of the battlefield parks you have probably visited. In a sense, like Bruce Catton, T. Harry Williams and Bell I. Wiley he is part of the modern history of the Civil War.

Unfortunately, despite all his fame, Ed's last name is frequently mispronounced, even by those who should know how to pronounce it. The most common mispronunciation is **BAIRSS**. This makes sense. After all, the name is spelled like the plural of "bear" with an extra **'s'** on the end. Just remember that Ed's name rhymes with "parse." When saying the name, I recommend putting a slight hiss on the double **'s'** at the end.

<u>Beaufort</u> -(BOH-furt)

as in <u>Beaufort</u>, North Carolina.

<u>Beaufort</u> -(BYOO-furt)

as in <u>Beaufort</u>, South Carolina.

In the course of your Civil War readings and Civil War touring you are bound to come across one, or the other, or both of these towns. Beaufort, North Carolina figures in Civil War history because of Burnside's Expedition to North Carolina from February to July 1862. Beaufort is located near Fort Macon, which was besieged by Burnside's force and surrendered on April 25, 1862. The whole area around Beaufort, North Carolina is dotted with historic sites. It is also not too far from New Bern, North Carolina where many important Civil War events took place.

Beaufort, South Carolina was captured very early in the war. On November 9, 1861 Federal forces under Brigadier General Thomas W. Sherman occupied Beaufort following the Battle of Port Royal Sound on November 7th. This Union toe-hold in the Port Royal-Hilton Head area of South Carolina, though never fully taken advantage of, furnished a base for coaling and supplying Federal blockading squadrons.

The different pronunciations of these two places with the same name, about three hundred miles apart, is strictly a matter of local preference. Beaufort, North Carolina is pronounced with a French inflection on the first syllable, while Beaufort, South Carolina takes the anglicized pronunciation.

Berdan -(bur-DAN)

as in Hiram Berdan, Colonel, Ist U.S. Sharpshooters.

Hiram Berdan is a name synonymous with sharpshooter regiments in the Union Army. He was a mechanical engineer from New York City before the war, and was ranked as a top amateur rifle shot. When the war came, Berdan, who was not above self promotion, organized Berdan's Sharpshooters. This unit eventually became two regiments of U.S. Sharpshooters. Berdan was commissioned colonel of one of the regiments, the 1st U.S. Sharpshooters, in 1861. Though the Sharpshooters performed valuable service at several battles, including Gettysburg, Berdan himself seems to have spent most of his time wrangling for government contracts for his various inventions in weaponry. Many of his fellow officers found him unscrupulous and, at least one, described him as being totally unfit for command.

As for the pronunciation of his last name. The tendency of many people is to pronounce it **BUR-din**. This is just one of those cases where you have a two syllable name and a fifty-fifty chance of picking the right syllable to stress. In the case of Berdan's name I picked the wrong one, and used it until corrected by a helpful Park Service guide at Gettysburg. Further checking in standard references confirmed what I had been told.

Biloxi -(buh-LUK-see)

as in Biloxi, Mississippi.

This is one of those pronunciations lots of people take great pride in knowing. Evidently, Biloxi is a town many World War II GI's got to, for one reason or another, during their training. In addition, there is a large Air Force base there to this day. So, many otherwise ignorant Yankees know how to properly pronounce the name of this very Southern town. However, there are still those who do not, and many are Civil War buffs.

Biloxi was captured by a Federal landing party from nearby Ship Island in December 1861, but not occupied. The name Biloxi is derived from the name of one of the area Indian tribes and means "broken pot." Pronunciation as given above is the traditional local way of saying the name.

Birdseye -(BERD-zee *or* BAIRD-zee)

as in James Birdseye McPherson, Major General U.S.V.

James McPherson, who will be more fully discussed under the entry "McPherson," was commander of the Army of the Tennessee, one of Major General William T. Sherman's "Army Group." He was killed during the Atlanta Campaign.

General McPherson's middle name appears both familiar and easily pronounced. However, despite the fact that James McPherson's middle name is spelled exactly like the last name of Clarence Birdseye, a name nearly everyone who has ever eaten frozen food is familiar with, it is not pronounced the same way. The frozen food brand is pronounced **BERD-zie**. The McPherson family of Clyde, Ohio pronounced it with a **'zee'** at the end, not an **'zie.'**[22] In addition, you will notice I have given two pronouncers for this one. Either one should suffice as a proper way of saying the name. It is one of those situations where it is said both ways, depending on who says it.

Boatswain -(BOH-sun)

as in Boatswain's Swamp, Virginia.

Boatswain Swamp is another name for the Battle of Gaines's Mill, which took place on June 27, 1862. Gaines's Mill was the third of the Seven Days Battles during McClellan's Peninsula Campaign. Boatswain's Swamp was a small sluggish stream that curved around a plateau upon which the Union Fifth Corps had assumed a defensive position. The banks of the stream were heavily overgrown and extremely boggy.[23] Several assaults on this position by the Army of Northern Virginia finally carried the day, but the cost in casualties was high.

I realize that many, many people know how to pronounce the word "boatswain," despite its absolutely ridiculous spelling. However, there are those (and for many years "those" included me) who do not, or who may think that since Boatswain is being used as a proper name, a proper place-name in Virginia, it may have some really unusual pronunciation. Well, it doesn't. By the way, the word "boatswain" is derived from the late Middle English, Bote Swayn, or boat servant. I don't imagine there are many boatswain's mates who see themselves defined as such. In modern usage it means a warrant or petty officer on a fighting ship, or a merchant ship in charge of rigging, anchors, cables, and the deckhands.

Boeuf -(buuf *or* boof ['oo' as in "book"])

as in Bayou Boeuf, Louisiana.

Bayou Boeuf is another one of those names that show up in studies of the Red River Campaign. Many skirmishes are connected with the name, but no major battle. Bayou Boeuf is, of course, a French name. The word "boeuf" in French means "ox" or "beef."

Pronunciation of this name presents some unusual problems. There is no real equivalent in the English language for the French **'oe'** sound. One must resort to such facial gymnastics as forming the lips as though one were about to make the long **'o'** sound, while at the same time saying the **'e'** sound. This is the reason I have given two pronouncers. The first one contains **'uu,'** which I was reluctant to use because it can be confusing. The use of **'uu,'** however, is the only way I could translate the sound. The second pronouncer is an attempt to clarify and simplify the first pronouncer. The choice is up to you.

Bonham -(BONE-um)

as in Millidge Luke Bonham, Brigadier General C.S.A.

South Carolina-born Luke Bonham was a lawyer prior to the Civil War. A graduate of South Carolina College, his early legal and political career in the Palmetto State was interrupted by military service during the Second Seminole uprising of 1836 and the Mexican War. Bonham was elected to the state house of representatives in 1840 and to the U. S. Congress in 1857. When South Carolina seceded he resigned from Congress. Since Bonham had always been active in the state militia he was appointed commander of the South Carolina Army around Charleston with the rank of major general.

After the war broke out and South Carolina troops were mustered into Confederate service Bonham was appointed to the rank of brigadier general. He led a brigade at the Battle of Manassas in July of 1861. Bonham resigned from military service in January of 1862 to fill a seat in the new Confederate States Congress. He remained in this office until elected governor of his state in December 1862. He was governor until the end of 1864. In February 1865 he was again appointed brigadier general and served under Joseph Johnston until the end of the war.

The automatic pronunciation of the name Bonham tends, even in South Carolina, to be **BON-um**. However, the Bonham family traditionally has answered to **BONE-um**.[24] Certainly, during the life of Millidge Luke Bonham it was pronounced that way. It is doubtful you will be corrected for pronouncing General Bonham's name **BON-um**, but think of how superior you will feel saying it correctly.

<u>Bolivar</u> -(BAHL-i-vur)

as in <u>Bolivar</u> Heights, Harpers Ferry, West Virginia.

The name Bolivar Heights, one of the three commanding elevations overlooking the town of Harpers Ferry, West Virginia is often mispronounced. Many people say **BULL-i-ver**, which is perfectly understandable since a well known brand of wrist watches with a similar name, and similar spelling, is pronounced almost the same way. However, the local pronunciation in the town of Harpers Ferry, as well as the nearby town of Bolivar, makes the first three letters rhyme with the word **doll**.[25]

<u>Boteler</u> -(BOHT-lur *or* BOT-lur)

as in <u>Boteler's</u> Ford or A. R. <u>Boteler,</u> Confederate Congressman.

Boteler's Ford was not a Civil War-era car dealership, but one of the shallow crossing places or "fords" on the Potomac River. When Robert E. Lee withdrew his Army of Northern Virginia from Maryland at the conclusion of the Antietam Campaign he crossed the army at Boteler's Ford on the Potomac. Just to make things interesting as well as confusing, Boteler's Ford was also called Blackford's Ford.

Alexander R. Boteler was a member of the Confederate Congress and a staff officer for Stonewall Jackson. Boteler was also a confidante of Jackson's and was often assigned to act as a liaison between the Mighty Stonewall and the government in Richmond. Prior to the war Boteler had served in the U. S. Congress representing the district that included Jefferson County, Virginia (now West Virginia). Boteler's home, Fountain Rock, just outside Sheperdstown was not too far from Boteler's Ford on the Potomac River. The house was burned by troops under Major General David "Black Dave" Hunter in July 1864.

I have given the two most common correct pronunciations of Boteler's Ford.[26] However, pronunciation of the Boteler name as though it were spelled **Butler** came to my attention during research. This pronunciation was confirmed by the staff at the Duke University Archives where Alexander Boteler's papers are deposited. Members of the archives staff had extensive personal dealings with the family[27] However, this pronunciation seems to apply to the family only. The ford that takes its name from the family is most often pronounced **BOHT-lur** or **BOT-lur**.[28] I found that many people, myself included, were unsure of the pronunciation of Boteler. I once heard it pronounced **BOH-TEL-ur** and the seed of doubt was planted in my mind.

Botetourt -(BOT-uh-tot)

as in Botetourt County, Virginia.

Botetourt County is at the upper, or southern end of the Shenandoah Valley just south of Rockbridge Country and north of Roanoke County. No military engagement of any significance took place in this county during the Civil War. A number of Confederate military units came from this county however, including the Botetourt Artillery. The Botetourt Artillery was the only Virginia unit to participate in the 1863 Vicksburg Campaign. They fought at Port Gibson, Champion Hill and the forty-seven-day siege at Vicksburg. Upon returning to Virginia they participated in the Battle of Lynchburg in 1864.

Botetourt County takes its name from Norborne Berkeley, Baron de Botetourt, who was colonial governor of Virginia from 1768 to 1770. The peculiar pronunciation of the name is undoubtedly an English attempt at French that failed or, more likely, an English simplification of one of those old Norman titles.

I first encountered the mysterious name "Botetourt" when I was in college. I was passing through the Virginia county of that name on the way to a social engagement at Roanoke College.[29] My first impulse upon seeing the name on a road sign was to pronounce it **BOT-tuh-TORT** (after that, I promptly forgot about the whole thing). Years later, I came across the name again, this time in a footnote in one of Douglas Southall Freeman's volumes in which he indicated the proper pronunciation. When I came to include Botetourt in this book I verified Freeman's pronouncer with Park Service historians and Virginia residents. However, I discovered that aside from the pronouncer I have given above, there is an alternate one, **BOHT-uh-TORT**, which is not unlike my first attempt at the name years ago.

Boudinot -(BOO-duh-not)

as in Elias Cornelius Boudinot, Cherokee Confederate congressman.

Prior to the Civil War Elias Boudinot was a railroad engineer in Ohio, and a lawyer in Arkansas. Like his father, also named Elias Boudinot, he was also a skillful journalist. Boudinot was a well known politician in Little Rock and chairman of Democratic State Central Committee in 1860. In 1861 he was secretary of the state's secession convention and after Arkansas seceded he helped his uncle, Stand Watie, organize a Cherokee regiment for the Confederacy. He served briefly with the 1st Cherokee Rifles before his tribe elected him to the Confederate Congress. By 1863 he had been appointed to the powerful Military Affairs Committee, which permitted him to introduce a number of bills to benefit the Indians. Boudinot, because he was half Cherokee, was a non-voting member of the congress. He served two terms and apparently was known to resort to some shady political practices to achieve his aim. After the war, he helped negotiate peace between the Cherokees and the Federal Government.

Elias Boudinot was named for his father, who had been the editor of the *Cherokee Phoenix*. Boudinot, Sr. had adopted the name of Elias Boudinot, the American patriot, and president of the Continental Congress. This patriot was also a philantropist who funded a mission school in Cornwall, Connecticut that Boudinot, Sr. attended.

The Boudinot name is French in origin. In searching the usual sources for the proper pronunciation I noticed that current biographical dictionaries sometimes list the pronunciation as **BOO-duh-noh**, which is the French way of saying it. The older sources, the ones printed in the 19th century, list the pronouncer with a hard **'t'** ending. I decided to go with the older sources. After all, they were around when the real Boudinot was there to correct them. It was a wise decision as further research disclosed.[30]

Bowdoin -(BOHD-un)

as in Bowdoin College, Brunswick, Maine.

Bowdoin College in Brunswick, Maine is the alma mater of Brigadier General Josuah L. Chamberlain and Major General Oliver Otis Howard, among others. The college was named in honor of James Bowdoin, Governor of Massachusetts from 1785 to 1787, and founder of the American Academy of Arts and Sciences (no, not the same outfit that gives out Oscars every year).[31]

The name "Bowdoin" is included in this dictionary because I have discovered, not to my great surprise, that lots of people not familiar with Bowdoin College mispronounce the name. After all, why on earth would anyone spell Boden, B-O-W-D-O-I-N?

Breathed -(BRETH-ud)

as in James Breathed, Major C.S.A.

Maryland born James Breathed joined Company B of the 1st Virginia Cavalry in August 1861 as a private. By the following March he had been promoted to lieutenant and was serving with Pelham's Battery of Stuart's Horse Artillery. Breathed made captain in August of 1862, and was a major by 1864 assigned to the Horse Artillery Battalion. Breathed was wounded at the Battle of Yellow Tavern, where his boss Jeb Stuart was mortally wounded. After the war he was a medical doctor in Hancock, Maryland.[32]

Breathed's name turns up quite often in histories that cover the Army of Northern Virginia. I always thought it a peculiar name. After all, it is spelled the same way as the word, "breathed" as in, to have inhaled and exhaled. I checked with various NPS historians on this name and the consensus was the pronouncer given above.[33]

Brockenbrough -(BRO-ken-broh)

as in John Mercer Brockenbrough, Colonel C.S.A.

John M. Brockenbrough was a brigade commander in Lee's Army of Northern Virginia. His big moment in Civil War history probably came when his brigade participated in the Pickett-Pettigrew Charge at Gettysburg. However, Brockenbrough provides us with a an opportunity to take a look at the career of a Civil War officer who wasn't a general. So often those of us who read about and study the Civil War forget about the line officers who did the dirty work of fighting the war, the average guy who never got into the history books by performing some act of extraordinary bravery, the guy who just did his job.

John Brockenbrough was born in Richmond County, Virginia in August 1830, graduated from Virginia Military Institute in 1850, and was made colonel of the 40th Virginia in May 1861. When brigade commander Brigadier General Charles Field was severely wounded at Second Manassas Colonel Brockenbrough took over and served as acting commander for ten months. When a permanent commander of Field's Brigade was announced it wasn't Brockenbrough who was named. Instead, Henry Harrison Walker, a colonel with little combat experience, became the permanent brigade commander, causing Brockenbrough to submit his resignation on January 21, 1864. Why he never got permanent command of the brigade is somewhat of a mystery.

It is possible that a blunder made during the fight at Falling Waters on July 14, 1863 during Lee's retreat from Pennsylvania led to Brockenbrough being viewed with disfavor. Confederate forces were retreating from the engagement and Brockenbrough ordered his brigade forward.. For whatever reason, Brockenbrough then put the brigade under the command of his aide, Captain Wayland Dunaway, and left the field with the main force. Dunaway was captured along with many others and the brigade was badly mauled; three regiments lost their flags.[34] Why Brockenbrough left the field is a mystery. The man's courage in battle was well established, and Brockenbrough was never officially blamed for anything. In any event, his active military career was finished.

Pronunciation of Brockenbrough's name is one of those cases of family choice. I was told by historian Robert K. Krick that present day members of the Brockenbrough clan insisted that the name was said as though it were spelled "**Brokenbrough**." He cites as his authority no less a personage than the granddaughter of John Mercer Brockenbrough, the late Miss Eleanor B. of the Museum of the Confederacy.

Buford -(BYOO-furd)

as in John Buford, Brigadier General U.S.V.

The name Buford may seem an unnecessary inclusion in this dictionary. Most people don't seem to have any problem with this one. However, for a number of years I found I had a tendency to pronounce the name of this famous Union cavalry general as though it were spelled "Bufford"--**BUFF-urd**. I was happy to discover a few other people who made the same mistake. Stupidity shared becomes only half stupid. Anyway, it is important to get John Buford's last name right. He was one of the important players in the first day's action at Gettysburg. Buford's cavalry division held off a goodly portion of Henry Heth's Division of the Army of Northern Virginia in the very first hours of the big battle before help arrived in the form of the Union First Corps.

Bussey -(BUS-ee)

as in Cyrus Bussey, Brigadier General U.S.V.

Born in Ohio and raised in Indiana, Cyrus Bussey's is a familiar story for the Old Northwest. He started as a clerk in a dry goods store, eventually opened his own business, moved to Iowa, entered state politics and by the time the war came had some militia experience. Bussey put together a creditable enough war record. He fought at Pea Ridge and Arkansas Post and was in command of a cavalry brigade during the Vicksburg Campaign. After the war he returned to business and politics, and was appointed Assistant Secretary of the Interior in 1889 by President Benjamin Harrison.

Obviously, Cyrus Bussey was nothing more than a typical young man on the make, a sort of 19th century Yuppie. But, as has been the case of several of the entries in this dictionary, his name is mentioned often enough to merit consideration. Also, the man was a general. Pronunciation of the name Bussey, at first glance, seems not to be an insurmountable obstacle. However, I found that it was one of those names that gave me pause, and made me wonder if it might be pronounced differently, like **BYOO-see**, for example. So, to remove my own doubts, I checked it out and found more confusion: It seems that the name Bussey can be pronounced either, **BYOO-see, BUS-ee** or **BUZ-zee**. Thus, with three possible pronouncers to choose from and no known expert on Cyrus Bussey in evidence I called the folks in Bloomfield, Iowa, the town Bussey lived in.[35] **BUS-ee** is the correct pronouncer.

Major General James Birdseye McPherson

C

<u>Cabell</u> -(KAB-ul)

William Lewis <u>Cabell</u>, Brigadier General C.S.A.

William Lewis Cabell, nicknamed "Old Tige," spent most of the war in the west. Cabell performed valuable service at the Battle of Elkhorn Tavern (Pea Ridge) under Major General Earl Van Dorn. Later, he commanded a brigade of cavalry under Sterling Price in Arkansas and Missouri and finally in Kansas where he was captured in October 1864. He was not released until July of 1865.

Cabell was a West Point graduate from Virginia. At the outset of the war he was on General P. G. T. Beauregard's staff and fought at Manassas. According to Warner's *Generals in Gray*, Cabell assisted Generals Beauregard and Johnston in designing the Confederate battle flag. After the war he moved to Texas where he served four terms as mayor of Dallas, was a U. S. marshal and dabbled in railroading.

Pronunciation of Cabell can cause problems for those not familiar with the name. **Kuh-BELL** was the way I was saying it until I knew better. I happened upon the name accidently while going through a biographical dictionary and discovered the error of my ways. After checking with the helpful staff at the Museum of the Confederacy, I had my verification.

<u>Cairo</u> -(KAIR-roh)

as in <u>Cairo</u>, Illinois *or* USS <u>*Cairo*</u>

Cairo, Illinois is located at the confluence of the Ohio and Mississippi rivers. During the Civil War it became an important supply base and base of operations, especially to General Ulysses Grant. Pronunciation of the name is merely a corruption of Cairo, Egypt, which of course is pronounced **KIE-roh**. There was also an ironclad that plied the Mississippi River during the war called the USS *Cairo*, pronounced just as the Illinois town is.

Cannae -(KAN-ee)

as in the Battle of Cannae.

Every once in a while you will come across a reference to the Battle of Cannae in your Civil War reading. For example, at the Battle of Frayser's Farm (or Glendale) on June 30, 1862 Lee failed in an attempt to achieve a double envelopment, "..the gray army proved unready for a *Cannae* maneuver..."[36] The battle being referred to here took place in 216 B.C. during the Second Punic War. It was fought between a Roman army of 80,000 men under Terentus Varro and the Carthaginian Army under Hannibal consisting of half that number. Hannibal, with his back to the Aufidus River, drew the superior Roman force into an attack on the thinly manned center of his line. The Romans were convinced that they were driving the Carthaginians into the river as the center of Hannibal's line fell back, but as they pushed farther and farther they were being enveloped by his heavily manned flanks. Once the envelopment was complete the hemmed in Romans were annihilated. This battle is considered a prime example of tactical perfection.[37]

Pronunciation of this ancient battle is made difficult by that 'ae' at the end of the name. For a long time I thought it was pronounced **kan-NAY** or **CAY-nuh**, I used both. Luckily, it was one of those names that didn't often come up in conversation, and when I did have a chance to make mention of it, I don't think anyone knew what the hell I was talking about anyway. So, correct pronunciation of Cannae is not particularly vital to your future as an erudite Civil War buff. Just think of it as yet another weapon in your arsenal for Civil War Conference One-upmanship.

Carondelet -(ka-RON-da-LET)

as in USS *Carondelet*.

The USS *Carondelet* was one of seven armored, or ironclad gunboats designed by Samuel Pook in 1861, thus the nickname, "Pook Turtles." Pity this gunboat wasn't called USS Pook, a much easier name to contend with than the *Carondelet*. The *Carondelet*, which was indeed turtle-like in appearance (and probably pook-like as well), was used in the Tennessee and Cumberland rivers during operations against Fort Henry and Fort Donelson, it also saw service in the ill-fated Red River Campaign. The cumbersome vessel weighed more than nine hundred tons, had five boilers, two engines and thirteen guns. Like the other "Pook Turtles," the *Carondolet* was a flat bottomed scow, 175 feet long, with a fifty foot beam and a six foot draft. She was clumsy, slow and more dangerous to her own crew than to any adversary. She finally met another clumsy, slow and dangerous armored vessel called the CSS *Arkansas* in July 1862 and the resulting engagement left the *Carondolet* disabled and grounded.

The great temptation when one sees the name *Carondolet* is to say the last syllable as one would say the last syllable of "Chevrolet." Carondolet, by the way, is the location of the boatyard where the ironclad was built. In 1861 it was a "muddy, sprawling, roistering little community between St. Louis and Jefferson Barracks... Missourians, with their genius for distorting the French names in which the region abounds, have always pronounced the name with the **'a'** nearly swallowed and a hard **'t'**."[38]

Catharpin -(kuh-*TH*ARP-un)

as in Catharpin Road, Chancellorsville, Virginia.

The Catharpin Road runs in a south-westerly direction from the Orange Plank Road near Chancellorsville. In its course it meanders past Piney Branch Church, crosses Brock Road at Todd's Tavern and continues southwest until it hits the road to Verdiersville. All this makes Catharpin Road an important map reference in the battles of Chancellorsville, The Wilderness and Spotsylvania. After Catharpin Road crosses Brock Road it is paralleled by Catharpin Run, a small winding creek.

Catharpin is a strange name. It is also a name of very obscure origins. The word shows up in the dictionary as a nautical term meaning, "any of a number of short ropes or rods for gathering in shrouds near the tops."[39] This doesn't help explain why the word "catharpin" was used to name a road in the Virginia Wilderness. Possibly an extension of the road once existed that ran to one of the Rappahannock or Potomac ports.[40] This road may have reminded local seamen of those short ropes the dictionary mentions. This explanation will have to suffice. In any event, it is the pronunciation we are primarily concerned with.

One of the mispronunciations I had heard was **kuh-TAR-pin**, the other was **KAT-har-pin**. The staff at Fredericksburg and Spotsylvania National Military Park gave me the proper local pronunciation.

Catoctin -(ka-TOK-tin)

as in Catoctin Mountain, Maryland.

Catoctin Mountain is simply an extension of the Bull Run Mountains of Virginia into west-central Maryland. The Bull Run Mountains are basically a chain of very large hills. They run from southwest to northeast, parallel to the much loftier Blue Ridge

Mountains. Between Leesburg and Harpers Ferry the mountain chain gaps for the Potomac River, then continues on into northern Maryland where it eventually merges with South Mountain, which is the Maryland extension of the Blue Ridge Mountains. During the Antietam Campaign both armies, Confederate and Federal, passed through Frederick, Maryland and then marched west over Catoctin Mountain and South Mountain.

Catoctin Mountain is an important landmark, especially for students of the Antietam Campaign. The name derives from the Algonquian language meaning "speckled mountain." Pronunciation guidance is abundant in the form of reference books and Park Service people, not to mention local Marylanders.

Chapultepec -(chuh-POOL-tuh-pek)

as in the Battle of Chapultepec, Mexican War.

Among the many Civil War notables who fought at this battle were U. S. Grant and Stonewall Jackson. You cannot possibly read the biographies of Civil War generals without coming across at least some reference to the Mexican War (1846-1848). It was in this conflict that many of the great captains of the 1860s learned their first practical lessons in wartime soldiering.

The storming of Chapultepec, a fortified hill about three miles southwest of Mexico City, took place on September 13, 1847 and was one of the last major actions of the Mexican War. The palace atop the rocky hill was built in the late 18th century and by 1847 housed the Mexican Military College.

Chartres -(SHAHR-truh)

as in Robert Phillipe Louis Eugène Ferdinand d'Orléans, Duc de Chartres, Captain U.S.V.

Now that you have had an opportunity to read the above name I would like to be able to tell you that this guy was called "Bob" by his pals. It would certainly simplify matters. As it turns out, this French noble visitor to the United States, who served briefly on General George McClellan's staff, did have his name simplified by his American hosts. His fellow officers referred to him as, "Captain Chatters."[41] Chartres was one of those characters who became part of the Union army at the beginning of the war. There was a genuine shortage of staff officers with experience and many of these foreigners, whether soldiers of fortune or exiled nobility like Chartres, were welcomed with open arms in Washington. Duc de Chartres and his younger brother, the Comte de Paris, exiled princes of the House of Orléans, along with there middle aged uncle, Prince de Joinville, made for an exotic addition to McClellan's staff. All three served with McClellan during the Peninsula Campaign.

chasseur -(sha-SOOR)

as in, "The men of the 14th Brooklyn wore the uniform of the French chasseur."

One of the many dazzling varieties of uniform worn during the Civil War was that of the French chasseur, or light infantryman. This type of uniform, which had gained favor with a few pre-war militia outfits, was a sort of restrained zouave costume. As worn by the 14th Brooklyn, for example, a regiment whose official Federal designation was the 84th N. Y. Volunteers, it consisted of straight red trousers, white leggings, blue blouse, and red cap trimmed in blue. Though dressed like a juggling troupe, that in our own time might have appeared on the Ed Sullivan Show, this regiment won a reputation as courageous fighters. The 14th Brooklyn earned the nickname, "The Red Legged Devils."[42]

The word "chasseur" means "chaser" or "hunter" in French. It is one of the easier French words, but nonetheless a cause of some pronunciation difficulty for many people. The pronouncer I have given is a reasonable facsimile of the original French.

chevaux-de-frise -(shuh-VOH-duh-FREEZ.)

The literal translation of this term is "Frisian horses." It was a portable defensive barrier developed by the Frisians (Friesland and the Frisian Islands are mostly part of The Netherlands) in the 17th century. The usual construction of a chevaux-de-frise was a length of timber, or iron, six to nine feet long studded with long, pointed stakes. Most of us have seen pictures of these things; they look like deadly saw horses. Military units in a fortified position often used these contraptions to stop an assaulting enemy force, or at least impede its progress. The chevaux-de-frise was made obsolete by the invention of barbed wire. Ah, the wonders of progress!

<u>Chickahominy</u> -(CHIK-uh-**HOM**-uh-nee)

as in <u>Chickahominy</u> River, Virginia.

It occurs to me that many new Civil War buffs might be reading this little dictionary and inclusion of names like Chickahominy might be appreciated. The Chickahominy River is about ninety miles long and rises sixteen miles northwest of Richmond then flows in a southeasterly direction into the James River.[43] Many battles during the Peninsula Campaign of 1862 were fought in the vicinity of this sluggish stream. It is a name you will come across time and again when reading about the Civil War in Virginia. The name Chickahominy is derived from the name of an Indian tribe that was part of the Powhatan Confederacy which inhabited eastern Virginia.

<u>Chickamauga</u> -(CHIK-uh-**MAW**-guh)

as in Battle of <u>Chickamauga</u>.

The Battle of Chickamauga, which took place on September 18-20, 1863 was fought along the banks of a tributary of the Tennessee River called the West Fork of Chickamauga Creek. Confederate General Braxton Bragg and his Army of Tennessee defeated Union General William S. Rosecrans and his Army of the Cumberland. It was the largest battle in the Western theater of the war.

Many, if not most, buffs know how to pronounce the name of this battle properly. However, there are those who are either unfamiliar with the engagement (Is that possible?) or simply never took the time to learn the proper pronunciation. The most outrageous mispronunciation I've heard recently is **CHIK-uh-MONG-guh**, which sounds more like a popular dance craze of the late 1940s than a Civil War battle. Probably the most common mispronunciation is **CHIK-uh-MAW-gwha** as though the word were spelled with a **'gua'** at the end. I suspect people say it this way because it sounds more Indian-like.

Supposedly, Chickamauga means "river of death" in some local Indian dialect. Wow, what a coincidence! It seems to me that many locations where awful things have happened have Indian names that predispose the place to tragedy. The truth is that many of the Indian names a place originally had were first heard by Spaniards or Frenchmen, who then passed them along to English speaking settlers. The result of all this translating and re-translating was a complete loss of original meaning. Thus, Chickamauga could be some total corruption of the original name, a name that might have meant, "A good creek to cross without getting your moccasins wet."

<u>Chimborazo</u> -(CHIM-buh-**RAH**-zoh)

as <u>Chimborazo</u> Heights, Richmond, Virginia.

As incredible as it may seem, the Confederacy had one of the best military hospitals during the Civil War; it also had one of the largest. Chimborazo Military Hospital, on Chimborazo Heights in Richmond, had beds for some 8,000 men housed in thirty pavilions. It also had five soap houses, Russian baths (whatever they were), five ice houses, a bakery that could bake 10,000 loaves of bread daily and a 400 keg brewery. A farm adjacent to the hospital grew food and grazed more than three hundred cows and several hundred goats. Despite this remarkable effort on the part of Confederate medical authorities, 19th century medicine could do very little for most of the wounded men. In addition, Chimborazo quickly became overcrowded and this, combined with supply and personnel shortages, turned it into "that carnal house of living sufferers."[44]

Chimborazo Hill or Heights is east of downtown Richmond. Today it is where the headquarters for the Richmond National Battlefield Park is located. During the Civil War this site along the James River was at the edge of the city and the topography of the forty acre plateau had good water and drainage.[45] Pronunciation is easily accomplished phonetically from the regular spelling of the name. However, it is a long name that might cause people to wonder which syllable is stressed. It is for that reason I included it in the dictionary.

<u>Cheves</u> -(CHIV-vis)

as in Langdon <u>Cheves,</u> U.S. statesman, Southern secessionist; Langdon <u>Cheves</u> Jr., Captain C.S.A.

Langdon Cheves died before the Civil War began, so his inclusion in this dictionary might be questioned. However, there are a number of students of the war who simply aren't satisfied with studying the war itself, but insist on studying the events that led up to it. This being the case, I have included the name of Langdon Cheves.

Cheves was a South Carolinian who was a banker and politician. His political career was a distinguished one that led him to become Speaker of the U. S. House of Representatives from 1814 to 1815. But it was Langdon Cheves career as a banker that put him solidly in the history books. Cheves became known as "the Hercules of the United States Bank." His draconian methods of shoring up the bank's liquidity helped to plunge the country into a major economic downturn, but he saved the bank!

Captain Langdon Cheves, his son, was born 1814 and became a Confederate engineering officer. Prior to the Civil War he was a lawyer and judge in South Carolina. When the war came he served for a time as an aide to General Thomas F. Drayton.

Cheves saw action at Port Royal and took part in the defense of Forts Walker and Beauregard. He also worked on fortifications at Charleston and in Savannah. Captain Cheves was the man who constructed the most famous Southern observation balloon, the "Silk Dress Balloon," and for this he is worthy of our note.

The balloon that Cheves put together was a multicolored creation made from nearly every yard of dress silk that he could lay his hands on in Charleston and Savannah. It was not made from all the silk dresses of the Southern ladies in those two cities as the popular tale has always stated. All the silk was stitched together and filled with illuminating gas from the Richmond gas works and was used during the Seven Days Battles.[46] The name of this balloon was probably the *Gazelle*.[47] It was used until the boat towing it was captured on July 4, 1862. The balloon, by some accounts, was cut up by Union troops for souvenirs. Captain Cheves outlasted his balloon by a year. He was killed by a shell fragment fired by a Union gunboat on Morris Island in Charleston Harbor in July 1863.

Pronunciation of the Cheves name might be explained by the fact that it is a variation of the old Scottish name "Chivas." Now, anyone who has ever partaken of Scotch whiskey is familiar with the Chivas Regal brand of Scotch. "Chivy," as it is known by the more frequent imbibers, is pronounced **CHIV-vis REE-gul**. Much of the time the first name is pronounced **SHIV-vis**, but the proper way is with a hard **'c.'** What probably confuses many people when they see the name "Cheves" is the spelling and, as a result, you hear **CHEE-vis** quite often. Of course, if one drinks enough "Chivy," fine distinctions in pronunciation become irrelevant, and nearly impossible to make. But at that point, who cares?

Chillicothe -(chil-uh-KAHTH-ee)

as in USS *Chillicothe.*

USS *Chillicothe* was a river ironclad designed by James Eads and Samuel Pook. She was built in Cincinnati during the winter of 1862-63, was 395 tons and had two 11-inch guns, and two 9-inch guns. Like most of the other "Pook Turtles," she was slow moving, hard to maneuver, and not very well constructed. The *Chillicothe* participated in the Yazoo Pass debacle (one of four unsuccessful bayou expeditions during the Vicksburg Campaign) in February and March of 1863, during which she was badly damaged. *Chillicothe* also participated in the Red River Campaign of 1864.

The name Chillicothe is familiar to many readers, but a genuine mystery to others. There are at least three towns called Chillicothe in the middle west. The largest of these is in Ohio. Thus, we can safely assume that a goodly portion of middle America can properly pronounce this name. But, we must not forget about the countless Civil War buffs who live hundreds of miles from the nearest Chillicothe.

Chuubusco -(choo-roo-BOOS-koh)

as in the Battle of Churubusco, Mexican War.

Churubusco and Contreras were two strong points guarding the southern approaches to Mexico City. Mexican President and General Antonio de Santa Anna concentrated about 20,000 men in the vicinity of these points. On August 19, 1847 American troops under the command of General Gideon Pillow attacked the Mexican position at Contreras and were repulsed. The following day, at dawn, a renewed American attack under General Persifor Smith routed the Mexicans.[48] Later that same day, August 20, the Americans attacked the Mexican position at Churubusco and won the battle there as well. Contereas and Churubusco were about seven miles from each other. Thus, accounts of the two engagements are generally written as though they were parts of the same battle.

Clausewitz -(KLOW-zuh-vits [KLOW rhymes with "COW"])

as in Carl von Clausewitz, Prussian military theorist.

Von Clausewitz was dead nearly thirty years when the Civil War began. Born in 1780 in Magdeburg, Prussia he served with the Prussian Army in all the campaigns against Napoleon. After 1818 he was administrative director of the Kreigsakademie in Berlin. It was during his tenure there that he wrote his studies of military campaigns. His major work, *On War*, is one of the most influential books of military theory ever written. In the book he stated what he believed to be the fundamental laws of war. Clausewitz believed that none of these laws were to be applied dogmatically on the battlefield, but modified to suit external influences, including psychological and moral considerations.[49] Clausevitz's most widely quoted belief is that war is an extension of politics.

Unlike Antoine Henri Jomini, the Swiss born French theoretician, Clausewitz exerted little, if any, influence on Civil War era officers. One of the reasons for this is that Dennis Hart Mahan, from whom most West Point graduates, who fought in the Civil War, learned their military theory, tended to emphasize Jomini. Another reason is that there was no English translation of Clausewitz available. In addition, the French were much more influential on America, culturally, in the 19th century than the Germans.[50] However, the name Clausewitz pops up often enough in writings and discussions of the tactics and strategies used during the Civil War to merit inclusion in this dictionary. Clausewitz was, after all, the greatest philosopher of war. Anyone who studies military history should know how to pronounce his name.

Cleburne -(CLAY-burn)

as in Patrick Ronayne Cleburne, Major General C.S.A.

Many Civil War buffs mispronounce this man's last name. I suspect that **'e'** sitting in place of a good, sensible American **'ay'** in the first syllable of the name causes the problem. One finds oneself tempted to pronounce the name, **KLEE-burn** or **KLEB-urn.**[51] This, of course, is incorrect. Patrick Cleburne was a native of Ireland (where it is usually pronounced **kluh-BURN**) who came to America as a young man. He settled in Arkansas before the outbreak of the Civil War, where he was a druggist and lawyer (a lively combination of occupations which makes more sense today than it did back in the 1850s). Cleburne who had had previous military experience in the British Army organized the Yell Rifles in Helena at the beginning of the war and rose quickly thereafter. Patrick Cleburne became one of the great Confederate generals of the Civil War in the western theater of operations. He has been called "The Stonewall Jackson of the West." [52] He distinguished himself at almost every important battle fought by the Army of Tennessee as a brigade and division commander and at Jonesboro on August 31, 1864 as a corps commander. His death at the Battle of Franklin in November 1864 was a tragic loss to the South.

Quite often the contemporary misspellings of a name are a good indicator of how it was pronounced. In the case of Cleburne various records using "Clai-" and "Clay-" in the first part of the name seem to support the **KLAY-burn** pronouncer.[53] Since Cleburne was from Ireland he undoubtedly pronounced his name the Irish way, but eventually went along with the American corruption of the name that was closest to the original Irish. If I were to choose an alternate to the American pronunciation it would be **kluh-BURN. KLEE-burn**, however, is a variation of the name that bears very little phonetic relation to the original.

Clough -(kluff)

as in Joseph Messer Clough, Colonel, 18th New Hampshire Volunteers.

Born in Sunapee, New Hampshire, Joseph Clough was a machinist and mill operator before the Civil War. Clough started out the war as lieutenant of the 1st New Hampshire, then became captain of the 4th New Hampshire which participated in coastal operations in the Carolinas early in the war. He eventually became colonel of the 18th New Hampshire and was brevetted brigadier general in March 1865 for gallant and meritorious services.

After the war, Clough returned to New Hampshire and worked as a railway mail agent and also farmed. He lived until 1919.[54] There are Cloughs living in New Hampshire to this day.

<u>Cluseret</u> -(kloo-zuh-RAY)

as in Gustae Paul <u>Cluseret</u>, Brigadier General U.S.V.

French born Gustave Cluseret arrived in the United States in January 1862. Cluseret was educated at St. Cyr (sahn-SEER), the West Point of France. He was made a chevalier of the Legion of Honor for his courageous actions in the insurrection of 1848 against the Orleanist regime then in power. The balance of his French military career he served in Algeria and fought in the Crimea. Cluseret resigned his commission in 1858 to accept command of the French Legion in Garibaldi's army. This move clearly marked him a soldier of fortune. Thus, coming to America to fight in our Civil War was perfectly natural for such a man.

In March 1862 Cluseret managed to get an appointment to the staff of General George McClellan as an aide-de-camp with the rank of colonel. After a short while he transferred to the command of General John Frémont, who was becoming entangled in Stonewall Jackson's Valley Campaign at the time. Cluseret was given command of a brigade and fought with great ferocity at the Battle of Cross Keys. As a result of this exhibition of fighting ability he was rewarded with a commission as brigadier general.

It is after the conclusion of his service in the Shenandoah that Cluseret's American military career moves into the Twilight Zone. Ezra Warner, in his *Generals in Blue,* writes that as of January 1863 Cluseret was under arrest for unspecified reasons. He goes on to report that a request from General William Rosecrans to have Cluseret detailed to his command was responded to by General-in-Chief Henry Halleck with a telegram saying, "If you knew him better, you would not ask for him. You will regret the application as long as you live...."[55] This is pretty strong stuff. The plot thickens when we learn that Cluseret resigned his commission in March 1863. A year later he turned up in New York City editing a weekly that opposed the Lincoln Administration and favored John Frémont for president. After the war, in 1867, Cluseret returned to Europe, got involved in revolutionary politics in France and nearly got himself executed. Years later, when things had settled down, Cluseret served several terms in the French Chamber of Deputies. He died in 1900.

Cluseret's last name is French and is pronounced in the French manner. I included him in this dictionary because his name is liable to be mispronounced (**KLUS-uh-RET**, which sounds like a brand of candy you might buy in a movie theater).

<u>Colquitt</u> -(KOL-kwit)

as in Alfred Holt <u>Colquitt</u>, Brigadier General C.S.A.

This Georgia-born lawyer and politician graduated from Princeton in 1844. He fought in the Mexican War and was a member of the Georgia legislature and the U. S. Congress. Colquitt became colonel of the 6th Georgia in May 1861, fought in the Peninsula battles and commanded a brigade under General D. H. Hill at Antietam. He also led his brigade at Fredericksburg and Chancellorsville. He then transferred to North Carolina, once again under D. H. Hill, and later fought at Olustee in Florida. He rejoined the Army of Northern Virginia in time to fight at Cold Harbor, and commanded his brigade at the Siege of Petersburg.

Colquitt's last name is not so unusual as to demand a pronouncer. It is, in fact, pronounced exactly as it is spelled. However, there is always a possibility that someone will spot that **'Q'** in the middle of the name and put a Spanish pronunciation on it. It is for that reason I have included the general's name in the dictionary. Colquitt is a well known name in Georgia; there is even a Colquitt County.

<u>Combahee</u> -(KUM-BEE)

as in <u>Combahee</u> River, South Carolina.

The Combahee River is a name you will come across in connection with Sherman's Carolinas Campaign, which followed his March to the Sea. The Combahee is 140 miles long and is formed by the confluence of the Salkehatchie and Little Salkehatchie rivers and flows southeast into the Atlantic Ocean at St. Helena Sound.

Obviously, the spelling of the name is at odds with the pronunciation. The natural tendency upon seeing the word is to say it as **COM-bah-HEE** or **com-BAH-hee**. However, in South Carolina they drop out that **'a'** in the middle and stress both syllables. Combahee is derived from an Indian word, probably meaning "small risings."[56]

<u>Congaree</u> -(KON-guh-REE)

as in <u>Congaree</u> River, South Carolina

The Congaree River is formed by the confluence of the Broad and Saluda rivers near Columbia, South Carolina. The river is about sixty miles long and empties into Lake Marion. You are likely to come across this name while studying Sherman's Carolinas

Campaign of 1865. The name Congaree is derived from an Indian word meaning "scraping bottom."[57]

Cony -(KOH-nee)

as in Samuel Cony, Civil War-era Governor of Maine.

A lawyer-politician, who prior to the Civil War was a state legislator, probate judge and state treasurer. Cony was a prominent Democrat who split with his party during the secession crisis and became a War Democrat. His warm support of the Lincoln Administration eventually got him elected governor. He served three terms starting in 1864.

The name Cony is pronounced the same as that bizarre little extension of land on the southern coast of Brooklyn, New York that has become famous over the years for amusement parks and hot dogs. It is included in this dictionary because unlike the name Coney, as in the above mentioned Coney Island, there is no **'e'** before the final **'y.'** This can lead to some confusion and the possibility that it might be mispronounced.[58]

Corps D'Afrique -(KOR-dah-FREEK)

Federal troops under the command of General Benjamin Butler occupied New Orleans on May 1, 1862. Butler thereafter acted as military governor of the captured city. One of his more controversial moves during his administration was the raising of the first black regiments in the U. S. Army. He called them the Louisiana Native Guard or Corps D'Afrique. The 1st Louisiana Native Guards was mustered into service on September 27, 1862 and several more regiments were later raised. Before the war ended there were to be more than 150 black regiments serving in the Union army. Usually, these regiments were designated "U. S. Colored Troops." The term Corps D'Afrique was confined those regiments mustered in as Louisiana Native Guard.

Corps D'Afrique is of course a French term and its pronunciation is governed by the peculiar rules surrounding utterances in that language. One must admit, however, that Corps D'Afrique sounds lot more romantic and inspiring than "U. S. Colored Troops."

Couch -(kowch)

Darius Nash Couch, Major General U.S.V.

Darius Nash Couch is best known for his service as commander of the Second Corps, Army of the Potomac in the Fredericksburg and Chancellorsville Campaigns. He was so disgusted with Joe Hooker's performance as commander of the army at Chancellorsville he resigned his own command and spent the rest of the war in relative obscurity. Like many, many other Civil War buffs, I assumed that his last name was pronounced **kowch**, like that giant upholstered thing in your livingroom. This assumption was correct, but.

The shocking discovery that I might be mispronouncing General Couch's last name came about as a result of watching the Ken Burns Civil War extravaganza on public television. When I heard narrator David McCulloch say, "Darius **Kooch,**" I leapt to my feet and shouted triumphantly, "There you go! This guy messed up! They never get it right, do they!" My sense of superiority over this "mere film-maker" soared to new heights when I found other buffs who had noticed the same mistake. We all chortled at the sheer magnitude of Ken Burns' ignorance. After all, we knew better. Darius Couch had lived most of his postwar life in our home state. He was at one time Adjutant General of Connecticut. Yet, despite our Yankee nativity and supposedly vast knowledge of the state's history we found out that we might be wrong. Ken Burns, who, after all, did a lot research, caused us to ask questions and the answers that started coming in seemed to support his version of the general's last name.[59]

For many months the correct pronunciation of Darius Couch's name was such a mysterious thing that all mention of the man's name was dropped (not that he was mentioned all that often, anyway). Some of us took to referring to him as "Kooch-Kowch" just to play it safe, most simply avoided the whole awful subject. Finally, some checking around was done; the sort of checking that should have been done in the first place. General Couch, as it turned out, had once run for governor in the state of Massachusetts. Since he lived in the town of Taunton, Massachusetts during this time I thought it wise to check with local historians there. Lisa Compton of the Old Colony Historical Society in Taunton told me that Leonard Couch, the general's grandson lived in town well into the 20th century and pronounced his name **kowch**. She added that there had never been any question of correct pronunciation of the name until the Ken Burns series. Everyone in Taunton just assumed that Burns & Company had made a mistake.[60]

A collective sigh of relief has greeted the news that the "Kooch-Kowch Controversy" has finally been settled. We can all now resume saying the general's name again with the swaggering confidence of years past. Never again will we be vexed by riddles like whether or not a guy who spends most of the time sitting around watching Civil War videos is called a "**Kooch** Potato."

coup-de-main -(KOO-duh-MAHN)

as in "General Lee decided that a coup-de-main by Longstreet's Corps was the only way to dislodge the Federals."

According to Mark Boatner's *Civil War Dictionary*, a coup-de-main is "a sudden and vigorous attack for the purpose of instantaneously capturing a position."[61] Other definitions use phrases like, "surprise attack" and "unexpected blow." In the course of reading books about the Civil War you are bound to run into these French military terms. The generation of professional soldiers who comprised a good part of the officer's corps in both armies were heavily exposed to the Napoleonic tradition. Military theoreticians like Jomini, an officer in Napoleon's army, were widely read. This is understandable since Napoleon was the most famous military figure up to that time. His influence on theories of strategy and tactics was pervasive. In addition, he was European. Americans were intellectually and culturally insecure and almost anything European in the fields of art, literature, philosophy and military theory was considered superior to the home grown product. You might think of French military terms as the buzzwords of the 19th century military establishment.

coup d'oeil -(KOO-DOY)

as in "Stonewall Jackson's grasp of tactics and coup d'oeil are two reasons for his success in the Shenandoah Valley."

Coup d'oeil means "a comprehensive glance; literally, stroke of the eye" in French.[62] As a military term from the Civil War-era it means the ability to evaluate a situation with speed and accuracy, especially regarding terrain. For example, at the Battle of Brawner's Farm, the opening engagement of the Battle of Second Manassas, Stonewall Jackson's taking advantage of the unfinished railroad cut showed his **coup d'oeil.**

Unlike **coup-de-main**, it is not likely you are going to run into **coup d'oeil** that often in either your reading or your dealings with fellow Civil War buffs and historians. In fact, I would seriously question the intellectual modesty of anyone who used **coup d'oeil** with regularity. Those of us who have had to struggle through the ordering process at a very expensive French restaurant under the eye of an overbearing waiter will always avoid the gratuitous use of French when English will suffice. Those who don't are, quite simply, show offs. In addition, there is another good reason why **coup d'oeil** rarely gets widespread use. It has to be one of the silliest sounding phrases ever given voice to when uttered as part of an English language sentence. Imagine, your listening to this perfectly sensible statement being made by someone when suddenly they toss in **coup**

d'oeil. It completely breaks up the flow of the sentence and seems to make the speaker appear as though something had gotten caught in the his windpipe. I recommend avoiding this French phrase altogether unless you wish to have the Heimlich Maneuver performed on you by some do gooder.

The problem with **coup d'oeil** is trying to achieve the French **'oe'** sound, yet not speak fluent French. In order to truly pronounce **coup d'oeil** properly one must form one's mouth as though he were about to make the **'o'** sound while at the same time saying the **'e'** sound, as previously mentioned in the entry on Bayou Boeuf. The pronouncer I have given is the simplest way of dealing with this term and comes closest to the French pronunciation. Anyway, do you really think a French speaking person is going to slap you on the back, or give you the "high five" if you get it absolutely right? Don't hold your breath.

<u>Crapo</u> -(KRAY-poh)

as in Henry Howland <u>Crapo</u>, Civil War-era Governor of Michigan.

Born in 1804, Henry Crapo grew up in Massachusetts. He worked at a number of different occupations before becoming involved in land speculation in the newly settled middle western states. Crapo had both business and government experience when he moved to Michigan in 1858. He had already made sizable investments in lumbering and sawmill operations in Flint, Michigan prior to his move. He became Republican mayor of Flint in 1860 and Governor of Michigan in 1864. Crapo was a Radical Republican and a strong supporter of the 13th Amendment. His strong performance in office got him reelected in 1866.

The name Crapo is pronounced somewhat differently than its spelling might indicate.[63] The name derives from the French name Crapaud, which is pronounced **kra-POH,** with the emphasis on the second syllable. The Anglicized spelling of the name lends itself to the non-euphonious alternative pronunciation, **KRAP-oh**, which is both amusing and dreadful. I am more than happy to clarify this matter with the pronouncer I have given.

<u>Cruikshank</u> -(KROOK-shank)

as in Marcus Henderson <u>Cruikshank</u>, Confederate Congressman.

Prior to the Civil War, Alabamian Marcus Cruikshank was a lawyer-politician who had been a member of the Whig Party and a strong opponent of secession. However, he did lend his support to the Confederate cause when the war came and ran a saltworks during the early part of the conflict. In late 1863 he was elected representative of Alabama's 4th District in the Confederate Congress, and in February of the following year was Chairman on the Committee on Enrolled Bills. Almost from the outset Cruikshank was an anti-administration obstructionist who opposed most measures put forward by President Jefferson Davis. The only thing Cruikshank supported was the occasional peace proposal.[64]

After the war, Cruikshank resumed his legal career and became a newspaper owner. He died in 1881. Pronunciation of the name is readily obtained in any good biographical dictionary.

Cupola -(KYOO-puh-luh)

as in the cupola of the Lutheran Seminary in Gettysburg.

A cupola is defined as "a light structure on a dome or roof, serving as a belfry, lantern or belvedere."[65] Some cupolas are bigger than others. The important one, the one that most Civil War buffs are most familiar with is on the roof of the Lutheran Theological Seminary building in Gettysburg. It was from this cupola that General John Buford observed the early stages of the first day's battle, and where Robert E. Lee observed the later stages. There were other cupolas in Gettysburg at the time of the battle, many of them are still with us. There is a large cupola atop Pennsylvania Hall on the Gettysburg College campus, that was in existence during the battle. There was a cupola, as well, on the roof of the German Reformed Church at the corner of Stratton and High Streets (that one has been turned into a bell tower). Another cupola sits on the roof of Christ Lutheran Church on Chambersburg Street, as it did during the battle, and let's not forget the cupola on the roof of St. James Lutheran Church at York and South Stratton streets. When it came to bell towers and cupolas, or cupolas that were also bell towers, Gettysburg had a goodly number for a town its size in 1863.

Many of the mispronunciations of cupola sound even more amusing than the correct pronunciation. My personal favorite is **KAH-poh-la**, sort of sounds like a type of Italian ice sold by old fashioned street vendors. The other one is **KUP-ula** which sounds like a Yiddish term of endearment.

<u>Czolgosz</u> -(CHAWL-gawsh)

as in Leon <u>Czolgosz</u>, assassin of William McKinley, U. S. President and famous Civil War veteran.

O. K., I'll admit that this one is a stretch. But when you consider that William McKinley was a sergeant in the Union army at the time of the Battle of Antietam, the size of his monument on the battlefield is such a remarkable phenomenon that some mention of the man's assassin in a Civil War pronouncing dictionary seems justified.[66] Anyway, Leon Czolgosz is the only presidential assassin who is practically forgotten. His obscurity has nothing to do with his dastardly act. William McKinley was an enormously popular U. S. President. His assassination in 1901 plunged the nation into profound grief. Yet, Leon Czolgosz, the unemployed wire mill worker from Detroit who put an abrupt end to McKinley's second term as president, has faded so far into obscurity that his name is unfamiliar to most Americans. The reason for this is simple: his name.

Czolgosz is a Polish name that invites all sorts of mangled pronunciations for those of us limited to speaking English. Unlike Lee Harvey Oswald and John Wilkes Booth, who have easily understood English names, or even Charles Guiteau, with his relatively easy French name, Leon Czolgosz is one presidential assassin nobody bothers discussing because no one wants to take a stab at saying his name. The likelihood that most Americans would know that **'cz'** in the Polish language takes a **'ch'** sound, or that **'sz'** is sounded as though it were **'sh'** is very remote. Add to this the fact that **'o'** sound in Polish is pronounced like the **'a'** in "saw" and "all," and the chances that an English speaking person would get Leon's name right become next to nothing. That's too bad really, because Czolgosz was an interesting character. He was an anarchist and believed that McKinley was an enemy of the people. His inclusion in this dictionary is pure whimsy on my part. However, never overlook the possibility that you may one day be on a battlefield tour of Antietam with your round table group and upon reaching the McKinley monument you'll have the opportunity to stun and amaze the crowd by knowing how to pronounce the name of the man who shot the noble commissary sergeant who later became our 25th President.[67]

USS <u>*Carondelet*</u>

D

<u>Daguerre</u> -(dah-GAIR)

as in Louis Jacques <u>Daguerre</u>, photographic pioneer.

Louis Daguerre was dead ten years before the Civil War began. An artist by occupation, he was a scenery painter for the opera in France. Collaborating with Joseph Niepce (nee-EPS), beginning in 1829, he worked on recording permanent pictures on sensitized metal plates by the action of sunlight. Daguerre finally perfected the process in 1839. Daguerreotypes, as they came to be called, were made on a silver coated surface sensitized with iodine and developed by exposure to mercury vapor. It was a cumbersome, primitive process, but it was the birth of photography. Had it not been for Daguerre and Niepce the study of the American Civil War would have been much less interesting.

By the time the guns fired on Fort Sumter in April 1861 the Daguerreotype process was already obsolete. The invention of the collodion wet-plate process had come into use by then. Once the image was fixed on the glass plate, prints could be made on paper. Though there were still many limitations to this method it provided the American public with readily available photographic prints. Photography was a booming novelty business when the war began. By the time the war was over, it had become a medium of communication. The documentary photography of men like Mathew Brady, Alexander Gardner, George Barnard and Timothy O'Sullivan possesses as much dramatic power today as it did 130 years ago.

Daguerre is, of course, a French name (as are many of the problem names we encounter in this little work). Pronunciation usually isn't too much trouble for most people when it comes to the word, "Daguerreotype." It is when the "otype" is removed that the word becomes a bit of puzzle. I suppose it's like removing the "Donut" from "Dunkin' Donut." "Dunkin," all alone seems odd, like walking into an all night donut shop and finding no cops drinking coffee.

Dahlgren -(DAL-gren *or* DAHL-gren)

as in John Adolph Bernard Dahlgren, Rear Admiral U.S.N.

I included the admiral's name in this dictionary at the behest of a number of people. Evidently the name Dahlgren which is pretty much pronounced as it is spelled looks mysterious enough to require some sort of guidance. The first pronouncer given is the common American way of saying the name. This pronouncer would be used in most cases, especially when referring to the Dahlgren gun. The second pronouncer is closer to the original Swedish pronunciation of the name. Either pronouncer will suffice. I suspect that many people are tempted to pronounce this name, **DAWL-gren**. This is somewhat off the mark, but will still be understood as referring to the admiral, his son Ulric, or his famous gun.

John Dahlgren was born in Philadelphia while his father was posted there as Swedish Consul. His naval career spanned nearly twenty years prior to the Civil War. In 1847 he was posted to the Washington Navy Yard and while there he established the Navy's ordnance department. He also invented several different types of naval artillery. Among these creations was the smoothbore iron shell gun we are most familiar with called the "Dahlgren."

When the Civil War began Dahlgren became Chief of the Bureau of Ordnance. In the summer of 1863 he applied for sea duty and was assigned to command the South Atlantic Blockading Squadron. After the war he returned to the Bureau of Ordnance where he died of heart disease while on active duty in 1870.[68]

John Dahlgren's son, Colonel Ulric Dahlgren, did not survive the war. He was killed during the famous cavalry fiasco called the Kilpatrick-Dahlgren Raid of early 1864.

Darius -(duh-RIE-us)

as in Darius Couch, Major General U.S.V.

We have already discussed General Darius Nash Couch at some length under the entry explaining the pronunciation of his last name. However, the good general crops up again in our little dictionary, this time because of his first, or Christian name. Darius the First was king of Persia around 500 B.C., so the name had been around for awhile when Couch's parents named him. The big problem in pronouncing the name is rooted in the fact that we don't come across it that often anymore. The great temptation upon seeing the name is to say it, **DAR-i-us** or some variation of that with emphasis on the first syllable. I suspect this is because we in America have names like Darryl and Darlene and we simply assume that all names starting with **D-A-R** are pronounced the same way.[69]

<u>Deas</u> -(daze)

as in Zachariah Cantey <u>Deas</u>, Brigadier General C.S.A.

Zachariah Deas was a wealthy cotton broker in Alabama before the Civil War. Deas had fought in the Mexican War so he had some military experience when hostilities broke out between the North and South. He was commissioned colonel of the 22nd Alabama in 1861 and personally laid out more than $25,000 in gold to arm his regiment with new Enfield rifle-muskets. He fought a Shiloh, where he succeeded to brigade command and was wounded. He became a brigadier general in December 1862 and fought at Stone's River, Chickamauga and Missionary Ridge. In fact, Deas was with the Army of Tennessee right up to its virtual extermination at Franklin and Nashville under John Bell Hood in 1864. After the war Deas went back into the cotton trade and also bought a seat on the New York Stock Exchange. He died in New York City in 1882 and is buried there.

The Deas family came from Scotland and settled in South Carolina during the Colonial period. Zachariah Deas was born in Camden, South Carolina in 1819 and ended up in Alabama because his father moved the family to Mobile in 1835.[70] Pronunciation of the family name could conceivably cause problems for people who think it might be two syllables, as in "Diaz." It is interesting to note that there is a swamp in the South Carolina low country on what was originally the Deas family property called "Daisy's Swamp," a corruption of the family name.[71]

<u>DeBow</u> -(duh-BOH)

as in <u>DeBow's</u> Review.

In the years before the Civil War *DeBow's Commercial Review* was one of the most influential periodicals in the South. Established in 1846 by James Dunwoody Brownson DeBow and published in New Orleans, it was the leading journal of commerce, agriculture and secessionist politics in the South. *DeBow's* was often strident in its editorial support of slavery and Southern expansionism. After the Federal occupation of New Orleans in April 1862 DeBow moved his magazine's operations to Columbia, South Carolina. Only one issue was published during the remainder of the war. The *Review* was revived after the war, but never again exerted the influence it had had during the antebellum years. James DeBow died in 1867 and his *Review*, after a checkered career of sporadic publication, followed him to the grave in 1880.

I almost didn't use the DeBow name in his dictionary, until I realized I had heard it mispronounced on a few occasions as **duh-BOW** (to rhyme with "cow").

D'Epineuil -(DAY-pee-noy)

as in D'Epineuil's Zouaves.

D'Epineuil's Zouaves, officially known as the 53rd New York Infantry, was the creation of one Lionel Jobert D'Epineuil. D'Epineuil is variously described as a confidence man, trickster and scoundrel, depending on which source you read. He was a recent immigrant to New York when the Civil War began. He conned Federal authorities into believing that he had had many years experience in the French army and got permission to raise a regiment of Frenchmen. "D'Epineuil's Zouaves" was a mixture of ethnic groups. Drinking and brawling seemed to be the main combat skills the outfit possessed. Colonel D'Epineuil turned out to be a fraud who had no military experience. He was scheduled for court martial on a number of charges.[72] The trial, however, never took place and D'Epineuil fades from the records. General George McClellan ordered the regiment disbanded in February 1862. Colonel D'Epineuil and the 53rd New York are just one of those bizarre footnotes to Civil War history.

D'Epineuil is a French name, and pronunciation is approximated to accommodate the rules of that language. The **'euil'** ending of the name is pronounced in French with a sound that is difficult for English speakers to emulate. Thus, I resorted to a more practical and pronounceable phonetic re-spelling. I could find no one in the Civil War history business who would venture a definitive pronunciation of this name. Using the French pronunciation is accurate and reasonably close to the way the colonel himself probably said it.

Des Arc -(DEZ-ARK)

as in Des Arc, Arkansas.

Situated along White River in east central Arkansas, Des Arc was captured by Federal forces on January 13, 1863. This was part of a Federal expedition up the White River which continued until January 19 and led to the capture of a number of Arkansas towns. Only a few days before the expedition up White River, the Army of the Mississippi under Major General John McClernand captured Fort Hindman at Arkansas Post on the Arkansas River.

Des Arc is not one the those names you will come across that frequently in your Civil War studies. But if you do, you want to be able to pronounce it correctly. As you can see, it is one of those French names. In French it would be pronounced, **day-ZARK**, or something along that line involving much use of the pharynx and resonating of the sinuses. The American pronunciation is not too far removed from the French, we've just eliminated all the phlegm.[73]

DeSaussure -(DES-suh-soh *or* DES-suh-SOH)

as in William Davie DeSaussure, Colonel, 15th South Carolina.

William DeSaussure was born and raised in Columbia, South Carolina. Prior to the Civil War he was a lawyer, but he was also an off again, on again professional soldier. He fought during the Mexican War and achieved the rank of captain and then did a stint in the South Carolina state legislature. In 1855 he rejoined the army and served until 1861 as a captain with the First Cavalry. With the coming of the war he became colonel of the 15th South Carolina. At the Battle of Gettysburg he fought as part of Kershaw's Brigade in McLaws' Division and was killed in the second day's fighting.

Colonel DeSaussure's loss was mourned by his comrades, who felt his military talents were equal to those of his brigade commander Joe Kershaw. DeSaussure was called by some the "Bayard of South Carolina."[74]

Given the immense popularity of the Battle of Gettysburg among Civil War buffs, in any extensive reading on the subject DeSaussure's name is bound to turn up. DeSaussure is one of those Huguenot names that are so often associated with South Carolina. Obviously, the South Carolinians started pronouncing these names there own way a long time ago. Thus, DeSaussure, as it is most often pronounced, bears very little resemblance to the original French. The only variation to the pronunciation I have given for this name is **DES-suh-SOH**. This second pronouncer merely gives equal stress to the first and last syllables. It is simply an alternate way of pronouncing the name, but not a substantial alteration.[75]

DeTrobriand -(duh-TROH-bri-AHN)

as in Philippe Regis Denis de Keredern DeTrobriand, Brigadier General U.S.V.

General DeTrobriand was born a French aristocrat. His father was a baron, but young Phil was not in line to inherent the old man's title and, as a result, he decided to make his own way in the world. After studying at the Universities of Tours (toor) and

Poitiers (pwah-TYAY) he became a lawyer. DeTrobriand, however, was a romantic soul and in addition to practicing law, he wrote poetry and even published a novel. While visiting the United States in 1841 he met and married an American heiress named Mary Jones (what a nice sensible name!). The newly married couple settled in New York City where DeTrobriand wrote and edited various French language publications. He became a citizen in 1861. When the war came he got an appointment as colonel of the 55th New York.

DeTrobriand turned out to be a very good soldier and he rose in rank quickly. His career in the Army of the Potomac is an exceptional one: He fought in the Peninsula Campaign as part of Erasmus Keyes' Fourth Corps, commanded a brigade of the Third Corps at Fredericksburg, Chancellorsville and Gettysburg. He performed competently and gallantly in all these engagements. He was commissioned brigadier general in January 1864 and assigned to divisional command in the Second Corps. He fought with the Army of the Potomac all the way to Appomattox Court House.

After the war DeTrobriand stayed in the army, accepting a regular commission as colonel. He retired in 1879 as colonel of the 13th U. S. Infantry. He wrote one of the better histories of the Army of the Potomac in the years after the war. The book, *Four Years With the Army of the Potomac,* published in 1889, still makes good reading and is considered a valuable source. General DeTrobriand died at his summer home in Bayport, Long Island in 1897 and is buried there.

Philippe DeTrobriand's last name is a long and complex one. Sounding it out is relatively simple, however, deciding which syllable, or set of syllables, is stressed is another matter. Pronouncers are readily available in a number of standard references, *Lippincott's Universal Pronouncing Dictionary* (the bulky 1915 Fourth Edition) and *The Century Dictionary & Cyclopedia, Volume IX* to name two of the older ones.

de Vecchi -(duh-VEK-kee)

as in Achille de Vecchi, Captain, 9th Massachusetts Battery.

Because of the fame achieved by the 9th Massachusetts Battery under the command of Captain John Bigelow at the Battle of Gettysburg, Achille de Vecchi has become an obscure footnote to Civil War history. Nonetheless, the man's name does turn up in books and magazine articles.

Captain Achille (ah-KEEL-ee) de Vecchi was the first commander of the Ninth Independent Battery, Massachusetts Light Artillery. The unit was formed in July 1862, mustered into Federal service in August and assigned to the Washington defenses in September. The men were well trained by de Vecchi, who was on a leave of absence from the Italian Army. Some sort of friction must have developed between the Massachusetts men and the Italian captain, because morale in battery was bad. In

January 1863 de Vecchi resigned and John Bigelow took over as commander.[76] There are no arcane sources for finding out how to pronounce the name de Vecchi. It is an Italian name, Captain de Vecchi was from Italy, and Italian names are pronounced a certain way.

Dilger -(DIL-gur)

as in Hubert Dilger, Captain U.S.V.

Captain Hubert Dilger, known affectionately as "Old Leatherbreeches" by his men, may have been one of the best artillerists the Army of the Potomac had. Dilger was courageous to the point of foolhardiness, though much admired by his commanders. He was known as a "man who fought his guns at times as though they were pistols."[77] Dilger, a native German, wore leather breeches into battle, thus his nickname.[78] Attached to Company I of the First Ohio Light Artillery, part of Carl Schurz's Division of the Eleventh Corps, Dilger performed heroically at the Battle of Chancellorsville.

Having heard rumors all afternoon on May 2, 1863 that the Federal right flank, manned by the Eleventh Corps, was about to be attacked by Confederates he decided to check out the situation personally. Riding west of the Eleventh Corps position with an orderly he ran into the troops of Stonewall Jackson. After managing a hair's breadth escape, he headed back to corps headquarters at top speed. Once there, he was sent along to Hooker's headquarters at Chancellorsville where he reported his findings to a cavalry major who found the intelligence laughable and refused to let Dilger see the General. There is no record of the identity of this cavalry major, which is too bad as his name might have become a word synonymous with the behavior of a jackass.

When Jackson's attack struck, the Eleventh Corps line was quickly routed. Dilger's Battery, posted near the Wilderness Church, did not join the retreat but maintained its position, pouring canister into the oncoming Rebels. The Confederates came within eighty yards of Dilger before he ordered the battery limbered up. After withdrawing a short distance, the battery stopped and again began firing at Jackson's advancing hordes. Despite this heroic effort, the Confederate advance continued and eventually overwhelmed all opposition, including Dilger's. Many years after the war Dilger was awarded the Medal of Honor for his efforts at Chancellorsville.

Pronunciation of Hubert Dilger's last name is a relatively simple matter if one realizes that the letter **'g'** is almost always given a hard pronunciation in the German language. There is a tendency amongst English speakers to pronounce the name as **DIL-jur**, with the soft **'g.'**

Duffié -(DOO-fee-YAY)

as in Alfred Napoleon Alexander Duffié, Brigadier General U.S.V.

French born "Nattie" Duffié was a professional soldier prior to coming to America in 1859. The son of a French count, he was a graduate of the military college of St. Cyr (SAN-SEER) and served with the cavalry in Algiers, Senegal, the Crimea, and Italy. Duffié won several decorations for valor in the Crimea and in 1859 was wounded at the Battle of Solferino. It was while he was recovering from this wound that he took a leave of absence from the French army and came to the United States. While he was here, he met and married the daughter of a wealthy and prominent family from Staten Island, New York (Hey, maybe it really was love).

With the outbreak of the Civil War, Duffié resigned his commission in the French army and received a commission as captain in the 1st New Jersey Cavalry, he then transferred to the 2nd New York Cavalry (also known as the Harris Light Cavalry). By July of 1862 he was colonel of the 1st Rhode Island Cavalry. Duffié was a very competent cavalryman and under his guidance the 1st Rhode Island became a first class outfit.[79]

Duffié fought with distinction at Second Manassas, and his performance at Kelly's Ford in March 1863 led to his promotion to brigadier general in June of that year. Eventually, he commanded a cavalry division under Alfred Pleasonton at Brandy Station. After that he transferred to operations in West Virginia and saw service under Franz Sigel and David Hunter. In the autumn of 1864 Duffié was captured by Confederate partisans at Bunker Hill, Virginia. He was finally paroled in February 1865 but never again received an important assignment. His capture incurred the wrath of the unforgiving General Philip Sheridan who wanted Duffié dismissed from the service.

In the postwar years Duffié served as U. S. Consul in Cadiz, Spain. He died in 1880 and is buried in Staten Island.

Pronunciation of Duffié's last name is in the French manner. I have included it in this dictionary for the same reason I have included certain other foreign names. In researching Duffié's name I ran into a surprising number people, some of them in the history business, who pronounced the name **doo-FEE** or **doo-FAY**. If there were no acute accent over the final **'e'** there would be a good case for **doo-FEE,** and if the final two letters were **'ee'** with no accent over either letter a case could be made for **doo-FAY**. The fact that the name ends with **'ié'** with an accent over that final **'e'** changes everything, at least in the French language.

Dumfries -(DUM-freez)

as in Dumfries, Virginia.

Just after Christmas in 1862 Confederate cavalryman Jeb Stuart conducted one of those raids he was famous for, and for fame often undertook. Taking advantage of the demoralized and idle Army of the Potomac after its ignominious defeat at Fredericksburg, Stuart led 1,800 horsemen on a raid of Federal supply bases. Stuart hoped to interrupt the flow of supplies to General Ambrose Burnside's army and also cause him to detach troops to pursue the raiders. On December 27th Stuart's cavalry ran into unexpectedly strong opposition by Federals at Dumfries, Virginia twenty-two miles north of Fredericksburg. It is this engagement that gives the raid its name.

The name Dumfries is taken from that of a county in southern Scotland. In Scotland the name is pronounced **dum-FREESS** with the emphasis on the second syllable. I found out, however, from the folks at the Dumfries, Virginia town hall that visitors from Scotland, they have encountered, pronounce it pretty much the same way they do. Since time and budget constraints prevent me from going to Scotland to find out what "pretty much the same" means, I will offer no opinions. Dumfries, Virginia was originally settled by Scottish immigrants and during the 18th century was a thriving tobacco port just off the Potomac River on Quantico Creek. The growth of other towns with better harbors and the build up of silt in the harbor bottom sent Dumfries into decline by the end of the colonial period. The 1882 edition of *Lippincott's Pronouncing Gazetteer of the World* describes the town as "a decayed post-village of Prince William Co., Va...It has 2 churches and was formerly a shipping port. Pop. 167." A much improved Dumfries survives to this day.

Duryée -(dur-YAY)

as in Abram Duryée, Brigadier General U.S.V.

Abram Duryée was a wealthy New Yorker and mahogany importer prior to the Civil War. He was extremely active in the local militia until 1859, so much so that he reached the rank of colonel. Duryée got to see some combat before the Civil War in the form of the Astor Place Riot of May 10, 1849. He was wounded twice during this black day in the history of New York City.[80]

When the Civil War came Abram Duryée raised a regiment that became known as "Duryée's Zouaves." This elaborately dressed, well drilled, well equipped outfit was mustered into Federal service as the 5th New York and saw its first fighting in one of the war's earliest engagements, Big Bethel. Duryée was promoted to the rank of brigadier general in August 1861 and assigned to training duty. He did his job well, but was anxious to get an active field command. He was finally made a brigade commander in Ricketts' Division of McDowell's Third Corps during the Second Manassas Campaign. Duryée was wounded twice during Second Manassas, and three more times during the Antietam Campaign. He took some well earned leave at this point, but when he returned to duty after a 30-day absence was disappointed to find a junior officer had been promoted over him to division command. He resigned in January 1863.

After the war, Duryée served in various municipal offices in the City of New York, including Police Commissioner and city dockmaster. He died in 1890. On the whole, Duryée was a very competent civilian soldier who apparently couldn't crack the West Point Old Boys Network.

The name Duryée presents some pronunciation problems for those not familiar with the name. That double 'e' at the end, plus the accent mark on the first 'e' could be a source of confusion.

D'Utassy -(doo-TASSY)

as in Frederick George D'Utassy, Colonel, 39th New York Volunteers.

Frederick D'Utassy was described by contemporary journalist Henry Villard as "nothing but a swaggering pretender."[81] Villard was probably right about this mysterious soldier of fortune who showed up in New York when the Civil War broke out. D'Utassy, according to himself: was of Hungarian birth, had served in the Austrian army, then became involved in 1848 revolution that swept Hungary and the rest of Europe. Wounded and taken prisoner, D'Utassy continues, he escaped and finally ended up in Constantinople where he did a spell in the Turkish cavalry. From there he went to Greece and worked for the British authorities as an interpreter. After a time, he made it to America where his reduced circumstances forced him to teach fencing and foreign languages in order to earn a living.[82] General George McClellan had his own opinion of this character. The Young Napoleon claimed that D'Utassy was a onetime rider in the Franconi Circus whose real name was Strasser. What all this adds up to is that D'Utassy's real background is probably an unsolvable mystery. One thing is certain, he was a superb confidence man.

D'Utassy was colonel of the 39th New York, better known as the "Garibaldi Guard." The Garibaldi Guard was one of those ethnic regiments that were raised early in the war. Unlike the Irish and German regiments, the 39th New York was a polyglot agglomeration of ethnics. In the ranks of this "picturesque collection of foreign scamps"[83] were Hungarians, Swiss, Germans, French, Italians, Spanish, Croats, Sepoys, Cossacks and a few English deserters. It was also claimed that Sicilian robbers and murderers were included in the ranks. Whatever the exact ethnic makeup may have been, the

Garibaldi Guard was formed in May of 1861. By the end of the month they were encamped at the nation's capital, and by July they were part of Louis Blenker's brigade.

Meanwhile, Colonel D'Utassy was having problems. In a regiment where more than six languages were spoken, a breakdown in communication was bound to result, not to mention a loss of unit cohesion. There were rivalries between officers of different ethnic companies, there were charges of ethnic prejudice, there were also ugly rumors that D'Utassy was mishandling regimental funds. During the Battle of Manassas on July 21, 1861 the regiment was held in reserve and didn't see any fighting. Back in camp, after the Union defeat, the 39th New York resumed its constant infighting. In September of 1862, during the Antietam Campaign, the 39th was captured by Stonewall Jackson's forces at Harpers Ferry. The captives were immediately paroled.

D'Utassy's troubles, however, were only beginning. In December an investigation by the War Department was begun to look into mishandling of government monies by officers of the 39th New York. Ultimately, D'Utassy was arrested, court-martialed and cashiered from the service. He was sent to Sing Sing prison in the spring of 1863, spent a year and disappeared after his release. D'Utassy resurfaced again in Cincinnati, Ohio in the mid-1870s working as a manager for the Phoenix Insurance Company. In 1891 he moved to Baltimore, Maryland to work at the Phoenix operation there. He died in Wilmington, Delaware on May 2, 1892, his body found in a gas filled hotel room. The local coroner determined the death was accidental.[84] A strange ending for an even stranger character. As for the 39th New York, under a new commander, the regiment eventually straightened out and managed to get through the rest of war.

Pronunciation of D'Utassy's name presents some unique difficulties. In the first place, the name is probably made up. Assuming his real name was Strasser, probably an Austrian name, it appears that the good colonel Italianized it. Whether he did this while in Europe or after arriving in the United States is not known. Since the name looks sort of Italian, the best I can do for a pronouncer is one that is sort of Italian too. Research continues on this one. I have included the name in this dictionary because D'Utassy's story is too good to pass up.

Rear Admiral
John Adolph Bernard Dahlgren

Major General
Darius Couch

E

Eads -(eedz)

as in James Buchanan Eads, engineer, Civil War boat-builder.

One of the more remarkable engineers to appear on the American scene in the 19th century was James Eads. If he is remembered at all today it is because of the Eads Bridge, one of many that crosses the Mississippi River in St. Louis. The Eads Bridge wasn't always just another river crossing. When it was completed in 1874 it was considered one of the engineering marvels of the age.

Producing marvels was something James Eads seemed to do with relative ease. Born in Indiana in 1820, his family moved to St. Louis when he was thirteen years old. Young James quit school early on to help out with family finances. One of his earliest jobs was selling apples on the street. From apple selling he went on to become a dry goods clerk at the establishment of Williams & Durings. While working at the store he caught the eye of Mr. Williams who let the boy use his personal library. Eads studied hard and by 1838 he became the purser on a river boat. One of the things Eads noticed about life on the big river was the number of boats lost. Recognizing an opportunity here for a bright young man, he developed a diving bell in his spare time and by 1842 had given up his purser's job and gone into the steamboat salvaging business. He was very successful. By 1857 Eads had amassed a fortune, and thanks to his study of hydraulics and his experience with riverboats, knew more about the Mississippi than almost anyone alive.[85]

When the Civil War came the Federal government was in a big hurry to gain control of the western rivers, especially the Mississippi. This meant that boats were needed fast, especially the newly developed ironclads. Eads contracted with the government to build seven ironclads, 900 tons each, in sixty-five days, a nearly impossible undertaking. However, James Eads was as good as his word and delivered the first boat, the *St. Louis*, in just sixty-six days with the other six following in quick succession. During the course of the war Eads constructed fourteen armored gunboats, converted seven transports into "tinclads" and built four heavy mortar boats.

Of course, anyone who is from St. Louis will know immediately how the name *Eads* is pronounced. However, those of us from other parts of the republic may not be all that familiar with it. I conducted my own survey on the *Eads* name, with a random selection of Civil War buffs at a recent conference, to pronounce the famous engineer's name. The results were mixed (meaning, that I didn't bother doing a statistical profile of correct and incorrect answers) and most of those who got it wrong pronounced the name as "**adz**" rhymes with "**cads.**" This confirmed my opinion that inclusion in this dictionary was called for. Pronouncers are in abundant supply in standard reference works, not to mention residents of St. Louis.

Edisto -(**ED-is-TOE**)

as in Edisto Island, South Carolina.

This is one of those entries you may be looking at and saying, "What! I can't believe I've had this one wrong all these years!" Well, that was my reaction too when I first discovered that **ed-IS-toe** or **eh-DIS-toe** was dead wrong. Edisto Island is a fifty-four-square-mile chunk of land that sits at the mouth of the Edisto River in southeast South Carolina. The island is part of the Atlantic Ocean coastline of the state.

No great battle or engagement took place at Edisto Island, but it was occupied off and on, early in the war by Union troops and there were skirmishes there from time to time. However, both Edisto Island and the Edisto River are important reference points to know the pronunciation of for those of us who study Civil War history. Another important geographic point to remember is that Edisto Island is one of the so-called "Sea Islands" that run in a chain off the coasts of South Carolina and Georgia, noted for the production of sea island cotton.

Pronunciation of Edisto didn't seem to be a problem that required an entry in this dictionary. It was then that I discovered in the course of my research that my assumption was wrong. Quite by accident, I came across an entry for "Edisto" in the Claude and Irene Neuffer (NIFE-ur) book I was using to look up something else. The Neuffers are experts on words concerning South Carolina, and they say in their book, *Correct Mispronunciations of Some South Carolina Names*, that they have found the name "Edisto" mispronounced in their own state! I didn't feel so stupid after that.

Egloffstein -(**EG-lahf-SHTIEN**)

as in Frederick Wilhelm von Egloffstein, Colonel U.S.V.

Colonel Egloffstein was a baron and prior to the Civil War was a topographical artist in his native Germany. During the war he became colonel of the 103rd New York, which fought at South Mountain and Antietam, as well as being part of Sherman's March. Egloffstein was breveted brigadier general for his services in the conflict and after the war returned to Germany. Here he became a engraver and also developed the half-tone process of engraving.[86]

Von Egloffstein is a German name, of course. Pronouncing the **'st'** in **'stein'** with the **'sch'** sound is proper, however, just saying it as **stine** will suffice.[87]

Ely -(EE-lee)

as in Ely's Ford on the Rapidan River.

Ely's Ford, a shallow crossing spot on the Rapidan River, figures prominently in both the Battles of Chancellorsville and The Wilderness. The ford was used by elements the Army of the Potomac as it moved south in the opening phases of the spring campaigns of 1863 and 1864. The Ely family farm was situated just south of the ford, thus the source of the historic river crossing's name.

Usually, the name "Ely" does not present too much difficulty for people. The rule of thumb that applies to the name is that it is pronounced **EE-lee** when it applies to a place, and **EE-lie** when it is a given name, in most cases. Park Service personnel and historians give this as the correct pronunciation at the Fredericksburg-Spotsylvania National Military Park.

Elon -(EE-lon)

as in Elon John Farnsworth, Brigadier General U.S.V.

One of more unnecessary tragedies of the Battle of Gettysburg was the death of Elon Farnsworth. After the failure of the Pickett-Pettigrew Charge on the afternoon of July 3, 1863 cavalry division commander Judson Kilpatrick thought he saw an opportunity to further disrupt Robert E. Lee's fragmented lines. He ordered newly minted Brigadier General Elon Farnsworth to attack Longstreet's position on the Confederate right flank. Farnsworth, quite properly, protested the attack as suicidal. Kilpatrick insisted and as a result Farnsworth was killed.

Elon Farnsworth was from Michigan. His only pre-war experience was as a civilian foragemaster with Albert Sidney Johnston's Mormon Expedition. When the war came he enlisted in the 8th Illinois Cavalry and by the end of 1861 was a captain. Farnsworth served with distinction in the 8th Illinois as well as on the staff of General Alfred Pleasanton. His sudden promotion from captain to brigadier general on June 29, 1863 was probably because his uncle John Farnsworth, former colonel of the 8th Illinois

Cavalry, was at that time a powerful member of the U. S. House of Representatives. Elon Farnsworth was a general for less than a week when he was killed.

The name Elon is an odd one. For many years I was calling this guy **EE-lon** and was never really sure I was right. It sounded wrong, but there was no other way to pronounce the word, short of making up sounds that weren't there. As it turned out, I was correct all along.[88] Elon is a biblical name and according to *Nelson's Bible Dictionary*, "the name of three men and one town in the Old Testament" is Elon. Pronunciation for the name Elon is given as "EE-lahn" in *Nelson's*.[89]

enfilade -(EN-fuh-LAYD)

Most people tend to think of the word "enfilade" as a verb when in fact much of the time it is used as a noun. In its most strictly dictionary defined sense enfilade means, "a position of works, troops, etc., making them subject to a sweeping fire from along the length of a line of troops, a trench, a battery, etc."[90] The fire thus directed is "enfilade fire." Like many dictionary definitions it seems to shed light on the subject, but in reality creates more darkness than light. So, the key to understanding this word lies in the category of "parts of speech." If we define enfilade as a verb transitive rather than a noun, we come up with, "To fire or be in a position to fire down the length of a trench or a column of troops." There.

During the Civil War, as in many other wars, getting into a position where you could subject your enemy to enfilade fire was most definitely to your advantage. Linear tactics being what they were, a column of troops, deployed in line of battle, facing a charging enemy in one direction could not easily be turned. Should the charging enemy overlap the end or flank of the column they could direct fire down the length of the column, causing the flank to give way.

Pronunciation of enfilade is no great mystery. Most sources use the long **'a'** in the last syllable. However, a few dictionaries list **EN-fuh-LAHD** as an alternate pronunciation. Nothing wrong with this. It's sort of like the lyrics from that old song that go, "you say tuh-MAY-toe, I say tuh-MAH-toe."

Enroughty -(en-RUFF-tee *or* DAR-bee)

as in Darbytown Road.

For those of you wondering whether the pronouncers given above are a misprint or some sort of incredible writing error, let me assure you they are not. During the Seven Days' Battles on the Virginia Peninsula in 1862 both sides in the conflict were plagued with inadequate maps of the area. Confederate Major General John Magruder ran into serious problems because of this during the Battle of Glendale (or White Oak Swamp) on June 30, 1862. Specifically, the problems Magruder had concerned two names that were used interchangeably.

Ordered to send reinforcements to Major General Theophilus Holmes, who was heavily engaged with Porter's Fifth Corps on Turkey Run in the Malvern Hill area, Magruder became lost. The maps showed that a family named "Enroughty" lived on several farms in the area. Since roads were mostly unmarked, farms made for a handy way of referencing the map. However, the only family farms Magruder ran into were owned by people who called themselves "Darby." In fact, one of the main roads in the area was called "Darbytown Road." Magruder lost a lot of valuable time seeking the farms of the Enroughty family only to discover that he had, unknowingly, already located them.

Thus, here is Enroughty's Conundrum; the Enroughty family pronounced their name "Darby." Because of some arcane inheritance dispute many years before, the Enroughty family was forced to adopt the name Darby. But the Enroughtys were a proud and stubborn lot and insisted that "Darby" be spelled as though it were Enroughty. That is one version of why there is such confusion over this name. I found another, even more complex, explanation in J. N. Hook's, *The Book of Names.* According to Dr. Hook, after H. L. Mencken published *The American Language* in 1919 he received a letter from one F. W. Sydnor who told him about the confusion caused by the Enroughty name in Virginia. When Mencken published his *American Language: Supplement II* in 1948 he included Sydnor's information as follows:

> "The records show one **Darby Enroughty** (pronounced En-ruff-tee) to have been living near Fourteen Mile creek in 1690. He had a son named **John** and one named **Darby.** Later there were two **John Enroughtys** living in the same locality, cousins, whose name was frequently found in the records. Double Christian names were rarely used in those days, and it became necessary to distinguish between the two **Johns**. **John Enroughty**, the son of **John**, was known by his Christian name, but **John,** the son of **Darby Enroughty**, was designated **John Enroughty the son of Darby,** and at least once as **John Darby**. The **Enroughtys** of Henrico and those known as **Darby** (real name **Enroughty**) are all descendants of **Darby Enroughty**. Those bearing the name **Enroughty** are the descendants of his son **John**, and those bearing the name of **Darby** are the descendants of his son **Darby.**"

Frankly, I would tend to believe Mencken's information. If you read it several times, very slowly, preferably aloud, it will start to make some kind of sense to you. Now, many of you may be wondering how all this knowledge of the Enroughty-Darby riddle will contribute to your understanding of the American Civil War. The answer is that it won't. However, picture yourself at a Civil War conference when the question of the Darbytown Road comes up, assuming it does. You may be the only person there with a complete explanation, an explanation that will make the eyes of all within your hearing glaze over.

Erysipelas -(ER-uh-SIP-uh-lus)

Erysipelas is defined as "an acute, febrile infectious disease, caused by a specific streptococcus, characterized by diffusely spreading deep-red inflammation of the skin or mucous membranes."[91] During the Civil War, this hospital disease had a mortality rate of forty percent. It was thought that it might be airborne, so victims of the affliction were isolated from the other wounded in separate wards or tents.[92] The only treatment for erysipelas was to paint iodine around the edges of the wound, which seemed to prevent its spreading. Erysipelas was just one more horror in the Grand Guignol that was Civil War medicine.

However, to be fair and accurate, there was much that was commendable about medical treatment in the 1860s. The use of anesthetic was new at that time, and it undoubtedly saved many lives. In addition, many surgical techniques were developed during the war that also saved lives. Unfortunately, the picture that remains with most of us who have studied the Civil War extensively is the one showing piles of amputated limbs lying next to the field hospital tent. War is still the same bloody shambles it always was, but the medical treatment has made remarkable strides.

Esten -(ES-ten)

as in John Esten Cooke, Southern writer.

John Esten Cooke is not remembered because of any military exploits he performed during the Civil War. A friend and relative of General Jeb Stuart, he served as an ordinance officer on Stuart's staff. His fame comes about as result of his role as Boswell to Stuart's Dr. Johnson. Cooke was a writer, the type of writer who, had he lived today, would write the sort of novels Danielle Steele churns out. Unlike the glitzy, blow dried heroes and heroines who slither through Steele's novels, Cooke's protagonists are the bold dragoons of Stuart's Cavalry. Indiscriminately blending fact and fiction, Cooke wrote wartime columns for the *Southern Illustrated News.* He also wrote a biography of Stonewall Jackson shortly after Jackson's death in 1863 and several other books and articles that lionized his hero, Jeb Stuart. After the war, his two novels, *Surry of Eagle's Nest* and *Mohun* sold quite well.

The tendency I have found among people in pronouncing Cooke's middle name is to say it as, **EAS-ten**, as one would pronounce Easton, Pennsylvania. Perhaps the absence of the letter **'a'** between the **'E'** and the **'s'** in the name is automatically filled in by people. This is understandable, since Esten appears somewhat incomplete. Just one of those things.

Ewell -(yool)

as in Richard Stoddart Ewell, Lieutenant General C.S.A.

Undoubtedly there are many of you, if not most, who know how to pronounce this not uncommon name. However, as a boy I had problems with it and found that I had a tendency to say "**E-well.**" The reason for this was my lack of familiarity with the name, but also the perfectly sensible assumption that most words are pronounced as they are spelled. As you can see, I was new to the fine points of the English language and didn't realize that logic and common sense have no place in it. Anyway, for that reason I have included Dick Ewell's name in the dictionary. After all, there may be new Civil War buffs out there who need to be shown the proper way.

Richard Ewell was a corps commander in Lee's Army of Northern Virginia. He is an important enough figure in Civil War history to have had a book or two written about him alone, so I will not attempt to capsulize his career in this book. Suffice it say, if you seek information on General Ewell you will find it in abundance in many books.

Evander -(i-VAN-dur)

as in Evander McIvor Law, Brigadier General C.S.A.

General Law was educated at the Citadel in South Carolina and after graduating in 1856 taught at a military school he helped found in Tuskegee, Alabama. When the war broke out he raised a company of troops and was elected lieutenant colonel of the 4th Alabama. Law fought in every major campaign of the Army of Northern Virginia until the final year of the war. He was wounded at Cold Harbor and after recovering, commanded a force of cavalry in the army of Joseph E. Johnston in the Carolinas campaign of 1865.

Evander Law's moment of limelight in the history books comes about at Gettysburg. Law was a brigade commander in Hood's Division and held a key position on the extreme right of the Confederate line on the second day of the big battle. It was Law's Brigade that attacked the Union left at Little Round Top and became an unwitting accomplice to the 20th Maine's rise to fame and glory. After the war, Law became prominent in establishing the educational system of the state of Florida. Law was a journalist who wrote many postwar articles on Civil War campaigns and was a big-shot in the United Confederate Veterans. He lived until 1920.

General Law's first name was almost as big a source of fascination as his middle for me over the years. I always thought the name had a nice flow to it. However, like many buffs I was unsure of the correct pronunciation of his first name. Had I been a professional boxing fan I would have known the pronunciation of the name immediately since Evander Holyfield, a prize fighter of some repute, has been prominent in television sports coverage in recently.

Lieutenant General Richard Stoddart Ewell

F

Fascine -(fuh-SEEN)

as in, "The bristling tops of numerous fascines made the fortification look treacherous."

A fascine is basically a long bundle of sticks bound together and used to reinforce earthworks. Fascines were usually buried inside the earth wall to reinforce the interior slope of the parapet. Thus, the fascine acted as a substitute for the sandbag.

The word is French, derived from the Latin, "fascis," meaning bundle or pack.

Fauquier -(FAW-keer)

as in Fauquier County, Virginia.

Incredible as it may seem, for one of the largest counties in Northern Virginia, no major battle of the Civil War took place in Fauquier County! Neighboring Prince William County hosted First and Second Manassas, Stafford County boasts Fredericksburg and Culpeper County had Brandy Station and Cedar Mountain. To be sure, there were plenty of engagements in Fauquier County and the opposing armies went back and forth across the county many times during the war, but still, no major battle. Like many of Virginia's counties, Fauquier County was named after one of the state's more popular governors. Francis Fauquier was one of last colonial governors of Virginia; he died in 1769.

Fauquier is a French word and unless you are familiar with either the name, or the French language you are going to have serious trouble with it. It is, after all, one of those words which if mispronounced can make you sound very foolish, or get you arrested. Pronunciation guides are available in a number of reference books. I also checked with several residents of that part of Virginia and NPS personnel. An acceptable variation on the pronouncer I have given above might be **FAW-kee-ur.**

Fessenden -(FESS-en-den)

as in William Pitt, Francis and James Deering Fessenden, U.S.

The Fessenden family of Maine figured prominently in some aspects of our country's Civil War history: William Pitt Fessenden, born 1806, was in the U. S. Senate, while his two sons, Francis and James Deering were generals in the field during the war. Senator Fessenden, who left the Whig Party in the 1850s to help found the Republican Party, was an expert on public finance. As a member of the Senate Finance Committee he was a self appointed watchdog of excessive Federal spending during the war. He was appointed Secretary of the Treasury by President Lincoln after Salmon Chase's appointment to be Chief Justice of the Supreme Court. The senator's two sons had good war records, both reaching the rank of general.

Francis Fessenden was a graduate of both Bowdoin College and Harvard. Before the war he was a lawyer. Francis spent the early part of the war on garrison duty and eventually saw active service at Shiloh under Major General Don Carlos Buell. After he recovered from a wound he received there he was appointed colonel of the 25th Maine and served in the Washington defenses. He was mustered out of the volunteer service in July 1863 then reactivated again in January 1864. Fessenden ended up taking part in Nathaniel Banks' Red River Campaign, where he was again wounded; this time it cost him his right leg. He was promoted first to brigadier and then major general. Immediately after the war he served on the military commission that tried Henry Wirz, the former commandant of Andersonville. After he left Federal service in 1866 Fessenden returned to Maine to resume his law practice. He died in 1906.

His older brother, James Deering Fessenden, was also a Bowdoin College graduate and a lawyer prior to the Civil War. With the outbreak of hostilities he raised a company of sharpshooters, which became part of the 2nd U. S. Sharpshooters. In the spring of 1862 James Fessenden was appointed to the staff of General David Hunter, who was then commanding operations in the Carolinas. Fessenden organized the first regiment of black soldiers in the national service, "an action subsequently disavowed by the government."[93] After this he served under Joseph Hooker at Chattanooga and the Atlanta Campaign. He eventually ended up working for Phil Sheridan in the Shenandoah Valley and at the Battle of Cedar Creek he commanded a brigade. For the remainder of the war he served on garrison duty in Winchester, Virginia. He reached the rank of brigadier general before leaving the service. After the war, Fessenden practiced law and served in the Maine legislature. He died in 1882.

Neither of the Fessenden brothers will ever become the subject of a television mini-series, but they had nothing to be ashamed of, and plenty to brag about. Pronunciation of the name Fessenden is made difficult, for those not familiar with it, by having at least two syllables that one is tempted to emphasize. I found myself, and others, saying the name as, **fez-ZEN-den**, or **FEZ-n-DEN**, in both cases using a **'z'** sound instead of an 's,' and in both cases pronouncing it incorrectly. Several standard reference works are consistent in giving the pronouncer I used at the top of this entry.

Finis -(FIE-nis)

as in Jefferson Finis Davis, President of the Confederate States of America.

Jefferson Davis was born in Kentucky in June 1808, the tenth child of Samuel and Jane Davis. The oldest child, Joseph, was already in college when Jefferson Davis was born. Jane Davis was forty-seven years old at the time of the birth, and it was perhaps a combination of whimsy and resolve that prompted Samuel to give the child the middle name "Finis." Finis in Latin means "the end," "the conclusion." Samuel chose Jefferson for the boy's first name, in honor of Thomas Jefferson, who was then serving in the White House.[94]

Many people upon seeing this peculiar middle name pronounce it **FEE-NEE**. This is probably because they've seen a few foreign films made in France. When a French motion picture finally concludes (quite often with the enthusiastic support of its American audience) the word "finis" appears on the screen, or at least it used to. "Finis" in French means the same thing it does in Latin, the language they borrowed it from. However, the French pronounce it their own inimitable way. Since we are much more exposed to French, a language still in wide use, than to spoken Latin (even the Catholic Church dropped it), we automatically assume the "finis" is pronounced with a silent 's.' Had we all been exposed to motion pictures with a Latin soundtrack this problem would not exist. But even a Latin soundtrack would not help with Jefferson Davis' middle name. In Latin the name Finis would be pronounced **FEE-nis**. The traditional Southern pronunciation of the name, however, makes it part of a language all its own.[95]

Frémont -(fruh-MONT)

as in John Charles Frémont, Major General U.S.V.

No one is going to dispute you when you pronounce John Frémont's last name as **FREE-mont**. This is one of the commonest improper pronunciations of the man's name. There are towns and counties named after the old "Pathmarker of the West" and that is how they are often pronounced. However, for years and years, I kept noticing that accent mark over the letter **'e'** in the first syllable of the name, and for years and years it bothered me. When I began putting together this book I found that it bothered other people as well.

John Charles Frémont was born in Savannah, Georgia in 1813. Since his parents were not legally married at the time of his birth, he was an illegitimate child (remember, this was back in the days when that sort of thing meant something). General Frémont's father was a dashing and handsome French émigré named Charles Frémon (that's right, no final 't') who fell in love with a married woman while he was teaching French at an academy in Richmond, Virginia. The married woman, Frémont's future mother, Mrs. Anne Pryor finally left her husband and eloped with Charles Frémon. After moving from place to place they stayed in Savannah, Georgia for a time; long enough to have a child, John Charles. From there, they headed for Nashville and eventually ended up in Norfolk, Virginia where, apparently learning of the death of Mrs. Pryor's estranged husband, they were married. In 1818 Charles Frémon also died, leaving his young wife and three children in poverty. Evidently, economic reasons impelled Mrs. Frémon to move to Charleston, South Carolina.[96] And so, it is in Charleston that the real beginning of any biography of John Charles Frémont commences.

There is not sufficient room in this book to even capsulize the life of John Frémont. Suffice it say, he was a great explorer and a terrible Civil War general. Writer-historian Bernard DeVoto has called him "Childe Harold's American heir."[97] Charley (that's what friends and family called him) Frémont is one of those legendary figures forever attached to the story of the winning of the West.

Pronunciation of the Frémont name would be **fray-MON** in French because of the acute accent over the letter **'e'** and the unpronounced **'t'** (final consonants are usually silent in French). The Americanization of the name has led to a sort of linguistic compromise. The accented **'e'** is not pronounced as a long **'a'** but rather as an indistinct vowel. However, primary emphasis is still on the second syllable of the name.

Major General
John Charles Frémont

G

<u>Galena</u> -(guh-LEE-nuh)

as in <u>Galena,</u> Illinois or USS <u>*Galena*</u>.

Galena, Illinois was the hometown of Ulysses Grant. Grant was born in Point Pleasant, Ohio but his family finally settled, after several moves, in Galena. It was from here that Grant, the unsuccessful ex-army man who was working as a clerk in his brother's leather goods store, went off to the Civil War and into the pages of history.

The USS *Galena* was an ironclad launched in Mystic, Connecticut in February 1862. Unlike the monitor type warship, which was basically an armored raft with a revolving turret supported by a lower hull of wood, the *Galena* was a small, wooden steam driven corvette, plated with iron with a single-tier gun deck. Flag Officer Louis M. Goldsborough called her, "a most miserable contrivance."[98] The *Galena* was rigged as a schooner, with most of the masts removed and the upper portion of her sides curved inward at an angle to deflect incoming fire. Iron plates were bolted to iron bars on its sides[99] The *Galena* was far more vulnerable to getting hit by hostile fire than a monitor. This was proven beyond any doubt in May 1862 when the *Galena* steamed up the James River along with the USS *Monitor* and three other ships, and took on the Confederate battery at Drewry's Bluff. During the three hour engagement the *Galena* was struck over forty times and sustained eighteen perforations. Thirteen crew members were killed and eleven were wounded. The *Monitor* was undamaged and sustained no casualties. The *Galena's* armor plates were later removed and she served during the rest of the war as a wooden gunboat on blockade duty.

Most people are cognizant of the proper pronunciation of Galena. However, I found when I was younger I wasn't sure just how the name was pronounced and had a tendency to either avoid saying it or, if I did, said, **ga-LENA**. I was a mere boy at the time. So, for those among my readers who are still "mere boys" or "mere girls," and aren't so cocksure about Galena, I have included it. Anyway, you got to find out about the USS *Galena.*

<u>Galusha</u> -(guh-LOO-sha)

as in <u>Galusha</u> Pennypacker, Brigadier General U.S.V.

Talk about your strange names! Actually, I've always been rather fond of this general's name. Galusha Pennypacker always sounded to me like the Northern equivalent of the fictional character, Jubilation T. Cornpone. The name has great theatrical potential. "Galusha Pennypacker-The Musical," would look perfectly natural emblazoned on the marquee of a Broadway theater. However, Galusha Pennypacker is not a made-up name created for the amusement of people who attend the theater.

According to Ezra Warner in *Generals in Blue*, Pennypacker was "the only general in the history of the U. S. Army who was not old enough to vote for or against the President who appointed him." This remarkable young man came from a well established Philadelphia family and was educated in private schools. He enlisted in the 9th Pennsylvania within days of the firing on Fort Sumter. He was sixteen years old when he became quartermaster sergeant. The 9th Pennsylvania was a ninety-day outfit and after it was mustered out, Pennypacker recruited a company for the 97th Pennsylvania and got a commission as captain in August 1861. He was promoted to major in October. Serving in the Department of the South, he fought at Fort Wagner in July of 1863. In 1864 his regiment was transferred to the Army of the James under Benjamin Butler. Pennypacker was appointed lieutenant-colonel in April 1864 and fought at Drewry's Bluff and Cold Harbor. In August 1864 he was appointed colonel and commanded a brigade in the Tenth Corps of the Army of the James. Later he was moved south again, this time commanding a brigade in North Carolina. He participated in the action at Fort Fisher and was severely wounded. For his gallant action in this operation he was promoted to brigadier general in February 1865 and later given the Medal of Honor.

Pennypacker continued in the army after the war, serving in the South and on the frontier. He retired in 1883 at the regular rank of colonel. He was 39 years old. Galusha Pennypacker was active in Civil War veterans affairs until his death in Philadelphia in October 1916.

Galusha is no longer a widely used first name. I seriously doubt that it ever was. Perhaps the best known Galusha in American history is Galusha Grow, who was speaker of the U. S. House of Representatives during most of the Civil War. According to one source, Galusha means, "one who is loud and noisy."[100] Somehow, this doesn't seem to fit the gentlemanly, unassuming General Pennypacker. The general's last name is German in origin; Pennypacker is an anglicized version of Pannebakker[101] or Pfannenbecker.[102]

Garesché -(GAR-uh-SHAY)

as in Julius Peter Garesché, Colonel U.S.A.

Colonel Julius Garesché is one of those unfortunate men whose manner of death is the single biggest reason for his inclusion in so many Civil War histories: Garesché was General William Rosecrans' Chief of Staff at the Battle of Stones River at the end of December 1862. While riding along the battle front on the 31st checking his units, Rosecrans was accompanied by Garesché. As Rosecrans and his staff passed within view of a Confederate battery a shot flew in their direction and decapitated Garesché, spattering Rosecrans with a considerable quantity of blood and brain tissue. Garesché's horse ran for about fifty feet before its headless rider fell to the ground.

After the battle Colonel William B. Hazen (later general) set out to search for his friend Garesché's body. Just as he found it, the corpse, apparently going into rigor mortis, moved with muscle contractions causing Garesché's hand to lift toward Hazen as though reaching out to grasp him. I don't know about you, but this Civil War buff would have run in the opposite direction with uncharacteristic celerity at such a sight. Hazen, however, was accustomed to the horrors of the battlefield and removed Garesché's West Point ring and his other personal effects, then attended to the burial of his friend in a secure place.[103]

Aside from his leading role as the Headless Horseman of Stones River, Julius Garesché was obviously a man of some ability. Prior to the Civil War he had had a twenty-one-year career in the army, and was for many years in the adjutant general's branch. Rosecrans had known him since his days as a cadet at West Point and Garesché was instrumental in Rosecrans' conversion to Roman Catholicism. In fact, Julius Garesché's brother was a Catholic priest who predicted a tragic end for the colonel (with friends and relatives like this, who needs enemies?).

Pronunciation of Colonel Gareshé's name gave me problems for a long time. The name has an acute accent over the final 'e,' which usually means an 'ay' sound in a French name. Yet, the name does not appear to be French; it looks Germanic. In addition, the first name Julius seemed somewhat German as well. I had neither the time nor the resources to do a thorough check of Colonel Gareshé's ancestry (perhaps in a second edition). My best guess would be that the name is Alsatian. I checked with a number of Civil War historians, Ed Bearss among them, for a correct pronunciation and you see it at the top of this entry.

<u>Garnett</u> -(GAHR-nit)

as in Richard Brooke or Robert Selden <u>Garnett,</u> Brigadier Generals C.S.A.

The cousins, Richard and Robert Garnett, were members of an old Virginia family. Both attended West Point, and both graduated with the class of 1841. When the Civil War came both joined the Confederacy, both became generals and both were killed in action. To this day we have not been able to determine if the two photographs, the only ones incidentally, of the Garnett cousins are properly identified. The picture used in Ezra Warner's *Generals in Gray* for Richard Brooke Garnett has been disputed by some authorities and Garnett family members, and said to belong under the name Robert Selden Garnett. The photograph of Robert Selden Garnett in the Warner book is said to be that of Richard.[104] Another theory floating around has it that the two photos are of the same person--whether that person is Richard or Robert is a moot point. All this confusion illustrates the mystery that surrounds Richard and Robert Garnett.

Here's another mystery; what happened to the body of Richard Brooke Garnett? He was killed in the Pickett-Pettigrew Charge at the Battle of Gettysburg and his body was never recovered. Was he buried with the Union or Confederate unknowns (there is a story that his uniform was stripped of insignia by souvenir hunters after the battle), or was his body found and interred at Richmond's Hollywood Cemetery? What about the story that Garnett's sword, which he reportedly wore during the Charge, turned up in a Baltimore pawn shop decades after the battle?[105] This is probably true. But, what does it mean?

Luckily we are not interested here in what happened to the Dick Garnett's body, or how and why his sword ended up in Baltimore. Our interest is in another mystery; the proper pronunciation of the Garnett family name. On the surface this would appear to be a simple matter to resolve. Unfortunately, that **'ett'** at the end of the name tempts one to pronounce the name as **gahr-NET**. This makes sense when you consider that the name Barnett is pronounced **bahr-NET**. Over the years I have heard speakers at Civil War conferences pronounce the name with the emphasis on the last syllable. On the other hand, I have heard speakers pronounce it the correct way. Whatever your own experience has been with the Garnett name, be assured that it is pronounced the same as the semi-precious gem, the garnet, though this pretty little stone has only one **'t'** at the end of it.[106]

Gettysburg -(GET-iss-burg)

as in Battle of Gettysburg and Gettysburg, Pennsylvania.

You may find it hard to believe that I have included the name "Gettysburg" in this dictionary. But consider the fact that countless people mispronounce this most famous of Civil War names. The most common mispronunciation is **GET-eez-burg** and this makes sense, since that is how the name is spelled. Spelling notwithstanding, the proper pronunciation is as I have indicated above. I realize that attempting to correct some people on the pronunciation of Gettysburg is going to be a hopeless task. I, myself, say it incorrectly most of the time. I suspect that saying **GET-eez-burg**, with that long **'e'** sound in the middle, is a natural tendency among those of us who reside in the Northeastern part of the country, especially the New York metropolitan area. However, if I am willing to make a sustained effort to correct myself, I feel it is only fair that my fellow Yankees make the same effort. Who knows, with time and application we may succeed in saying this venerated name properly. The town of Gettysburg was founded by James Gettys, who most say pronounced his name **GET-eez**, while others say **[GET-is]**.[107]

Gist -(gist [with a hard 'g' as in "goofy"])

as in States Rights Gist, Brigadier General C.S.A.

States Rights Gist is one of those Southern generals everybody always remembers because of his unusual given name. Could there be any doubt which side of the war a man with such a name fought on? The other thing that many Civil War buffs remember about States Rights Gist is that he is one of the six Confederate generals killed or mortally wounded at the disastrous Battle of Franklin, Tennessee in November 1864.

A graduate of Harvard Law School, he practiced law before the war and was active with the South Carolina militia. When the war broke out he served with the South Carolina Army at Fort Sumter. Gist then became a volunteer ADC on General Bernard Bee's staff and fought at First Manassas. After Bee's death in the battle, Gist succeeded him in command of the brigade. He was promoted to brigadier general in March 1862 and was sent to South Carolina to serve under the command of General John Pemberton. By May of 1863 he was near Vicksburg, Mississippi where he was part of Joseph E. Johnston's intended relief column for the besieged fortress. Gist was then assigned to the Army of Tennessee. With his brigade part of Walker's Corps, he fought at Chickamauga, Chattanooga and the Atlanta Campaign. He was part of John Brown's Division in Benjamin Cheatham's Corps at Franklin in November 1864. Gist was killed while leading his brigade against Union breastworks.

Civil War buffs and others beyond count have been saying this man's last name wrong for years. As one of that legion of mispronouncers, it never occurred to me that I was saying the name wrong. After all, my reason for saying the name wrong makes sense. The word "gist," as in "the gist of what he said was..." is spelled exactly like the family name is. To quote Claude and Irene Neuffer, "Though the common noun meaning the main point of the matter, *gist*, follows the pronunciation rule that **'g'** followed by **'i'** has a **'j'** sound, the family name still present in South Carolina, and Gist Street in Columbia are properly pronounced with a hard **'g'**."[108]

Gouverneur-(GOO-vur-NOOR)

as in Gouverneur Kemble Warren, Major General U.S.V.

Gouverneur Warren's moment in the Civil War limelight came on Little Round Top on the afternoon of July 2, 1863. It was Warren who discovered that Little Round Top, on the extreme left of the Union line, was virtually unoccupied by Federal troops just as Longstreet's Corps of Lee's Army of Northern Virginia was about to launch its attack on the Union left flank. His quick action in getting troops deployed on this key hill probably averted disaster for the Federals. Every buff worth his salt, knows the story of Vincent's Brigade of Sykes' Fifth Corps rapidly making its way to Little Round Top, arriving only minutes before the Confederate attack hit. Subsequent heroic efforts by the 20th Maine, on the extreme left of the line, are part of Gettysburg legend.

Gouverneur Warren, despite his moment of glory at Gettysburg, ultimately did not fare well in the Civil War. This West Point graduate and lifelong professional soldier put together a creditable war record, but fell afoul of the very capable, but very nasty playground bully, General Philip Sheridan at the Battle of Five Forks. Warren, who was disliked for various obscure reasons by Sheridan, Grant and George G. Meade was summarily relieved of command of the Fifth Corps during the battle for not deploying his troops rapidly enough. That, at least, was the gist of Sheridan's charge. This action by Sheridan effectively ruined Warren's military career, though he remained in the service after the war. A court of inquiry in 1879 finally exonerated him. The findings of the court were published in November 1881, but it was too late to do poor Warren any good. He had died in August of that year, according to some, "of a broken heart."[109] Three years later, in 1884, General Sheridan became commanding general of the army and though he was a good general, he was not a nice man.

General Warren's first name is pretty much pronounced as it is spelled. However, its similarity to the word "governor" is close enough to cause problems for people.

Govan -(GUV-en)

as in Daniel Chevilette Govan, Brigadier General C.S.A.

Born in North Carolina and raised in Mississippi, Daniel Govan attended the University of South Carolina as part of the class of 1848, though he left before graduating. When he was twenty years old he joined his relative, Ben McCulloch (another future Confederate general) and headed for the gold-fields in California. By 1850 he was a deputy sheriff, under Sheriff Ben McCulloch, in Sacramento County, California. In 1853 he returned to Mississippi and became a planter, like his father. Later that year, he married and moved to Arkansas, where he established a plantation.

When the Civil War came, Govan raised a company of volunteers which ultimately became Company F, 2nd Arkansas. Govan was promoted to colonel and took over command of the regiment in January 1862. As part of Albert Sidney Johnston's Army of the Mississippi he saw action in Kentucky and fought with his regiment at Shiloh. Govan also led the 2nd Arkansas at Stones River and commanded a brigade at the Battle of Chickamauga. He was promoted to brigadier general in February 1864. Govan commanded a brigade in General William Hardee's Corps during the Battle of Atlanta and was captured at Jonesboro on September 1, 1864. After being exchanged three weeks later, he resumed his brigade command and participated in John Bell Hood's disastrous Tennessee Campaign, being wounded at the Battle of Nashville. He recovered and rejoined his brigade in February 1865, which by that time was with Joe Johnston in Greensboro, North Carolina. When Johnston surrendered on April 26th the war finally ended for Daniel Govan.

After the war, he returned to his plantation in Arkansas. In 1894 he was appointed an agent for the Tulalip Indian Agency in the state of Washington. Two years later he moved to Tennessee where he died in March 1911. General Govan left behind fourteen children!

Pronunciation of the name "Govan" leads to a number of possibilities at first sight: **GOH-van** is one, **goh-VAN** is another, then there is always the possibility of **GAH-vin**. I avoided saying this name for years, only to discover that its correct pronunciation was available in any good biographical dictionary.

Grimké -(GRIM-kee)

as in Sarah and Angelina Grimké, Southern abolitionists.

The Grimké sisters were an unusual pair. Daughters of a wealthy Charleston, South Carolina judge, they were raised amid the pomp and circumstance of the best Southern society. In middle age, however, the two spinsters moved to Philadelphia and were converted to Quakerism and abolitionism. Both sisters were very articulate and both had their views published. Angelina wrote an *Appeal to the Christian Women of the South*, and Sarah wrote an *Epistle to the Clergy of the South*. The postmaster of Charleston had copies of both books promptly burned when they arrived in the city.[110] The Grimké sisters were also active in the women's suffrage movement.

Grimké is an unusual name to find connected with Charleston, South Carolina. It becomes even more unusual when you find out that it is a name that figures quite prominently in the abolition movement. Pronunciation could prove difficult for those not familiar with the name.[111] I have included it in this dictionary for those who study the events leading up to the Civil War as well as the war itself.

<u>guidon</u> -(GUY-din)

At the head of the cavalry column was a trooper carrying a <u>guidon</u>.

The guidon is that small, forked flag carried by cavalry units. Usually they are in two colors, the top fork one color, the bottom fork another. These flags, or pennants, also had the numerical designation of the unit on them as well. Probably the guidon most familiar to people is that of the Seventh Cavalry, seen in many historically inaccurate motion pictures portraying Custer's Last Stand. Guidons were used as a guide for column movements as well as a rallying point during the confusion of battle. The guidon is also used sometimes to describe the man carrying such a flag or pennant.

Guidon is often mispronounced. I have heard a variety of these mistakes: **GEE-don**, **GWEE-din**, **GIDD-n**, to name just a few. It is easy enough to remember the proper pronunciation by thinking of it as two separate words, "guide" and "in."

<u>Guinea</u> -(GIN-ee)

as in <u>Guinea</u> Station, or <u>Guiney</u> Station, or <u>Guiney's</u> Station, Virginia.

If you look at a modern road map or atlas of the state of Virginia you will find this location just south of Fredericksburg listed as "Guinea" or sometimes "Guinea Station." It is the site of the Stonewall Jackson Shrine, the place where Jackson died of the wounds he received at the Battle of Chancellorsville. In May of 1863 it was a stop, called "Guiney's Station," on the Richmond, Fredericksburg and Potomac Railroad. Near the railroad line was the twelve hundred acre plantation of Thomas Chandler called "Fairfield." The Chandler family had gotten to know Jackson the previous winter during the Fredericksburg Campaign. After Stonewall was wounded he was brought to Fairfield and died there on May 10, 1863.

Normally, a place name from the Civil War era that is still listed on modern maps would not raise any questions. After all, lots of people have visited the site of Mighty Stonewall's death over the years. However, for those who have not, but only know of Guinea or Guiney Station from their reading, the multiple spellings of the place name may cause pronunciation problems. It seems that all the old maps, including those of Jed Hotchkiss, and also maps accompanying the *Official Records*, list the place as "Guiney's Station." Using that spelling, it is possible the place might be pronounced **GUY-nee**. For years, I looked at this spelling and was convinced it was a family name, not a name taken, as the modern spelling would indicate, from the Guinea Fowl, or New Guinea, or Guinea Pepper. In the course of my reading, I came across an interesting footnote in Edward Stackpole's 1958 book, *Chancellorsville: Lee's Greatest Battle.* In the footnote following the mention of Guiney's Station, Stackpole says:

> The spelling used here is that shown in Confederate reports and correspondence given in the Official Records of the Rebellion, as well as on a number of contemporary maps, including those of Jed Hotchkiss. According to local citizens well informed on the history of the area, the site was named for the original colonial settler, one Michael Ginney or Guinney. Today the station is known as Guinea Station.[112]

I was very curious as to why the name of the place had changed to Guinea. It was, I discovered, a process that took place over a long period of time. As stated, the name of the location was Guiney's Station during the Civil War. This name became Guiney Station, apostrophe removed, in 1890. By 1910 the post office was listed as "Guinea."[113]

A pronouncer for the name Guinea is probably not necessary for most people. There are those, however, who may wonder whether there is some local pronunciation in Virginia they are unaware of. After checking with the Park Service people in Fredericksburg I found the name was said in the usual way.

<u>Gutzon</u> -(GUT-sun)

as in <u>Gutzon</u> Borglum (BOR-glum), sculptor of the North Carolina Monument at Gettysburg.

Borglum also did Mount Rushmore, but we all know that the North Carolina Monument is much more impressive. I have included Borglum in this dictionary because so many people seem unwilling to believe that his first name is pronounced pretty much as it is spelled. Actually, his full name is John Gutzon de la Mothe Borglum. In addition, you are bound to come in contact with his name if you visit Gettysburg and take a genuine interest in some of spectacular monumental statuary scattered over the battlefield park.

The North Carolina Monument is located in a grove of trees along Confederate Avenue on the Gettysburg Battlefield. It depicts a small group of North Carolina soldiers who had "just been ordered forward to charge across that very bloody battlefield" after they "had caught shelter in a group of trees....With them was a color bearer."[114] The five bronze figures are poised for action, leaning forward toward the Union line on Cemetery Ridge. The monument was unveiled on July 3, 1929. The total cost was $50,000.[115]

Brigadier General Galusha Pennypacker

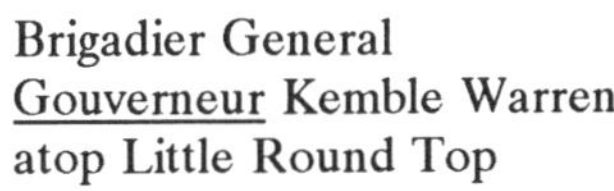

Brigadier General Gouverneur Kemble Warren atop Little Round Top

H

Hagerstown -(HAY-gurz-town)

as in Hagerstown, Maryland.

There was no Battle of Hagerstown in the Civil War, but both armies passed through this Maryland locale on the way to some big fights. There was some fighting within the city limits of Hagerstown, to be sure. In one such incident, Kilpatrick's Federal cavalry engaged Confederates who were retreating through Maryland after the Battle of Gettysburg.

Hagerstown in located in Washington County, Maryland, sixty-eight miles west of Baltimore. Any student of the Antietam or Gettysburg campaigns is familiar with the name of this strategically located town. The most common mispronunciation of Hagerstown is **HAG-urz-town**, omitting the long **'a'** that would make it correct.

Hamtramck -(ham-TRAM-ik)

as in the Hamtramck Guards and Hamtramck, Michigan.

Hamtramck is one of those names that crops up once in a while in Civil War history. Company B of the 2nd Virginia Regiment was named after Captain John Francis Hamtramck. Hamtramck had been colonel of the 1st Regiment of Virginia Volunteers during the Mexican War, then captain of a militia unit in Shepherdstown, Virginia in 1858. When he died in 1859 the Shepherdstown Light Infantry became the Hamtramck Guards. At the outbreak of the Civil War the Hamtramck Guard became part of the 2nd Virginia.[116]

Hamtramck, Michigan is a city in Wayne County, which lies entirely within the corporate boundaries of Detroit. It was in the Wolverine State that I first encountered the name Hamtramck, and naturally, I mispronounced it.

<u>Hardee</u> -(HAR-**DEE**)

as in William Joseph <u>Hardee</u>, Lieutenant General C.S.A.

In his mid-forties when the Civil War started, William Hardee had established a solid reputation as a knowledgeable, capable professional in the Old Army. Graduating from West Point in 1838, he served with gallantry in the Mexican War. After the Mexican War he did a stint as commandant of cadets at the Military Academy. In the mid-1850s Hardee wrote a textbook, *Rifle and Light Infantry Tactics,* which would be used as a primer for officers on both sides in the Civil War. When his home state of Georgia seceded in 1861 he resigned his lieutenant colonelcy in the U. S. Army and joined the Confederacy with the rank of brigadier general. Hardee fought as a corps commander at Shiloh, Perryville, Stones River, Missionary Ridge and the Atlanta Campaign; by October 1862 he had attained the rank of lieutenant general. As a battlefield commander he was reliable (just as his nickname, "Old Reliable," would indicate) but never an inspired leader. He had the misfortune of having his only son, William Joseph Hardee, Jr. die in the Battle of Bentonville while under his command. After the war he managed plantations in Alabama and was actively engaged in various businesses in the Selma. He died in 1873.

Hardee's name is pronounced with the emphasis on the last syllable. This is the traditional pronunciation of the name. Little information is offered in biographies of the general to indicate how this pronunciation evolved. Biographies of the Hardee show that the name was sometimes spelled "Hardy" among his ancestors,[117] which means that it is not a name that was derived or contracted from some longer, or entirely different foreign name.

<u>Hartranft</u> -(HAHRT-ranft)

as in John Frederick <u>Hartranft</u>, Brigadier General U.S.V.

Pennsylvania-native John Hartranft was a Medal of Honor recipient. Aside from that he was a fair general who put together a creditable war record. Hartranft was from Norristown, Pennsylvania, which is not too many miles northwest of Philadelphia. Prior to the war he was a civil engineer and a lawyer (an interesting combination). When the war began, he was colonel of a militia regiment that was mustered into Federal service as the 4th Pennsylvania Infantry.

The 4th was one of those ninety-day regiments so common at the outset of the Civil War. The 4th Pennsylvania's three months was up on July 20, 1861, the day before the Battle of Bull Run and despite pleas from Colonel Hartranft the men hit the road and headed home. Colonel Hartranft, no longer possessing a regiment to command, offered his services to Colonel William B. Franklin in the impending battle. The engineer-lawyer performed so well in this otherwise disastrous Union defeat that he was given the Medal of Honor for it in 1886. By November 1861 Hartranft had raised another regiment, the 51st Pennsylvania, was commissioned its colonel and joined the Burnside Expedition to the South Carolina coast in 1862. Hartranft finally got an appointment to brigadier general in May 1864 for his performance at the Battle of Spotsylvania Court House. By the time Grant's Overland Campaign ground to halt at Petersburg in June 1864, Hartranft had commanded at both the brigade and division level .

In the wake of Lincoln's assassination in April 1865, Hartranft was appointed special provost marshal for the trial of the assassination conspirators. He was defacto "jailer" of the conspirators. Hartranft was mustered out in 1866 and became involved in Pennsylvania politics. He eventually served two terms as governor of the state, was postmaster of Philadelphia and collector of the port of Philadelphia from 1881 to 1885. He died at Norristown in October 1889.

Pronunciation of Hartranft's name is pretty much phonetic. The key to saying it properly lies in the division of the two syllables. If you say, **HART** as a separate, distinct word and **RANFT** the same way, you should have no problem. Mostly, it is one those names that looks harder to say than it actually is.[118]

<u>Haverhill</u> -(HAY-vrul)

as in <u>Haverhill</u>, Massachusetts.

I had always hoped I would have an opportunity to put this name in a pronouncing dictionary. I was so proud of never having made the fatal error of mispronouncing it in the Boston area of Massachusetts. Massachusetts is one of those states that takes a perverse pride in its peculiar pronunciation of place names. People in the Bay State don't care if you've never been there before when you mispronounce a place name. You are supposed to know the correct pronunciation because Massachusetts has existed since the Garden of Eden, and Boston <u>is</u> The Hub of the Universe. When you do mispronounce one these sacred names, they will ALWAYS correct you.

What has this to do with the Civil War? As it turns out, the name Haverhill comes up once in a while in Civil War history. To cite an example; in E. B. Long's *Civil War Day by Day* under the entry for August 19, 1861 says, "Newspapers at West Chester and Easton, Pennsylvania, were raided by Unionists, and a publisher in <u>Haverhill</u>, Massachusetts, was tarred and feathered by a mob for alleged pro-Southern sentiments." The poor sap probably mispronounced Haverhill!

Hébert -(ay-BAIR)

as in Louis Hébert and Paul Octave Hébert, Brigadier Generals C.S.A.

Louis and Paul Hébert were first cousins. They were born in Iberville Parish, Louisiana; Louis in 1820, Paul in 1818. The Héberts were descendants of French settlers who came to Louisiana in the 17th century. Both grew up as part of the wealthy sugar planter class, both cousins attended Jefferson College, and both went to West Point. Louis graduated 3rd in the class of 1845, Paul graduated 1st in the class of 1840. Two years after graduating Louis resigned and took up the running of his plantation. Paul taught engineering at West Point after graduating and resigned five years later to become Chief Engineer for the State of Louisiana.[119] Paul also found time to get elected Governor of the state in 1852.

When the Civil War came Louis became colonel of the 3rd Louisiana, fought gallantly at Wilson's Creek and Pea Ridge where he was captured. After being exchanged he was promoted to brigadier general and given a brigade command in Sterling Price's Army of the West. He fought a Iuka, Corinth and Vicksburg, where he was again made a prisoner. Following his second exchange, he transferred to the Army of Tennessee and was sent to North Carolina. He spent the rest of the war in command of artillery around Fort Fisher.

Paul Hébert's Civil War career was somewhat less spectacular than his cousin's. He was elected colonel of the 1st Louisiana Artillery in 1861, and was commissioned a brigadier general a few months later. His only significant combat during the war was near Milliken's Bend in 1862. Most of the time he held administrative positions in the Department of Texas. He helped set up a system to implement General John Magruder's despised "Cotton Order."[120]

After the war, Louis Hébert became a newspaper editor and taught school. Paul pursued a career in engineering. Paul Hébert died in 1880, Louis followed him in 1901.

Hébert is a French name that is as common as Smith and Brown is among English names. It is pronounced in the French manner, the letter '**h**' being silent.

Henrico -(hen-RIE-koh)

as in Henrico County, Virginia.

Henrico County is the county in Virginia that in the 1860s contained the city of Richmond. It is not a name that crops up that often in Civil War reading, but once in a while it does, and it pays to be correct on the pronunciation. There is also the possibility that you may be visiting a number of historical sites in Henrico County and have cause to use the name. Why be embarrassed in front of locals? The first time I was in

Richmond I pronounced the county name **hen-REE-ko**, rhyming with Puerto Rico or Ron Rico Rum, and was immediately corrected by a native. This type of thing is always a bit upsetting. After all, I am not from Richmond, and can't be expected to know everything. Ultimately, I decided to stop into one of the local watering holes to ponder the whole thing. While there, I ordered myself a rum and coke. In case you're wondering; no, I did not ask for **"ron-RIE-koh"** rum.

The name Henrico is a shortening of "Henricopolis," a Greco-Latin form of "Henry City." In the case of Henrico County, the Henry involved was Prince Henry, Son of King Charles I of England.

Herr -(hur [rhymes with spur])

as in Herr Ridge or Herr's Tavern, Gettysburg.

Herr Ridge is one of the key geographic features of the first day's battlefield at Gettysburg. It is west of McPherson's Ridge, with Willoughby Run separating the two. Herr Ridge also figures as a location during the second day's battle, especially Longstreet's march and counter-march to get into position on the Union left. Herr Ridge is slightly higher in elevation than McPherson's Ridge.

Herr's Tavern is along the Chambersburg Road on Herr Ridge. The building still stands along modern day Route 30. Both Herr Ridge and Herr's Tavern are named after the Herr family (makes sense). It is a German name, as are many of the local family names in Gettysburg. Pronunciation is not as simple as it may appear. Though the name is spelled the same as the German word used as a form of address for men, it is not pronounced the same way. Local Gettysburg pronunciation is **hur**, as indicated above.

Heth -(heeth)

as in Henry Heth, Major General C.S.A.

A professional soldier, Henry Heth was born in Virginia and graduated from West Point in 1847. Heth spent the first part of the war in western Virginia, then served as a division commander in Edmund Kirby Smith's Army of Kentucky. He was assigned to the Army of Northern Virginia in January 1863. Most Civil War buffs remember Harry Heth as the division commander in A. P. Hill's Corps who opened the Battle of Gettysburg on the morning of July 1, 1863 by attacking John Buford's Federal cavalry. Heth was wounded in that action.

Pronunciation of Heth's name is no great mystery. Numerous sources, including Boatner's *Civil War Dictionary* give a pronouncer for it. The big thing with Heth's name is that long **'e'** which one must hear, or be told about, in order to get it right.

Hindman -(HINED-mun [HINED rhymes with "kind"])

as in Thomas Carmichael Hindman, Major General C.S.A.

General Hindman was born in Nashville, Tennessee in 1828. He was a lawyer and politician by occupation, having served in the Mississippi state legislature and the U. S. Congress as a representative from the Arkansas during the antebellum years. His only military experience before the Civil War was during the Mexican War when he served as a second lieutenant in the 2nd Mississippi Infantry.

With the coming of the war Hindman was appointed colonel of a regiment from his adopted state of Arkansas. He was promoted to brigadier general in September 1861 and major general in April 1862. He commanded the Trans-Mississippi Department for the Confederacy for a couple of months in 1862 until succeeded by General Theophilis Holmes. Hindman commanded Confederate forces at the Battle of Prairie Grove on December 7, 1862, a battle that ended up a tactical draw but a strategic defeat (Hindman had been unsuccessful in stopping the rendezvous of Union forces under Generals James G. Blunt and Francis Herron). Hindman requested a transfer and was given command at first of a division in Leonidas Polk's Corps of Bragg's Army of Tennessee. He fought at Chickamauga, Chattanooga and in the Atlanta Campaign. He was injured on July 4, 1864, (his eyesight impaired for several months) rendering him incapable of further field service.[121]

After the war, Hindman went to Mexico where he became a coffee grower. He returned to Arkansas in 1868, resumed his legal career and got caught up in Reconstruction politics. He was assassinated in Helena, Arkansas on September 28, 1868 by a person or persons unknown.

Thomas Hindman is included in this dictionary because a remarkable number of people I have talked with over the years in Civil War circles are unsure of the pronunciation of the name. Many, including myself, have wondered whether the name is said, **HIND-mun** (HIND rhyming with "wind" as in "trade wind") or **HINED-mun** (HINED rhyming with "kind"). The correct pronunciation is the second, and the one I have used at the top of this entry.[122]

<u>hors de combat</u> -(or-duh-kohn-BAH)

as in "General Hooker's division is <u>hors de combat</u>."

Given the reputation of General Joseph Hooker as a hard drinking, ladies' man you might think that a rough translation of the example cited above is, "General Hooker's division is comprised of fighting prostitutes." Undoubtedly, the high spirited "Fighting Joe" had fantasies along this line, but the real meaning of this French term is "out of combat" or "out of action." Every once in a while a Civil War historian will use the term "hors de combat" in his writing. Often this term will come up in a quote from some participant in a battle or engagement. It is almost always used to describe an individual or a unit that is unfit for combat, or unable to fight because of serious injury. During the Civil War, among the educated classes, French was the language of war, not love. Graduates of West Point were especially fond of French terminology to describe battlefield tactics and terms like "coup de main," "en échelon" and "coup d'éclat" were often used by officers when discussing tactics.

<u>Hotze</u> -(HOT-suh)

as in Henry <u>Hotze</u>, Confederate propagandist.

Swiss born Henry Hotze settled in Mobile, Alabama when he emigrated to the United States, and became a naturalized citizen in 1856. Hotze had talent as a journalist and was editor of the *Mobile Register* during the 1850s. He also spent a year as a secretary and chargé d'affaires at the U. S. Consulate in Brussels. In addition to all this talent Hotze was also a totally dedicated Southerner who believed in slavery. If Henry Hotze had lived in our own era he would have run one of the country's most successful public relations firms, or been the most effective lobbyist Washington, D. C. had ever known. Hotze was a genius as a publicity agent.

While working at the *Mobile Register,* Hotze became acquainted with Leroy Pope Walker. Walker was impressed with the obvious talent of the young man and when he became Confederate secretary of war he sent Hotze on a special purchasing mission to London. By the January 1862 Hotze was appointed a full time Confederate commercial agent in London. However, the real purpose of his job was to use his skills as a journalist to promote the Confederate cause in England.

The idea that sophisticated propaganda techniques are an invention of the our own time is obviously in error if we study the career of Henry Hotze. It would be no exaggeration to say that he was probably one of the most skillful operators for the Confederacy in Europe. Well educated, shrewd, and possessing a grasp of European politics that far exceeded other Confederate diplomats, Hotze did a superb job. As editor of the London based propaganda organ, *The Index*, he was able to favorably influence British public and political opinion in the South's favor. His subtle psychological methods and skillful pen performed great feats of public opinion molding. When the Confederacy lost Fort Donelson in February 1862 Hotze was able to put such a positive spin on the story that it began to look like a Southern victory.[123] Oh, how modern day Washington would love this man! Henry Hotze, America's First Spin Doctor!

Until the publication of his official papers in the early 1920s not many people had ever heard of Henry Hotze. Details of his postwar life are practically non-existent. It is known that he lived for twenty two years after the Civil War, but never returned to the United States, but remained in Europe as a journalist. He died in Zug, Switzerland in April 1887.[124]

To this day, few Civil War buffs know of the existence of this remarkable man. Thus, pronunciation of his name, which is not easy to begin with, is made more difficult by total unfamiliarity. Hotze is a German name and I have given the German pronunciation of it (or as close to it as I can using the respelling method). In checking around, I found the name is pronounced various ways by Civil War historians. Ed Bearss, Chief Historian of the National Park Service, says "hots," while at least two of other historians I spoke with said "HOT-zee." Undoubtedly, Henry Hotze ran into these mispronunciations during his lifetime.

Hough -(huff)

as in Daniel Hough, Private U.S.A.

Private Daniel Hough, Company E, 1st U. S. Artillery, has the unenviable distinction of being the first official fatality of the Civil War. After Fort Sumter had been bombarded on April 12-13, 1861 for thirty-two hours by Confederate forces, a formal surrender ceremony took place on April 14th. The fort's Federal garrison, under the command of Major Robert Anderson, was allowed to fire a one hundred-gun salute while the American flag was being lowered. On the fiftieth round Private Daniel Hough was reloading an artillery piece, which apparently had not been fully sponged after the previous shot. The round exploded prematurely, and Hough's right arm was blown off; he died almost instantly. A pile of shells beside the gun was ignited as well, and this, even larger, explosion wounded five men. One of those five, Private Edward Galloway, died five days later in a Charleston Hospital.[125]

Hough is pronounced "huff" for the same reason "rough" is pronounced "ruff" and "tough" is pronounced "tuff." Just another aspect of our often inscrutable language. A pronouncer for the Private Hough's name is also given in a number of sources, including Boatner's *Civil War Dictionary*.

Houghtaling -(hoh-TALING)

as in Charles Houghtaling, Colonel, 1st Illinois Light Artillery.

Mexican War veteran Charles Houghtaling was a New York-born, Illinois resident when the Civil War began. For most of the war he served as an artillerist. He was appointed captain of Company C of the 1st Illinois Light Artillery in July 1861, led this unit at siege of Island Number 10, and also during the siege of Corinth, Mississippi.[126] Houghtaling was also at the Battle of Stones River, and took part in the Atlanta Campaign, where he was Chief of Artillery, 14th Army Corps. He was promoted to the rank of colonel in August 1864, and participated in Sherman's March to the Sea. After the war, he resumed his occupation as a wagon manufacturer.[127]

Houghtaling is a scary looking name for those unfamiliar with its proper pronunciation. "Hough" is always a toss-up when it comes to pronunciation, sometimes it's **HUFF**, other times, as a prefix usually, it takes the **HOH** sound. Add to this the mysterious "taling" and you have a very difficult word to wrestle with. Since Colonel Houghtaling's name is not a household word in the Civil War history world I decided to contact the good people of Carmi, Illinois. Carmi was Houghtaling's last known residence; he died there in March 1883. It is a town of about seven thousand people in the southeastern part of the state near the Little Wabash River. Carmi is county seat for White County. Evidently, Carmi leaves responsibility for historical matters to the Edwards County Historical Society, a few miles north of Carmi in the town of Albion, Illinois. The pronouncer used above was finally confirmed in Albion.

Hovey -(HUV-ee)

as in Alvin Peterson Hovey and Charles Edward Hovey, Brigadier Generals U.S.V.

Alvin and Charles Hovey were distantly related. Alvin was born in Indiana, fought in the Mexican War, was a judge and politician. When the war came he was named colonel of the 24th Indiana, was promoted to brigadier general for gallantry at the Battle of Shiloh, and eventually became a division commander in the Thirteenth Corps of the Army of the Tennessee. Alvin Hovey was in the Vicksburg Campaign and did a splendid job at Champion Hill. After the war, he was appointed Minister to Peru and served in that post until 1870. He then returned to the practice of law, was elected to Congress in 1886, Governor of Indiana in 1888, and died in office in 1891.

Charles Hovey was born in Vermont, attended Dartmouth, moved to Illinois where he taught school, and eventually became Superintendent of public schools in Peoria. Hovey helped found the first state teacher's college at Normal, Illinois in 1857. When the war came, he recruited the 33rd Illinois, the "Normal Regiment," made up of teachers and students from the college. He was promoted to brigadier general in September 1862, though for whatever reason the appointment was never confirmed by the U. S. Senate. As a result, the commission expired in March 1863. Nonetheless, Hovey took part in the capture of Arkansas Post in January 1863 and was wounded in the process. He left the service because of the wound in May 1863. During the postwar years he was a successful pension lobbyist in Washington, D. C. and died there in 1897.

The last name Hovey could have a number of incorrect pronunciations, **HOH-vee** and **HAHV-ee** come immediately to mind. Just think of "a covey of quail" when you see the name and it may help you to remember the name's proper pronunciation.

Huger -(YOO-JEE)

as in Benjamin Huger, Major General C.S.A.

Benjamin Huger was a professional soldier who graduated from West Point in 1825, and was a few years older than Robert E. Lee when the Civil War began. Huger was not one of the great captains of military history. However, a quick look at a photo of him, and you realize that Hollywood would have seen him as the quintessential Confederate general. Huger looks like he came from central casting for a 1930s Hollywood Civil War epic. In all fairness to the late general, he had a bit more substance than that. Huger had a "most distinguished" record in the pre-war U. S. Army. He had commanded a number arsenals, was a member of the Ordnance Board and Chief of Ordnance under General Winfield Scott during the Mexican War. After the fall of Fort Sumter he entered the service of the Confederacy, was appointed brigadier general in June 1861 and major general in October of the same year.

During McClellan's Peninsula Campaign of 1862 Huger's fortunes began a steep decline. In command of a division in Joe Johnston's army defending Richmond, Huger was either never informed, or improperly briefed about Johnston's plan to attack the Federals at Seven Pines. His division was not in place on the right flank when the battle began, and he overslept on the morning of the battle.[128] His performances at Glendale (Frayser's Farm) and the Battle of Malvern Hill were also less than desirable. Add to this an investigation by the Confederate Congress of Huger's actions while in command of Roanoke Island, North Carolina in February 1862, and it is easy to understand why he was relieved of divisional command in July 1862. He spent the rest of the war as an inspector of artillery and ordnance, mostly in the Trans-Mississippi Department.

Huger came from an aristocratic Charleston family. The name is Huguenot French, but is not pronounced as the French would pronounce it. I spent years innocently pronouncing the name **HUG-gur**. As time went on, and I became more sophisticated, I realized that the name was probably French in origin, and started calling the man,

U-zhay. This proved quite satisfactory, since some of the sources I read confirmed that indeed was the way the name was pronounced. Then, one day I came across Mark Boatner's pronouncer in his *Civil War Dictionary*. According to the colonel, the name was pronounced **U-gee.** So much confusion over this name led me to avoid saying it altogether.

Most recently, I was reading Stephen Sears latest book, *To The Gates of Richmond*, and was informed by author that the name was pronounced **U-zhay,**[129] which was confirmed in Patricia Faust's *Encyclopedia of the Civil War*. I now became convinced that I had been right all along. Huger was French name, therefore, it is pronounced in a French way. Yet, after years and years of living with the agony of not being sure, absolutely sure, I still had lingering doubts.

Finally, this past year I wrote a letter to historian Robert K. Krick asking his thoughts on the proper pronunciation of various Virginia locales and personages. Almost as an afterthought, I included Benjamin Huger's name on my list. Lucky afterthought, for here is what Mr. Krick had to say about the old general's name: Citing a dandy little book by Claude and Irene Neuffer, *Correct Mispronunciations of Some South Carolina Names*, Krick says, "the author adduces testimony from a modern family member who recalls that the family linens (of the Huger family) bore the embroidered legend in a corner, for identification, of 'U. G.' In addition, a wartime poem in South Carolina rhymed a line ending in 'knee' with a line ending in 'Huger'." Thank you, Mr. Krick! That's good enough for me. This pilgrim's search is over!

Major General Benjamin Huger

I

Imboden -(IM-boh-den)

as in John Daniel Imboden, Brigadier General C.S.A.

John Imboden is primarily remembered as a cavalry leader. Born in Staunton, Virginia he was a lawyer and state politician before the war. After fighting at First Manassas, he organized a regiment of mounted infantry called the 1st Partisan Rangers, and took part in Stonewall Jackson's 1862 Valley Campaign. After that, he served primarily in the Shenandoah Valley until incapacitated by typhoid fever in 1864. Imboden is famous for the Jones and Imboden western Virginia Raid in April 1863. He also performed valuable service protecting the wagon trains and wounded on Lee's retreat from Gettysburg.

After the war, Imboden moved to Richmond where he set up a law practice. He entered the mining business sometime shortly after this and located a large vein of soft coal in Washington County in southwest Virginia. Busy as he was during this period, Imboden managed to find time to engage another former Confederate general, John McCausland, in a fist fight at a Richmond railroad depot.[130] He founded the town of Demascus at the site of his bituminous coal seam, and lived there until his death in 1895.[131] Aside from all this, John Imboden was married five times.

Up until recently the name Imboden seemed to present no problems to me. Pronunciation seemed a fairly clear cut matter. However, I began hearing a few people say the name with the emphasis on the first syllable and began to suspect that a little investigation might be in order. I found out during my searching that John Imboden has a descendent who lives in Kansas City. Mr. Wiley Imboden, who should know better than anybody else, pronounces his last name with the stress on the first syllable.[132] I must yield to the superior knowledge of the descendent.

Brigadier General John Daniel Imboden

J

<u>Jäger</u> -(YAY-gur)

as in <u>Jäger</u> Rifle.

Another name given the United States Rifle Model 1841. The Jäger or Mississippi model was the first general issue U. S. Army rifle manufactured for the percussion cap system. The Jäger weighed more than nine pounds and fired a .54 caliber lead ball. Many of these rifles were still in use during the Civil War. The model 1841 was considered so effective that it was given the name Jäger, the German word for hunter or huntsman. After the rifle was issued to Jefferson Davis' 1st Mississippi Regiment in the Mexican War it also acquired the nickname, "Mississippi Rifle."

<u>Joinville</u> -(*zh*wan-VEEL)

as in Prince de <u>Joinville</u>.

Immediately after the outbreak of the Civil War several foreign notables arrived in Washington to offer their services to the Union cause. Many of these men were soldiers of fortune, opportunists and exiled nobility from Europe. It is into this last category that the Prince de Joinville falls. Exiled by the regime of Napoleon III, the prince and his two nephews, the Comte de Paris and the Duc de Chartres were welcomed as exotic additions to the Washington social scene in 1861. De Joinville and his nephews soon became fast friends with General George McClellan, and by the time of the Peninsula Campaign became part of his military family. De Joinville wrote a book about his Civil War experiences with McClellan's army which was published in 1862.

Joinville is a French name, of course, and the thing to bear in mind when you use the pronouncer provided is to pronounce the final **'N'** in *Join* with the nasal passages open. In other words, the **'n'** sound should be the same **'n'** sound you would use for "garcon."

Jomini -(*ZH*JOE-mee-nee)

as in Baron Antione Henri Jomini.

Swiss-born Baron Jomini joined Napoleon's army when he was seventeen. Ten years later he was a colonel on the staff of Marshal Ney and went on from there to become a general on Napoleon's staff. Jomini was the foremost interpreter of the Napoleon's campaigns. His most influential published works were, *Traite des grandes operations militaires*, which translates to an infinitely more understandable, *Treatise on Grand Military Operations*, and *Precis de l'art de la guerre* (Come on, you can figure that one out!). Jomini had a profound influence on the tactical thinking of many Civil War commanders.

Jomini's emphasis on certain fundamental principles is reflected in much of the tactical thinking of generals like Robert E. Lee and George McClellan. Jomini thought that the use of tactics and strategy could limit the scope of war and control the level of violence. Jomini believed it was necessary for an army to concentrate superior numbers, with interior lines of operations, against opponents deployed on exterior lines. He believed in taking the offensive, the use of surprise and vigorous pursuit of a beaten foe. Jomini was also a big advocate of the turning movement.

Much of Jomini's military theory was put into practice during the Civil War. Some generals, like Henry W. Halleck and George McClellan, were deluded by Jomini into thinking they could win the war by maneuver. Others, like Robert E. Lee, made very effective use of Jomini's maxims concerning the use of the offensive, the exploitation of surprise and the turning movement. Still others like, Ulysses Grant and Nathan Bedford Forrest, never gave a damn about Jomini, or any other military theorist.

Pronunciation of Jomini's name is easily obtained in standard reference works. The most common error in pronunciation is usually made by giving an English sound to the letter **'J'** at the beginning of the name.

The Orléans Princes
from left: Captain Le Clerc
Duc De Chartres
Compe De Paris
Prince De Joinville
Standing ?
Captain Mohain

K

<u>Kanawha</u> -(kan-NOW-wha)

as in <u>Kanawha</u> Valley, West Virginia.

Both North and South began operations in 1861 to secure the area we now know as West Virginia. Robert E. Lee did rather poorly in this theater of operations, while George McClellan built himself a reputation that would lead to overall command of Federal forces before the end of the first autumn of the war. Battles with names like Corrick's Ford, Gauley Bridge and Rich Mountain, important at the time, are today all but forgotten. By 1862 new battles, with new generals took place. Much of the action centered on the Kanawha Valley, through which the Kanawha River runs. The capital of West Virginia, Charleston is along this river.

Kanawha is a word derived from the Algonquian language that may mean "hurricane." What this reflects about the nature of the Kanawha River is anyone's guess. Pronunciation by those of us who are not from West Virginia is often wrong. As a resident of New England, I tend to pronounce the word as, **kana-WHA**. I have noticed that New Yorkers and New Jerseyites do the same thing. Go figure.

<u>Kearny</u> -(KAR-nee)

as in Philip <u>Kearny</u>, Major General U.S.V.

Philip Kearny was the scion of a wealthy New York family, and a soldier of fortune (no pun intended). Prior to the Civil War, Kearny had studied law after graduating from Columbia. He traveled widely, and after inheriting several million dollars from his grandfather in 1836, decided to pursue his lifelong dream of a military career. His uncle, Stephen Watts Kearny of Mexican War fame, arranged a commission for young Phil in his regiment, the 1st Dragoons, in 1837. By 1840 Kearny had attended the French Cavalry School at Saumur, and had served briefly with French colonial troops in Algiers. After returning to the U.S., he served on the staff of General Winfield Scott and by 1846 was involved in the Mexican War. Kearny lost his left arm to a wound at Churubusco. After the Mexican War he was stationed briefly in California. He resigned from the army in 1851 and took a trip around the world (Oh, but the joys of great wealth are truly sweet!).

Philip Kearny's military career resumed again in 1859 when he joined Napoleon III's Imperial Guard and saw action in the Italian War. He was in cavalry charges at the battles of Solferino and Magenta. He was still overseas when the Civil War broke out in America. Offering his services to the Lincoln government, he was among the first to be appointed a brigadier general of volunteers. He took command of a New Jersey brigade in Franklin's Division of the Army of the Potomac, and during McClellan's Peninsula Campaign rose to division command in the Third Corps. He was promoted to major general in July 1862. At the Battle of Chantilly, a confused and indecisive engagement at the end of the Second Manassas Campaign, he was killed when he mistakenly rode into Confederate lines.

The pronunciation of Kearny's name as **KAR-nee** is fairly common for that name. There is a town in New Jersey, named after the general, and it too is pronounced **KAR-nee**.

Keitt -(kit)

as in Laurence Massillon Keitt, Colonel, 20th South Carolina.

Prior to the Civil War, Laurence Keitt had been a member of the U. S. Congress. In fact, Keitt accompanied Congressman Preston Brooks in 1856 when he caned Charles Sumner on the floor of the Senate. With the onset of war, Keitt raised the 20th South Carolina and was appointed its colonel in January 1862. The 20th was to spend most of the next two years on garrison duty around Charleston. During that time Keitt did a stint in the Confederate Congress. In the spring of 1864 Colonel Keitt and the 20th South Carolina were sent to Virginia to fatten the thinned ranks of Kershaw's Brigade of the Army of Northern Virginia.[132] They saw their first combat at the Battle of Cold Harbor and it was an unmitigated disaster for the green troops. On June 1, 1864, the inexperienced 20th was routed, and its colonel mortally wounded. Keitt died two days later in Richmond.

The Keitt family has been prominent for many years in South Carolina. Though some Keitt families pronounce the name **KEET**, most, including that of Colonel Laurence Keitt, prefer **KIT**.[133]

Keyes -(keez)

as in Erasmus Darwin Keyes, Major General U.S.V.

Erasmus Keyes is one of those Union generals I've always put in the category of "Early War Generals." If you have done any extensive reading on the Eastern theater of the war you know that Keyes name shows up time and again from the Battle of Bull Run through McClellan's Peninsula Campaign. Then, after McClellan leaves the Peninsula, he disappears from the books as completely as Jimmy Hoffa did from that restaurant parking lot in 1970. Well, perhaps not <u>that</u> completely. Nevertheless, Erasmus Keyes, a corps commander in the Army of the Potomac, is hardly ever mentioned again in the history of the Army. Not only is Keyes gone, but the Fourth Corps he commands is gone as well. What gives?

Actually, when McClellan pulled the Army of the Potomac out of the Peninsula, Keyes and the Fourth Corps were left behind so that there would be a Federal presence of at least some substance on the Peninsula. Keyes' Fourth Corps, which had been reduced in size just before the Seven Days' Battles,[134] became part of General John Dix's Department of Virginia. Eventually the corps was whittled away by reassignment of its troops until it was little more than "a paper organization."[135] In essence, General Keyes and his corps had been consigned to oblivion. The reason for this was largely political. Erasmus Keyes had not been George McClellan's choice for a corps commander, but one of the generals selected by the Lincoln Administration by seniority. McClellan did not even like the idea of dividing the army into corps, let alone the choice of Erasmus Keyes as a commander. In addition, McClellan had a personal antipathy for Keyes, whom he regarded as "very prissy & entirely unfit to command a corps."[136]

Keyes resigned from the army in the spring of 1864. He moved to the West Coast and became a successful entrepreneur. He died while on a trip to Europe in 1895 and is buried at West Point.

Pronunciation of General Keyes' name is problematic because of the prevalence of an alternate pronunciation. In the South the name is often pronounced **kize**. A popular American novelist, Francis Parkinson Keyes (1885-1970), who was from Virginia pronounced his name "Kize," for example. Erasmus Keyes, however, was from New England. I have encountered people at Civil War conferences, professional historians among them, who insist that **kize** is correct for this general's name. Every source I checked insisted it was **keeze.**[137]

<u>Knipe</u> -(nipe)

as in Joseph Farmer <u>Knipe</u>, Brigadier General U.S.V.

Before the Civil War, Pennsylvania-born Joseph Knipe was a shoemaker, an enlisted man in the regular army who fought in the Mexican War, and also worked for the Pennsylvania Railroad.[138] He became colonel of the 46th Pennsylvania in August 1861 and saw action in the Shenandoah Valley under the command of the hapless Nathaniel Banks. Knipe was wounded at the Battle of Cedar Mountain. During the Maryland Campaign of 1862 he led a brigade in the Twelfth Corps and at Chancellorsville the following year commanded his brigade as part of Alpheus Williams' Division.

General Knipe was still not fully recovered from his Cedar Mountain wound when the Gettysburg Campaign got underway. As a result, he was temporarily relegated to commanding a force of Pennsylvania militia, which had been hastily called up to meet the Rebel invader. He was sent, with his command of green troops, to Chambersburg. On June 22, 1863 the approach of Robert Rodes' Division of Lee's army was reported. This was too much for Knipe's militia troops and they immediately boarded the train for Harrisburg.[139]

Knipe was transferred to the War in the West, along with the rest of the Twelfth Corps, in the Autumn of 1863. He fought in the all the battles up to Atlanta with the Army of the Cumberland. In 1864 he transferred to a cavalry command and led a division under James Wilson's Cavalry Corps in Tennessee. He performed well at the Battle of Nashville.

After the war, Knipe was postmaster of Harrisburg, Pennsylvania, and filled a number of state and Federal posts thereafter. He died in 1901.

Knipe is a German name. Usually, the letter 'k' would be pronounced in the name Knipe, at least if the name were being said in the German manner. In the Harrisburg area of Pennsylvania, however, the 'k' is dropped and it is pronounced just like any other English word starting with 'kn.'[140]

Kossuth -(KAH-sooth)

as in Lajos Kossuth, Hungarian patriot, revolutionary and statesman.

Lajos (LAH-yosh, which translates to Louis) Kossuth spent many years after the failure of the Hungarian Revolt of 1848 wandering from country to country as a charismatic political exile espousing the cause of Hungarian independence. One of his stops was the United States, where he made a whirlwind tour of the country beginning in December 1851. For weeks America was caught up in a Kossuth craze: Kossuth clubs were started, Hungarian music became popular in restaurants, and people gave money to promote the cause of Hungarian freedom; there was even a fashion in Kossuth hats and coats.[141] Then, as suddenly as it had begun, it all ended, and by the end of 1852 Kossuth was all but forgotten (sounds like the pop music business).

But what has all this to do with the Civil War? Well, you might have noticed that in a few of the capsule biographies of some of the more prominent foreign born Civil War figures mentioned in this dictionary, and in other reference works, the name Kossuth pops up. General Julius Stahel, for example, was a follower of Kossuth in Hungary, and so was Sandor Asboth. Aside from that, Kossuth's name shows up in many antebellum histories detailing the country's gradual drift toward Civil War.

The standard pronunciation of Kossuth is actually anglicized version of the real pronunciation, which is more like KOSH-oot or KAH-shuut. The proper English pronunciation of Kossuth is available in a number of reference works, including the *NBC*

Handbook of Pronunciation, which gives the best respelling pronouncer and the one I used at the top of this entry.

Kryzanowski -(kzhi-zha-NOV-ski *or* krez-uh-NOV-ski)

as in Wladimir Kryzanowski, Brigadier General U.S.V.

According to H. L. Mencken, names like "Kryzanowski, Kosciuszko, Andrzejski...and Mikolajezyk still survive in American reference books and even in newspaper dispatches, though it is highly unlikely that more than one non-Polish-American in ten thousand can pronounce them."[142] That was back in 1948, and it seems likely that things haven't improved much since then. Hence, including General Kryzanowski's name in this dictionary seems necessary.

Wladimir Kryzanowski was born in Poland in 1824. At the time of his birth Poland was under Prussian, Russian and Austrian domination. When Kryzanowski turned twenty-one he joined the movement for Polish liberation. The revolt of the Polish nationalists took place in 1846, two years before the rest of Europe exploded into revolution, and failed. As a result, young Kryzanowski became a political refugee forced into exile. He arrived in the United States in 1847 and thanks to his educational background and mastery of English was able to start working as a civil engineer.

When the Civil War came, Kryzanowski was living in Washington, D. C., where he raised a company of volunteers for Turner's Rifles, District of Columbia Militia.[143] When this "three-month" unit was mustered out at the expiration of its service in July 1861, Kryzanowski went to New York to raise a Polish regiment. After he had raised four companies, they were combined with six other companies of Germans to form the 58th New York. He was appointed colonel of the new regiment in October 1861, and became part of Louis Blenker's Division.

Kryzanowski and his regiment ultimately became part of the Eleventh Corps, Army of the Potomac. This luckless organization, of which nearly half the regiments were made up of foreign speaking immigrants, met with disaster at Chancellorsville, and fared poorly at Gettysburg. It was finally combined with the Twelfth Corps to form the 20th after going west in the autumn of 1863. Despite the Corps' reputation, it contained many good fighting units and combat officers. Kryzanowski was among them.

After the war, Kryzanowski, who was a high profile Republican in the immigrant community, got an appointment with the Treasury Department, and worked for the IRS as well. Following that, he was a customs inspector in Central America, and held down the same job later on in New York City. He died there in 1887.

Pronunciation of General Kryzanowski's name, if we are to do it properly, means dealing with the Polish language. I have given two pronouncers; the first is as phonetically close as I could come to the Polish pronunciation,[144] the second is an Americanized version.[145] Since the 'kz' sound in the first syllable is close to impossible for most people to master without much practice, I have given the Americanized version of the name for reasons of practicality. You may find, as I have, that if you practice the Polish pronouncer you will want to do it alone. Attempting to say it to others may lead to the embarrassment of your inadvertently spitting on them. I have always tried to follow the advice of that old saying, "Never spit in a man's face unless his mustache is on fire."

Kyd -(kid)

as in Henry Kyd Douglas, Major C.S.A. and Confederate memorialist.

Henry Kyd Douglas is famous in Civil War history not for any battlefield exploit, but for the fact that he wrote a wonderful book after the war about his adventures as a member of Stonewall Jackson's staff. The book is called, *I Rode with Stonewall* and it is a well written memoir that contains many amusing and insightful anecdotes about Jackson. Though Douglas makes occasional factual errors, and probably has embellished some of incidents he describes, he provides us with a really good look at what life with Stonewall was like. In addition, Douglas gives his firsthand impressions of other notables of the Army of Northern Virginia, like Robert E. Lee and James Longstreet.

Over the years I have, on at least three memorable occasions, heard the name Kyd mispronounced. In a talk given by a park service historian in Virginia I heard Douglas' middle name pronounced, kie-d, rhymes with "hide." I had always assumed this was a wrong pronunciation. But there is a complication. At least one reliable source told me that locals in the Shepherdstown, West Virginia area, old-timers who knew the family, sometimes used this pronunciation, as did some members of the family.[146] Bearing this variation of the name in mind, I nevertheless recommend sticking with the conventional pronunciation of Douglas' middle name. As I have discovered during the course of researching this book, there comes a time with some of these names when so many variations surface that one must compromise and chose the likeliest, or most widely used pronunciation. It is either this or verbal anarchy.

Major General Erasmus Darwin Keyes

L

Lafayette and La Fayette -(luh-FAY-et)

as in Lafayette McLaws, Major General C.S.A. and La Fayette, Georgia.

Georgia born Lafayette McLaws graduated from West Point in 1842. He served in the Mexican War and on the frontier before the Civil War. He resigned from the U. S. Army in 1861, joined the army of the Confederacy and by June of that year was colonel of the 10th Georgia. He was appointed brigadier general on September 25, 1861 and major general the following spring after serving in the Peninsula Campaign. As commander of a division of the Army of Northern Virginia he fought in most of the major campaigns as part of Longstreet's First Corps. McLaws' big moment in Civil War history was the second day at Gettysburg, where his division was involved in heavy fighting at the Peach Orchard and in the Wheatfield. McLaws went west with Longstreet's Corps in the late summer of 1863 but did not fight at Chickamauga. After the Knoxville Campaign he was relieved by Longstreet for "failure to make preparation...and a lack of confidence in" the unsuccessful operations against Fort Sanders.[147] A court martial later exonerated McLaws, but he never forgave Longstreet. He was then assigned to the defenses of Savannah, Georgia and subsequently served under William J. Hardee and Joe Johnston in the Carolinas until the end of the war. After the war, McLaws was in the insurance business and also held down a couple of Federal posts (tax collector and postmaster) in Georgia. He died in 1897. On the whole, Lafayette McLaws was a competent and dependable commander.

In any study of the Chickamauga Campaign you are bound to come across La Fayette, Georgia. After Braxton Bragg had pulled his Army of Tennessee out of Chattanooga on September 7, 1863 he began reconcentrating it at La Fayette, Georgia which was about twenty miles to the south. This put Bragg less than five miles east of the West Fork of Chickamauga Creek, where on September 18th fighting would commence in one of the war's great battles.

Pronunciation of Lafayette McLaws first name and La Fayette, Georgia is a fairly typical Americanization of a French name.[148] There are other places named "LaFayette" that are locally pronounced the same as LaFayette, Georgia. I chose the one in Georgia because of its association with an important Civil War battle.

<u>Lamon</u> -(luh-MON)

as in Ward Hill <u>Lamon</u>, friend of Abraham Lincoln.

Ward Hill Lamon was an old friend, political crony and fellow attorney of Lincoln's. Lincoln and Lamon traveled the circuit in Illinois and acted as co-counsels in a number of cases. When Lincoln was elected President, Lamon, who had worked actively for his election, became Lincoln's self appointed body guard on the trip from Illinois to Washington.

Lincoln biographer Stephen Oates describes Lamon as, "a big, gruff fellow...a legendary boozer who spent much of his time in the saloon under his office, where he sang lewd and comic songs and got into brawls."[149] Though Lamon has many late 20th century counterparts among politicos in Washington, these modern day voluptuaries tend to conceal their more colorful behavior from the credulous electorate, and confine their lewd and comic behavior to non-election years. Despite his faults, Hill Lamon was well liked by the tolerant Lincoln. He saw to it that Lamon was made United States Marshal of Washington, D. C. during his presidency.

Lamon is one of those simple names that is often mispronounced (I guess). I have heard everything from **la-MON**, which sounds very much like the famous auto race on the Grand Prix circuit, to **LAY-man** and **LAM-un** in pronunciations of this five letter name. Pronunciation of Lamon, however, is apparently a relative thing. I got into a lively debate with several Lincoln scholars and Civil War historians over the correct pronunciation of Lamon. Gabor Borritt of Gettysburg College, a Lincoln scholar and editor of *Lincoln the War President* insisted that **luh-MON** was correct. This was confirmed by the fact that Ralph Newman of the Chicago Civil War Round Table and founder of the round table movement also uses this pronunciation.[150] Ultimately, summoning what small reserves of courage I still possessed, I decided to go with **luh-MON**. This pronouncer seemed to get the most votes in my little referendum in the groves of Academe and elsewhere.

<u>Lanier</u> -(luh-NEER)

as in Sidney <u>Lanier</u>, poet, Confederate soldier, spokesman for the Lost Cause.

Sidney Lanier was an 1860 graduate of Oglethorpe University in Georgia. In June 1861 he joined the Macon Guards and by the following spring was fighting in the Seven Days' Battles with Lee's Army on the Virginia Peninsula. Lanier transferred to signal duty late in 1862. By 1864 he had transferred to Wilmington, North Carolina and was a signalman aboard blockade runners. On November 2, 1864 he was captured at sea and ended up spending the rest of the war in Point Lookout Prison, Maryland. This imprisonment broke Lanier's health, turned him into an invalid and ultimately shortened his life.[151]

After the war, Lanier worked at various jobs. He was a tutor to a plantation family for a time, worked as a hotel desk clerk, and was even principal of an Alabama school. In 1873 Lanier, who was an accomplished musician, got a job with the Peabody Symphony Orchestra in Baltimore. Meanwhile, a novel he had begun writing during the war was completed and published in 1867. *Tiger-Lilies* was chivalric romance set in the South filled with "melodramatic incidents, stilted dialogue, and excessive literary allusions."[152] The book does give a graphic account of the main character's experiences as a prisoner of war based on Lanier's time at Point Lookout. More important, it was the beginning of a literary career that lasted until Lanier's death in 1881.

What Lanier is most remembered for is his poetry. He is considered by many to be the best poet of the American South in the latter part of the 19th century. His poems are structured in metrical patterns that are designed to achieve the same effect as music. His most famous works incorporating this musical quality are *The Marshes of Glynn* and *Song of the Chattahoochee.* His poetry also had a message. *The Symphony,* written in 1875, was an attack on post-Civil War industrialism. Lanier became known through his poetry as a voice of the defeated Confederacy, a bitter spokesman for the Lost Cause.

Lanier is French Huguenot name. Lanier's family tree had distinguished musicians going back to 17th century France and England.

Latané -(LAT-un-AY)

as in William Latané, Captain, 9th Virginia Cavalry.

In the early summer of 1862 many romantic delusions about the nature of warfare were still prevalent. The dimension and brutality of the conflict were yet not fully perceived by the participants. Despite the fact that by June of 1862 there had already been some major battles with much loss of life, the public at large in both North and South still retained a lot of romantic notions. Perhaps this explains the exaggerated public reaction in the South to the death of Captain William Latané.

Latané was the only battle death Jeb Stuart sustained in his famous "Ride Around McClellan." If you know your Peninsula Campaign history you know that in mid-June 1862, as part of his preparation for attacking McClellan's army before Richmond (thus opening the Seven Days' Battles), Robert E. Lee assigned his chief cavalryman, Jeb Stuart, the task of reconnoitering the position of the Army of the Potomac. Stuart's instructions were to reconnoiter the right flank and rear of McClellan's position. Old Jeb, however, far exceeded this by riding a complete circle around the Federals. The operation commenced on June 12, 1862 and ended on the 15th. Stuart and 1200 troopers rode more than one hundred-forty miles, destroying property, capturing prisoners and generally raising a lot of hell. The ride was a public sensation and a great morale booster for beleaguered Richmond residents. But what about Captain Latané?

William Latané was captain of Company F of the 9th Virginia Cavalry. Company F was also known as "The Essex Light Dragoons." On the second day of the ride, June 13, 1862, at a place just south of Totopotomoy Creek called Linney's Corner, Federal cavalry took a stand against Stuarts advancing troops. In the ensuing battle, Latané led a charge of the Essex Light Dragoons shouting, "On to them, boys!" Latané was a bit carried away by the excitement and got about fifteen yards ahead of his men. When he hit the Federal line, Latané ran smack into his Union counterpart, Captain William Royall of the 5th U. S. Cavalry. Flailing about with his saber, Latané managed to severely wound Captain Royall. Royall, however, was better armed and shot Latané twice with his pistol.[153] The Confederate was dead before he hit the ground. His body was brought, by his brother, to a nearby plantation, Westwood, where it was ceremoniously buried by the mistress of the house, Mrs Catherine Brockenbrough and her friend, Mrs. Willoughby Newton.

Before the war, Latané was a practicing physician who also ran his family's plantation. He was twenty-nine years old when he was killed. Because of his background, because it was early in the war and the South could still indulge in the ritual of heroic death, and because he was the only death on an otherwise bloodless undertaking, much was made of the untimely passing of Captain William Latané. You might say he became "The Cavalry Poster Boy of 1862." A month after his death, Latané was memorialized in a poem by John R. Thompson in the *Southern Literary Messenger* entitled "The Burial of Latané," and painter William Washington put the funeral scene on canvas. Prints of Washington's painting hung in Southern parlors for a generation.[154]

Latané's name is of French derivation. Pronunciation retains much of its French character because of that accent mark on the final 'e.' I had heard this name any number of times from various Park Service historians and academic historians, but never checked it out in any reference work. When the weighty tomes were perused they yielded up the same pronunciation I was familiar with.

Leister -(LIE-stur)

as in the Leister Farmhouse, Meade's Headquarters at the Battle of Gettysburg.

When Major General George G. Meade arrived on the Gettysburg battlefield a few hours prior to dawn on July 2, 1863 he selected the centrally located farmhouse of Mrs. Lydia A. Leister as his headquarters. Mrs. Leister would return after the battle to find her farm looking like a war zone, which is exactly what it had been for three days. She would complain bitterly for many years about the damage done to her farm.[155]

If you've toured the Gettysburg battlefield you have undoubtedly come across the Leister farmhouse. Located very near the Visitor Center and the Cyclorama, the Leister

House is a tiny one story, wooden building painted white. The most famous thing that occurred there during the battle was when Meade called a council of war. About ten o'clock on the evening of July 2, 1863 the commanding general called together all his wing and corps commanders to review the condition of the Army of the Potomac and decide what the next move should be. There had already been two days of brutal fighting at Gettysburg and Meade wanted to consider his options. One of those options was withdrawal and much controversy has developed over the years as to whether that was, in fact, what Meade had in mind. In any event, he and his corps commanders decided to stay put and fight it out.

Looking into the windows of the tiny Leister farmhouse today it is hard to picture even a small meeting taking place there. The rooms are the size of telephone booths. The house consists of two small rooms with a loft above them. The 1860 Census for Cumberland Township, Adams County, where the house is located, states that three adults and three children lived there![156] The Battle of Gettysburg must have been a peaceful interlude for the tiny dwelling. At the time of the battle Mrs. Leister was a widow, her husband, James Leister, having died in 1859 at the age of sixty-one.[157] The other people listed in the Census as living with Mrs. Leister were apparently relatives.

Pronunciation of the name "Leister" seems to present a difficulty to many people. Yet, it is simplicity itself. The 'ei' sound is almost always pronounced as a long 'i' in names. Over the years I have heard a variety of mispronunciations: **LEE-stur**, **LES-tur** and **LIS-tur** are the most frequently heard mistakes.[158]

Leonidas -(lee-ON-i-dis *or* lee-uh-NIE-dis)

as in Leonidas Polk, Lieutenant General C.S.A.

Leonidas Polk was one of more unique individuals to grace the officer's corps of the Confederate Army. Born in North Carolina, and graduated from West Point in 1827, he resigned his commission six months after graduation to study in the Episcopal ministry. By the time the Civil War came he was a bishop. His good friend Jefferson Davis persuaded him to accept a commission as major general in 1861.

Polk's Civil War career was in the western theater of operations, first under Albert Sidney Johnston, then under the command of Braxton Bragg, and finally under Joseph E. Johnston. Bishop Polk fought at Belmont, where he defeated Ulysses Grant, Shiloh, Perryville and Stones River. Bragg removed him from command after the Battle of Chickamauga for not attacking when told to, though he was reinstated by Jefferson Davis. Polk was finally killed by an artillery shell at Pine Mountain during the Atlanta Campaign of 1864.

Leonidas is one of those classical names people were fond of giving children in the 19th century. In fact, Greek and Roman classicism became such a rage in the earlier part of the last century that whole batches of towns in states like New York and Ohio were given names like Troy, Euclid, Sparta, Seneca and Athens. Thus, naming a male child after Leonidas, Spartan king and hero of the 5th century BC, was not unusual. These days, however, it is. As a result a lot people come to grief when they attempt to pronounce this name.

The correct way of pronouncing the name Leonidas is **lee-ON-i-dis**. There is a variation on this, however, which is so commonly used among Civil War historians that I have been compelled to put it in this entry as an alternate correct pronunciation. The use of **lee-uh-NIE-dis** is so frequent, especially among Southerners, that it is probable Bishop Polk himself said it that way.[159]

Liddell -(lid-DEL)

as in St. John Richardson Liddell, Brigadier General C.S.A.

General Liddell was born into a wealthy family near Woodville, Mississippi in 1815. He received an appointment to West Point in 1833, but resigned after a year, presumably because of poor grades. There is, however, an unsubstantiated story that he became involved in a duel and wounded a classmate. Whatever the case, he returned to Mississippi and became a plantation owner (his dad bought him one) in Louisiana. During the 1850s Liddell became embroiled in a feud with Charles Jones and was arrested for the murder of two of Jones' friends. There was a trial in 1854 and he was acquitted.[160]

The coming of the Civil War, if nothing else, legalized Liddell's penchant for shooting people. Using his important social connections (he was pal of General William Hardee and knew Jefferson Davis' family, to mention but a few) he secured a position as a volunteer staff aide to General Hardee with the rank of colonel. He worked on Hardee's staff in Kentucky and also acted as a confidential courier for General Albert Sydney Johnston. In May 1862 he was finally put on the payroll (the staff position had been an unpaid volunteer arrangement) and given command of a brigade at Corinth, Mississippi. Liddell was promoted to brigadier general in June 1862 and saw his first serious fighting as a leader of troops at the Battle of Perryville, Kentucky in October. His brigade performed well in the battle and he was commended by Generals Hardee and Polk.

St. John Liddell remained with Bragg's Army of Tennessee through the battles of Stones River Chickamauga and Chattanooga. He was transferred to Louisiana in December 1863 and was given command of a sub-district in the northern part of the state a month later. Liddell became involved in the Red River Campaign in April 1864 under General Richard Taylor, who he did not get along with. He requested a transfer and was put in command of Confederate forces in southern Mississippi.[161] Eventually he also was given responsibility for the defenses of Mobile Bay. Liddell took part in the defense of Mobile and was captured at Fort Blakely on April 9, 1865.

After the war General Liddell returned to his plantation in Louisiana and resumed his feud with Charles Jones. Liddell was aboard a steamboat on the Black River on February 14, 1870 when he met with Jones and his two sons. In the melee that ensued, Liddell was shot seven times and killed. Charles Jones and his sons were killed by a mob shortly thereafter.[162]

Pronunciation of St. John Liddell's last name puts the emphasis on the last syllable. As you will see in the next entry, pronunciation of the name Liddell does not always follow this rule. Standard reference works provided no answers on St. John Liddell's last name. I asked a number of Civil War historians and writers how they pronounced the name and **lid-DEL** prevailed in the most cases. The only printed reference I could come up with was in *Lippincott's Pronouncing Gazetteer of the World* (1882) detailing a 19th century hamlet in Montgomery county Mississippi named "Liddell" (containing a saw mill, a grist mill, and little else, I would imagine) which was pronounced **lid-DEL**. This at least established some sort of regional pronunciation of the name, but was still not definitive evidence. Further checking with Arthur Bergeron of the Department of State Parks in Baton Rouge, Jim Mundie of the Houston Civil War Round Table (and New Orleans native) and Nathaniel C. Hughes, Civil War historian and writer who specializes Trans-Mississippi Confederates, confirmed the **lid-DEL** pronunciation.

Liddell-Hart -(LID-ul-HART)

as Sir Basil Liddell-Hart, British military authority and writer.

Sir Basil Liddell-Hart, who died in 1970, was a major military historian. Among his better known works about the Civil War is *Sherman: Soldier, Realist, American*. If you do much reading in military history you are bound to run into the work of Liddell-Hart. Like J. F. C. Fuller, another Englishman, Liddell-Hart took a keen interest in the Civil War. There has always been a tendency on the part of English and European military historians to regard our war as nothing more than a bloody brawl between two armed mobs. Fuller and Liddell-Hart do not share this view.

For a number of years I was saying Sir Basil's hyphenated last name as **luh-DEL-HART**. What messed me up was that double 'l' in the first part of the name. I was recently listening to a talk at a Civil War conference at West Point when the speaker made reference to **LID-ul-HART** and I thought he might be referring to some famous Indian who was named for his lack of compassion. It slowly dawned on me who he was talking about. I was very happy no one had ever heard my own version of the name.

<u>Loudoun</u> -(LOW-din [LOW rhymes with cow])

as in <u>Loudoun</u> County, Virginia.

Loudoun County is one of the northernmost counties of Virginia. Though not the site of any major battle during the Civil War, Loudoun County is famous because of the activities of John Singleton Mosby and his Partisan Rangers. "Mosby's Confederacy," as it was called, is comprised mostly of locations inside Loudoun County. The county is also the location of Ball's Bluff, a major Union fiasco early in the war.

Loudoun is one of those names that will either trip you up on the first syllable or mess you up on the second if you are not familiar with the proper pronunciation. I heard one buff giving a talk on Mosby pronounce it, **LOO-down**. Both syllables got to him.

<u>Lovell</u> -(LUV-ul)

as in Mansfield <u>Lovell,</u> Major General C.S.A.

Lovell was born in Washington, D. C. in 1822. His father was Surgeon General of the Army at the time. He graduated from West Point in 1842 and served in garrison on the frontier until the Mexican War. During that conflict he was twice wounded and awarded a brevet promotion to captain for his gallantry at Chapultepec. In 1854 he followed his close friend Gustavus W. Smith in resigning from the army. Lovell and Smith headed for New York City. Lovell finally settled into a job as deputy street commissioner under his friend Smith. In September 1861 Lovell and Smith quit as street commissioners and accepted commissions in the Confederate army.

Thanks to lobbying efforts by his friend Smith, Mansfield Lovell was appointed major general in October 1861 and put in command of the defenses of New Orleans. General Lovell was a bit of a *bon vivant* and he managed to enjoy his short-lived command of the Crescent City. His defense against Federal invasion was inadequate because of shortages of men and matériel. Nevertheless, he was severely criticized for evacuating the city on April 25, 1862, after which it was captured with very little loss of life by Federal forces. Lovell was vilified so stridently that he called for a court of inquiry to clear his name. The court met the following year and more or less exonerated him. However, he never recovered his reputation after New Orleans.

His next assignment was a division command under Earl Van Dorn at Corinth, Mississippi in October 1862, and as a wing commander under General John C. Pemberton during the Confederate retreat in early December 1862 from the Tallahatchie to the Yalobusha. None of this mattered, however, since Lovell was relieved of command later that same month because of his loss of New Orleans. Much of this intense political pressure to make Lovell the scapegoat for the loss of New Orleans was probably exacerbated by the fact that Lovell came from a long line of Bostonians. Galvanized Yankees were good friends when the going was good, but pariahs when the tide turned against the South.

Pronunciation of the name Lovell is probably made difficult for some people because of that double **'l'** ending. Standard reference books give the proper pronunciation.[163] The most common mispronunciation I have heard is **loh-VELL.**[164]

Luray -(loo-RAY)

as in Luray Valley, Virginia.

Massanutten Mountain divides the Shenandoah Valley into two parallel valleys for a distance of about forty-five miles. The valley formed on the east by Massanutten and the Blue Ridge Mountains is called the Luray Valley. From the standpoint of the Civil War buff, this geographic fact is of some importance. During his famous Valley Campaign of 1862, Stonewall Jackson made good use of the Luray Valley to screen his movements. Another name for the Luray Valley is the Page Valley, taking its name from the county that comprises much of the area.

Many people in this country have been for a visit to Luray Caverns, near the town of Luray. Though they hear the proper pronunciation of the name when they are there, they apparently do not retain it too well. I have often heard it pronounced, **LOO-ree** or **LOO-ray**. The pronunciation I am using, as the proper one, is that used by the people who live in Luray, Virginia.[165]

Lunette -(loo-NET)

as in "Each of the artillery pieces was inside a lunette."

A lunette is a crescent shaped earthwork or fortification behind which an artillery piece is placed. The lunette provides the gun crew protection in the front and on both flanks. The open end of the crescent permits easy removal of the piece. When you visit battlefield sites you will often see the neatly landscaped remains of these fortifications wherever artillery was located on the original battlefield. Lunettes were dug out when no permanent, or semi-permanent fortification, was available.

Another definition of lunette is a towing ring on the end of a gun trail that drops over the pintle of the limber.[166] Lunette is also an architectural term.

Pronunciation of lunette puts the stress on the second syllable. The word is derived from the French for moon, which makes sense when you consider that it is crescent shaped. I always thought the word sounded like a term used to describe a very small lunatic.

Lysander -(lie-SAN-dur)

as in Lysander Cutler, Brigadier General U.S.V.

Lysander Cutler was more than fifty years old when the Civil War began. Born in Massachusetts, he moved to Maine in 1828 to teach school, became a successful businessman and eventually a state senator. However, the Panic of 1857 proved financially ruinous to Cutler and he moved to Milwaukee, Wisconsin where he became a grain broker. When the war came he was appointed colonel of the 6th Wisconsin, a regiment that was to become part of the famous Iron Brigade. Before the brigade got its name it did some serious fighting at the Battle of Brawner's Farm on August 28, 1862 the opening engagement of Second Manassas. Cutler was seriously wounded and when he returned to duty was given command of a brigade in the First Corps of the Army of the Potomac. He fought at Chancellorsville and Gettysburg, and assumed divisional command at the Battle of the Wilderness the following year. Cutler was relieved from active duty in September of 1864 at his own request. His health was shattered and he died a little more than a year after the war ended.

Lysander is one of those names taken from the classics. Lysander was a Spartan naval and military commander whose defeat of the Athenians in 405 B.S. ended the Peloponnesian War. Pronouncers for the name Lysander are abundant in dictionaries and other reference works.

Lieutenant General Leonidas Polk

M

McIvor -(muh-KEE-vur)

as in Evander McIvor Law, Brigadier General C.S.A.

You will find a full sketch of what General Law was all about during his long life under the entry for "Evander." What we are concerned with here is his middle name. McIvor is a spelling variation on the name McIver. It is a Scottish name and it is pronounced as I have indicated above in most parts of the country.

Mackall -(MAKE-awl)

as in William Wann Mackall, Brigadier General C.S.A.

Mackall is remembered primarily as Braxton Bragg's Chief of Staff. He was a West Point graduate and classmate of Bragg, served gallantly in the Mexican War and joined the Confederacy in 1861 as member of Albert Sidney Johnston's staff. Captured at Island No. 10 in April 1862 he was later exchanged and held various district commands until joining Bragg's staff in April of 1863. Later in the war he served as Joseph Johnston's Chief of Staff, but refused to serve under John Bell Hood when Johnston was relieved. He lived as a gentleman farmer in Virginia after the war.

I have run into people who absolutely insist that General Mackall's name is pronounced **muh-KAWL**. The late Bell I. Wiley, a well known Civil War historian, knew the General's family and he said it is pronounced **MAKE-awl**, as I have indicated in my pronouncer.[167]

McPherson -(muk-FUR-sun)

as in James Birdseye McPherson, Major General, U.S.V.

Civil War historian Ed Bearss has observed that one of the best things that could happen to a Civil War general's reputation (at least in the history books) is to be killed in a really important battle before he has made any serious mistakes. Two of the sterling examples of this phenomenon are General John Fulton Reynolds and General James McPherson.

Reynolds was killed on the morning of the first day of battle at Gettysburg. Since the moment poor Reynolds tumbled out of his saddle at the edge of Herbst's Woods there has been endless speculation on how things might have gone differently had Reynolds not been killed. Or, how if Reynolds had survived he might have gone on to become the greatest commander the Army of the Potomac ever had. Speculation like this is based on the debatable assumption that Reynolds was a great general. Reynolds was a good general. We have abundant evidence to support that. However, we will never know if he might have become a great general.

The same thing applies to James McPherson. McPherson was killed on July 22, 1864 during the Battle of Atlanta. The popular young general was an especial favorite of army commander William T. Sherman and he was utterly grief stricken at news of McPherson's death. His opinion of McPherson was so high that he had once predicted that if the war lasted long enough his charming friend's military reputation would eclipse both his and Grant's. Thus the groundwork was laid for another great might-have-been.

The real James Birdseye McPherson was no slouch. He was born in Ohio and attended West Point graduating first in the Class of 1853. He was assigned to the Engineers, of course, and after a brief stint of teaching at the Point did some work on river and harbor improvement, as well as seacoast fortifications. When the war came he first served as an aide to General Henry Halleck, then was assigned as chief engineer on the staff of Ulysses Grant. He was with Grant at Forts Henry and Donelson, Shiloh and the occupation of western Tennessee. He was promoted to brigadier general in August 1862, then major general two months later. Two months after his promotion, he became commander of the Seventeenth Corps of Grant's army during the Vicksburg Campaign. In February 1864 he led his corps in the Meridian Campaign under William T. Sherman and in March he became commander of the Army of the Tennessee. Let's face it, this guy was putting together a killer résumé. Unfortunately, McPherson died only a few months after he got his army command.

We will never know if James McPherson's military reputation might one day have eclipsed Uncle Billy's and U. S. Grant's. All we can say for certain is that James McPherson was a competent commander and a really nice guy. One other certainty is the pronunciation of his last name; as people with the old Scottish name McPherson are fond of saying, "there's no 'fear' in McPherson."

Madrid -(MAD-rid)

as in New Madrid, Missouri.

In the southeast corner of Missouri along an S-curve in the Mississippi River is a small town that got into the Civil War history books called New Madrid. Very early in the war Union forces started what turned out to be the long and arduous task of gaining control of navigation of the middle and lower Mississippi. In March of 1862 the recently organized Union Army of the Mississippi comprising five divisions of infantry, several cavalry brigades and a river flotilla all under the command of General John Pope, set out to capture New Madrid and Island Number 10 from the Confederates.

Pope began an eleven-day siege of New Madrid on March 3, 1862. Bombardment by siege artillery did not begin until March 13th, by which time the Confederate forces under the command of General John McCown were already evacuating the town. Pope occupied New Madrid the next day and turned his attention to the other Confederate position on the S-curve, Island Number 10. This operation, which involved gunboats and mortar boats, as well as the digging of a bypass canal, all climaxed in the Battle of Island Number 10 on April 7, 1862. Pope's victories at Island No. 10 and New Madrid not only opened the Mississippi as far south as Fort Pillow, Tennessee; it also captured the attention of Abraham Lincoln, who was desperate to find a general who took decisive action and could win on the battlefield. John Pope was brought east to command the newly formed Army of Virginia and was soundly defeated at Second Manassas in August 1862.

The name "New Madrid," at first look, seems a fairly straight forward name. But with different regions you get different syllable stresses. Thus, New Madrid, unlike Madrid, Spain is pronounced with the emphasis on the first syllable of Madrid.[168] Possibly the original settlers chose that pronunciation because they didn't want anyone getting their town mixed up with the capital of Spain, though the likelihood of this occurring, even <u>they</u> must have doubted.

<u>Magrath</u> -(muh-GRAW)

as in Andrew Gordon <u>Magrath</u>, Civil War Governor of South Carolina.

Andrew Magrath was a Federal district judge before the war and after his state, South Carolina, seceded from the Union he became a Confederate judge. He was elected governor of the Palmetto State in 1864 and served for the rest of the war. Magrath returned to the practice of law after the war.

The name Magrath is often pronounced **muh-GRAW**. It is also frequently pronounced **ma-GRATH**. The main problem, then, is determining which pronunciation the particular Magrath you happen to be dealing with uses. Unless one has heard the name, one is easily misled. In the case of Andrew Magrath the pronunciation used, according to historian Bell I. Wiley, is **muh-GRAW**.

Mahan -(muh-HAHN)

as in Dennis Hart Mahan, professor at West Point, military theorist.

Most of the important commanders, both North and South, received some of their military education in the classroom of Dennis Hart Mahan at West Point. Mahan taught at the Military Academy for more than forty years. He graduated from West Point at the top of his class in 1824 and with the exception of a four-year stint studying military science in Europe, he spent the rest of his army career as a teacher and theorist. Mahan was an advocate of defensive tactics, entrenchment and fortification and the use of the flank attack. He taught all the leading European military theories, but adapted them to the changing conditions and technologies of the times. Since he lived until 1871, he got to see his teachings put to practical use on the battlefield during the Civil War.

Pronunciation of Mahan puts the emphasis on the second syllable. The most common mispronunciation of this name is muh-HAN (rhymes with "can"). At the United States Military Academy at West Point all references to the late professor are pronounced as I have indicated above.

Mahopac -(MAY-oh-PAK *or* mah-HOH-PAK)

as in USS *Mahopac*.

Within weeks of the classic battle between the USS *Monitor* and the CSS *Virginia* (*Merrimack*) the pace of technological development in ironclads increased rapidly. Three weeks after the battle Ericsson (designer and builder of the *Monitor*) received orders for six improved versions of the boat. Contracts were also let for four additional the *Monitor* class boats from other builders. The ten boats that were finally built had thicker armor than the original the *Monitor* and more powerful armament. These were the *Passaic* Class of monitors. By September 1862 nine more Ericsson type monitors were ordered by the Navy, once again with significant design improvements. The USS *Mahopac* was among these. Like the original *Monitor*, the *Mahopac* had a single turret, but the addition of a defensive slope around the base prevented jamming. The hull was also stronger and the boat was more heavily armed, sporting a battery of 15-inch guns.[169]

The name Mahopac is one of those names that you will hear two pronunciations of. The town and lake in Putnam County, New York for which the vessel was probably named is pronounced MAY-oh-PAK. However, some older residents of the town say, mah-HOH-PAK. I have given both at the beginning of this entry. Since there seems to be no absolute certainty as to how the name was pronounced during the Civil War period, I would recommend going with the current pronunciation of the name as it is said in Putnam County.

Maney -(MAY-nee)

as in George Earl Maney, Brigadier General C.S.A.

Tennessee born George Maney was a graduate of the University of Nashville, a lawyer and a veteran of the Mexican War. He started the Civil War as a captain in the 11th Tennessee, was elected colonel of the 1st Tennessee and fought in western Virginia at Cheat Mountain. He went to the Western Theater in 1862 and was promoted to brigadier general for gallantry at Shiloh. As a brigade and division commander in the Army of Tennessee he fought at Perryville, Stones River, Chickamauga, Chattanooga and Atlanta. He was relieved of duty in August 1864 having been granted a leave of absence after being certified disabled by a doctor. Whatever the disability may have been it was not disclosed. Maney never again held a field command.

After the war, General Maney became president of the Tennessee and Pacific Railroad, served in the state legislature and vigorously campaigned for Republican national candidates in Tennessee. In 1881 he was appointed minister to Columbia by President Chester A. Arthur and was assigned to Bolivia in 1882. President Benjamin Harrison made him minister resident to both Paraguay and Uruguay in 1889 and minister plenipotentiary (Man, but wouldn't that fill up your old standard sized business card!) in 1890. Maney held this last position until 1894. He was in Washington, D. C. when he died suddenly in 1901.[170]

Pronunciation of Maney's name would seem a straightforward matter. Normally, a name with such a spelling would take the long 'a' sound as in, MAY-nee. This is the case with George Maney. Unfortunately, I heard the name pronounced MAN-ee and was thrown into confusion, since the person who said it knew his Civil War. I began to ask around and found others who were also in doubt. Thus, I have included George Maney in this dictionary.[171]

Manigault -(MAN-i-GOH)

as in Arthur Middleton Manigault, Brigadier General C.S.A.

A rice planter and exporter before the war, Arthur Manigault's military career for the Confederacy started in December 1860 when South Carolina seceded from the Union. Manigault was captain of the North Santee Mounted Rifles. He supervised the construction of batteries in Charleston Harbor and at the time of the firing on Fort Sumter was an ADC on General Beauregard's staff. Eventually, he became colonel of the 10th South Carolina, was ordered west with his regiment, and spent the remainder of the war as part of the Army of Tennessee. Manigault fought gallantly in the major campaigns of that army until a severe head wound at Franklin in November 1864 incapacitated him for further service. After the war he resumed rice planting and his commission business. He died from the lingering effects of his head wound in 1886.

Manigault is one of those French Huguenot names so common among the upper class families of Charleston, South Carolina. In fact, the Manigaults go back to the early 18th century in Charleston history. The family retained the French pronunciation of the name. There are some variations, however. At least one prominent black family in Columbia with the name pronounces it MAN-i-GAWLT, and there is a small community in Berkeley County called Manigault Lane, which is pronounced MAN-i-GOTE.[172]

Marais des Cygnes -(MAIR-duh-SEEN)

as in the engagement at Marais des Cygnes River, Missouri.

The engagement that took place at the Marais des Cygnes River on October 25, 1864 was a rear guard action by Confederates retreating after being defeated at the Battle of Westport, Missouri. All of this was part of Sterling Price's Raid in Missouri during September and October 1864. Marais des Cygnes is about sixty miles south of Westport, which is in the vicinity of modern day Kansas City. The delaying action at Marais des Cignes slowed the Confederate retreat and led to the rout of Price's rear two divisions at Mine Creek later in the day and the loss of more than a thousand men taken prisoner.

Marais des Cignes means "swan swamp" in French. It is easily one of most daunting of Civil War place names. Let us all be thankful that the major, decisive battle of the war did not take place at this location.[173] Can you imagine having to use that name frequently?

Marye's -(muh-REEZ)

as in Marye's Heights, Fredericksburg, Virginia.

The famous "sunken road" and "stonewall" of the Battle of Fredericksburg are located at the base of a ridge just west of the town of Fredericksburg called Marye's Heights. Confederates under the command of James Longstreet manned a fortified position on the left flank of Lee's line at the base of Marye's Heights on December 13, 1862. Two-thirds of the more than twelve thousand Federal casualties at Fredericksburg were the result of a series of frontal assaults against these heights.

Marye's Heights is named for the Marye family whose mansion still stands on the heights above the sunken road. John L. Marye, who lived in the house, was lieutenant governor of Virginia at the outbreak of the Civil War. The house and surrounding estate, known as "Brompton," is now part of the campus of Mary Washington College.

One of most common mispronunciations of Marye's Heights is when the first word is pronounced "Mary's," as though the extra 'e' at the end of that old fashioned name were silent. The other common error is to say it as, ma-RIZE Heights. I found that I had to be corrected any number of times on this one. Somehow the correct pronunciation just wouldn't sink in until I started saying to myself "Marye's, rhymes with breeze," every time I saw the name. Sounds crazy but it works.[174]

<u>Massanutten</u> -(MAS-a-NUT-en)

as in <u>Massanutten</u> Mountain, Virginia.

Massanutten Mountain runs down the middle of the central portion of the Shenandoah Valley in Virginia. This massive geographic protrusion creates a double valley between Strasburg and Harrisonburg. On the eastern side of Massanutten is the Luray, or Page Valley, on the western side is the Shenandoah Valley. The key gap to go from the Luray to the Shenandoah Valley is at New Market. During the Civil War the Massanutten provided Stonewall Jackson with excellent cover to move his little army up and down the valley.

The name Massanutten means "big mountain" in the local Indian dialect. People who don't come from Virginia, or who are unfamiliar with the proper pronunciation, tend to say, MAS-a-NOOT-en.

<u>Massaponax</u> -(MAS-uh-PON-uks)

as in <u>Massaponax</u> Church, Virginia.

There is a famous series of photographs, three of them taken by Timothy O'Sullivan, during the Overland Campaign, on May 21, 1864. Climbing up to the second story of Massaponax Baptist Church, located along the Telegraph Road south of Fredericksburg and east of Spotsylvania Court House, O'Sullivan captured General Grant and his staff in the midst of consultation. The three shots, taken only minutes apart, look like frames from a motion picture. O'Sullivan's camera is looking down on the yard in front of the church, where a bunch of pews have been set up in a circle. Members of Grant's staff are sitting there reading maps, discussing plans, smoking cigars. Grant is seated in two of the shots, writing orders, smoking his cigar, and in a third picture, leaning over the shoulder of General George Meade discussing a map in Meade's hand. The photographs have that haunting "captured moment in time" quality. Unlike most Civil War photos, these are not posed or set up. These pictures have a modern news photography look to them.

Massaponax Church was another stop on the road south for Grant. After the bloody Battle of Spotsylvania, he was moving his army once again in an attempt to sidle around Lee's right flank. The next stop, after this brief, wonderfully photographed stop at Massaponax Church, was the North Anna River, and from there to the horror of Cold Harbor.

Massaponax is pronounced as it is spelled. The only difficulty is deciding which syllable to stress. It is simply a long name that looks a lot harder to say than it is. I first heard the name properly pronounced years ago while on a battlefield tour of Spotsylvania led by Ed Bearss and Robert Krick.

Mattaponi -(MAT-uh-puh-NIE)

as in Mattaponi River, Virginia.

The Mattaponi rises in Spotsylvania County, Virginia, and flows southeast for 125 miles to join the Pamunkey River and form the York River. If you look at a map of Virginia you will see that the Mattaponi is actually formed by the combination of four smaller rivers, the Mat, the Ta, the Po and the Ni. The Mat and the Ta combine to form the Matta, which then combines with the Po and the Ni to form one river in the vicinity of Guinea Station, south of Fredericksburg.

The name Mattaponi is an important map reference for anyone studying the Virginia campaigns. There is no specific battle or engagement named after the Mattaponi River, but you are sure to run across the name. I have given the local pronunciation at the top of this entry.

Maury -(MAW-ree [MAW rhymes with "law"])

as in Dabney Herndon Maury and Matthew Fontaine Maury, C.S.A.

Dabney Herndon Maury graduated from West Point in 1846, fought in the Mexican War, and entered Confederate service as a captain of cavalry. He eventually became chief of staff for General Earl Van Dorn and fought with distinction at Pea Ridge, Iuka and Corinth. He was promoted to brigadier general in March 1862. In July 1863 he took command of the District of the Gulf and held this position till the end of the war. Maury is famous for his defense of Mobile.

Matthew Fountain Maury is the more famous of the two well known Maurys. Like Dabney, his nephew, he was born in Virginia and served the Confederacy during the Civil War. That is where the similarity ends. Matthew Maury founded the science of oceanography. At the age of nineteen he became a midshipman in the U. S. Navy though he had been raised many miles from the ocean in the state of Tennessee. An accident that partially crippled him had the unexpected benefit of permitting him to devote his time to studying the oceans and publishing his findings. His first published work was titled *A New Theoretical and Practical Treatise on Navigation*. Aside from a number of excellent works on navigation, his major contribution was a book called, *The Physical Geography of the Sea*.

During the Civil War, Matthew Fontaine Maury was in the Confederate Navy. His service included river and harbor defenses and research into new naval weapons. His invention of the electric torpedo led to his being sent to Europe by the Richmond government to do further research. While there he also became involved in preparing commerce raiders for Confederate service on the high seas.

After the war ended, Matthew Maury went to Mexico where he became part of the cabinet of Emperor Maximilian. When Maximilian was deposed and executed, Maury went to England. He taught meteorology until his death in 1873. His nephew Dabney Herndon Maury also became a teacher after the war. He wrote many articles for the Southern Historical Society, eventually, served the government as a diplomat in South America. He died in 1900.

Pronunciation of Maury is easily obtained in a number of standard references. The commonest pronunciation error is to say the name as MOW-ree (MOW rhyming with "cow").

Meagher -(marr *or* muh-HAR)

as in Thomas Francis Meagher, Brigadier General U.S.V.

Born in Waterford, Ireland in 1823, Thomas Meagher became involved in the Irish independence movement. In the summer uprising of 1848 he was captured, convicted of treason, and sentenced to be hanged, drawn and quartered. Fortunately, his sentence was commuted to exile in Tasmania. He escaped in 1852 and made his way to the United States. Meagher acquired U. S. citizenship and became a lawyer, noted popular lecturer and newspaper editor in New York.[175]

A political power among the Irish-Americans, Meagher raised the Irish Brigade in New York City after the war had broken out. He was commissioned a brigadier general in February 1862, and led his brigade in the Peninsula Campaign, Second Manassas, Antietam, Fredericksburg and Chancellorsville. In a dispute over reorganization of the brigade after Chancellorsville, Meagher resigned in May 1863. His political importance, however, caused the Lincoln Administration to shelve his resignation and reassign him to General William Sherman's command. Meagher was with Sherman at Atlanta, commanded a provisional division after Savannah and led it in the Carolinas Campaign.

After the war Meagher was appointed Territorial Secretary of Montana. In 1867 he drowned when he fell or was pushed off a steamboat into the Missouri River. The general was reportedly quite drunk at the time of his vertical insertion into the Missouri.

"Meagher of the Sword," as he was known to his Irish American supporters is one of those historical characters it is impossible to get an objective opinion about. To some of his contemporaries he was an untrustworthy, self aggrandizing drunk, and to others he was an Irish patriot. But whether Meagher was a cad or a colossus is not the concern of this book; pronouncing his name is.

Meagher is like many other Celtic names; it is derived from the Gaelic language, a language so completely incompatible with English it may as well be Japanese. You can get some inkling of how the pronunciation **MARR** came about when you realize that a variant pronunciation of the same name is **muh-HAR**. At least with the second pronunciation some attempt is being made to recognize the other letters in the name. Probably the name Meagher was pronounced with a great deal of guttural sound originally, employing lots of saliva in the process.

Meigs -(megz)

as in Montgomery Cunningham Meigs, Quartermaster General, U.S. Army.

It would be difficult to overstate the importance of Montgomery Meigs to the Union war effort. Born in Georgia and raised in Philadelphia, Meigs attended the University of Pennsylvania before entering West Point. He graduated with the class of 1836 and from then until the outbreak of the Civil War worked as an army engineer on a dazzling array of projects. Among the projects that Meigs had a hand in was the Potomac Aqueduct and the addition to the Capitol Building of the House and Senate wings, as well as the dome.[176] When the war came, his special talents were put to use by the Lincoln Administration in the office of Quartermaster General.

Considering the fact that when the war opened the standing army of the country was just over sixteen thousand officers and men, and the War Department had a smaller staff than the average medium sized modern retail operation, it is a tribute to Meigs organizational ability that he was able to meet the needs of an army of more than two million men. Yet despite the gargantuan size of the logistics task before him, Meigs managed it and got the dome of the Capitol finished as well.

Pronunciation of General Meigs name is made difficult by the 'ei' combination. Usually, the 'ei' is sounded as a long 'i,' as in the names Weiss and Heitman. For many years, I avoided saying the name because I wanted to say MIEGZ, but felt insecure about it. I had heard it said megz, but wasn't altogether sure that was correct. A quick look at any good dictionary would have cleared it up for me immediately. But like a man lost in his car, I was not willing to stop and ask for directions.

Metairie-(MET-uh-ree)

as in Metairie Cemetery, New Orleans.

Metairie Cemetery was originally the site of a racetrack. It was established after the Civil War, but is nevertheless the final resting for a few Confederate notables. Among those who find a permanent address at 5100 Pontchartrain Boulevard, New Orleans are General Pierre Gustave Toutant Beauregard, General John Bell Hood and General Richard Taylor.[177]

Pronunciation of this famous cemetery's name can be found in standard reference books; *Webster's New Geographical Dictionary* to cite just one. I first heard the name properly pronounced by a resident of New Orleans and later confirmed by Civil War historian Richard McMurry.

Monocacy -(muh-NOK-acy)

as in Monocacy Junction, Maryland *or* the Battle of Monocacy.

The Monocacy River in Maryland is a tributary of the Potomac River. It branches off the Potomac about thirty-five miles upstream from Washington and runs generally north until it splits into Rock Creek and Pipe Creek just south of the Pennsylvania border. About three miles south-east of Frederick, Maryland the Baltimore and Ohio Railroad crosses the Monocacy River. This is also the point on the river where the Georgetown Pike crosses and is called Monocacy Junction.

On July 9, 1864 General Lew Wallace, in command of 6,000 Federal troops, tried to block Confederates under General Jubal Early who were attempting to raid either Baltimore or Washington. Wallace didn't know which city Early had in mind, so he selected Monocacy Junction because this was where he could block the Confederates from crossing the Monocacy on both the National Road to Baltimore and the Georgetown Pike to Washington. Wallace suffered a tactical defeat in the battle that followed, but he did achieve a strategic victory. By delaying Jubal Early one day he bought precious time for the defenders of the capital. In that critical 24-hours reinforcements from the Army of the Potomac arrived in Washington.

Monocacy is one of those words you look at and decide you'd better wait for guidance from a local before attempting to say it. It looks like a term to describe some form of government, or some bizarre variation of the traditional marriage contract, or even some new board game. The proper pronunciation is confirmed by Park Service personnel.

Moultrie -(MOOL-tree)

as in Fort Moultrie, Charleston, South Carolina.

Fort Moultrie was already an old fort when the Civil War began. Situated on Sullivan's Island at the mouth of Charleston Harbor, it was originally constructed as a sea battery for protection of the city of Charleston. It eventually became a favorite post in the Old Army. Moultrie was regarded as "a veritable country club, with never an Apache or a bushwhacker to worry about and a cotillion every Saturday night."[178] By the end of 1860 all this changed. Charleston was the cradle of Southern secession and the Federal garrison at Fort Moultrie was about to become the enemy.

As we all know (or should know), Fort Moultrie was evacuated by the Federals on December 26, 1860 as they made their way to the uncompleted fort in the middle of the harbor, Fort Sumter. The rest, as they say, is history. One thing worthy of note here is that Fort Moultrie was ultimately used by some of the secessionist artillery that fired on Sumter.

Moultrie is a Scottish name. Colonel William Moultrie fought back the British in 1776 at the Battle of Sullivan's Island and the palmetto log fort he built on the island became Fort Moultrie. The name of the Moultrie family was always pronounced **MOOL-tree**. The Moultrie family survives to this day and that is still the way they pronounce their name. The most common mispronunciation of this name is **MOLE-tree**. This would be correct in the state of Georgia, where the town of Moultrie is pronounced that way.[179] Despite finding all this out, I still think **MOLE-tree** sounds better.

Mumma -(MOO-mah)

as in the Samuel Mumma Farm, Sharpsburg, Maryland.

Samuel Mumma, his wife and sixteen children had evacuated their farmhouse just north of Sharpsburg, Maryland a day or two before the Battle of Antietam got underway. It was a good thing they did, because the Mumma farm was smack in the middle of a good part of the action and the Mumma farmhouse was burned during the battle. Lying between the West Woods and East Woods on the battlefield, the Mumma Farm is one of more important landmarks at Antietam. It would be impossible in a book this size to enumerate all the details of the action that took place on and around the Mumma farm, but I can at least provide some useful information about the pronunciation of the name.

Mumma is a German name. For those of you who have toured the Gettysburg Battlefield extensively the Mumma name will seem familiar (Mummasburg Road). In Sharpsburg, Maryland the Mumma name is pronounced as I have specified above and Antietam National Battlefield Historian Ted Alexander will back me up. However, as you will find out in the next entry, things are decidedly different in Pennsylvania.

Mummasburg -(MUM-miz-burg)

as in the Mummasburg Road, Gettysburg, Pennsylvania.

The Mummasburg Road runs from Arendtsville, Pennsylvania in a southeasterly direction into Gettysburg. Along the way it passes through the small town of Mummasburg, from which it takes its name. As the road gets close to Gettysburg it passes over Oak Ridge, one of the important geographic features of the first day's battlefield. It was on this section of the Mummasburg Road that Confederates under General Robert Rodes hit the Union line where the First Corps connected with the Eleventh Corps, or almost connected (there was a gap about a quarter of a mile long).[180] The Federals holding the position right along the Mummasburg Road were commanded first by General Henry Baxter and then General Gabriel René Paul. This was the scene of some fierce fighting.

Pronunciation of Mummasburg is simple. The word is said exactly as it is spelled. However, if you've gone to all the trouble of learning how to properly pronounce the name of the Samuel Mumma (MOO-mah) farm at Antietam Battlefield, you may think that the "Mumma" in Mummasburg is pronounced the same way. To prevent this minor disaster from occurring, I have included Mummasburg in this dictionary. Both Park Service personnel and Licensed Battlefield Guides at Gettysburg will confirm my pronunciation.

Quartermaster General Montgomery Cunningham Meigs

N

<u>Nahant</u> -(nuh-HANT)

as in the USS *Nahant*.

The *Nahant* was a *Passaic*-class Ericsson type monitor. After the success of the original USS *Monitor* Ericsson received contracts for additional ironclads that were larger and improved. Among these was the *Nahant*. It had a single turret like the original *Monitor*, thicker armor and more powerful armament. The *Nahant* was part of the South Atlantic Blockading Squadron and participated in operations against Charleston in April 1863. The vessel is named for Nahant Bay, an inlet of Massachusetts Bay in the northeast corner of Massachusetts.

Pronunçiation guidance on Nahant was easily obtained in several printed sources (e.g. *Webster's New Geographical Dictionary*) and various present and former residents of Massachusetts with whom I am acquainted. Massachusetts provides the only variation on the pronunciation you may hear, **nuh-HAHNT**.

<u>Natchitoches</u> -(NAK-uh-TOSH)

as in Natchitoches, Louisiana.

Natchitoches is a town in northwest Louisiana that figures prominently in the Red River Campaign of 1864. Though never the site of a major battle, the name comes up frequently when reading about the campaign. If you are like most Civil War buffs you probably don't know a damn thing about the Red River Campaign of 1864 except that it was run by General Nathaniel Banks and was a total failure. It was mounted in the first place because Lincoln wanted the Federal flag flying over some part of Texas to combat the French threat (under the auspices of Emperor Maximilian) in Mexico.[181] The plan was to move up the Red River and seize Shreveport, Louisiana the gateway to Texas. In addition, Lincoln hoped to win the loyalty of planters along the Red River by having the military purchase their cotton. Nothing went as planned.

A most peculiar word, Natchitoches. The name is so peculiar that most good dictionaries include it and always give a pronouncer.

Norfolk -(NOR-fuhk)

as in Norfolk, Virginia.

For those of us from Connecticut, this is a tough one. There is a pretty little town in the northwest corner of the Nutmeg State with the name Norfolk, and it is generally pronounced **NOR-FAWK**. Naturally, upon seeing the same name in Virginia we are likely to say it the same way. There is also a Norfolk in Nebraska, and I haven't the faintest idea how locals there pronounce the name.

Norfolk is important in Civil War history because of the Gosport Navy Yard. This valuable ship building facility was abandoned by Federal troops just a few days after Virginia seceded in 1861. At that time, Gosport was the country's most important naval facility and fleeing Federals attempted to burn as much property as possible before they left so the yard wouldn't fall into Confederate hands intact. Several ships were burned and others were scuttled, including the steam sloop *Merrimack*. In addition, some of the navy yard's buildings were burned. However, when Confederates arrived the dry-dock was still usable and so were some 1200 cannon with accompanying gunpowder.[182] Letting all this drop into the lap of the Rebels was an embarrassing disaster for the U. S. The disaster became even more poignant when the *Merrimack* was salvaged and converted into the ironclad, CSS *Virginia*. Norfolk was recaptured by the Federals in May 1862 during McClellan's Peninsula Campaign.

Pronunciation as given above is the local way of saying Norfolk. If you are in Norfolk and say it wrong, you are likely to be politely corrected. If you visit Norfolk, Connecticut and say it wrong, chances are no one will say a word. Small town Yankees pretty much keep to themselves.

Nueces-(noo-AY-sis)

as in Nueces River, Texas.

The Affair at the Nueces River took place in August of 1862. Several large settlements of German immigrants in central and northeastern Texas were hotbeds of Unionist sentiment. Several hundred of the Germans had organized, calling their group the "Union Loyal League," to protect themselves against harassment by the local Confederate military. Military authorities in Texas considered them a threat to internal security. Sixty-five of the Germans, under the leadership of Fritz Tegener decided to flee to Union authorities in New Orleans by way of Mexico. They were intercepted by Confederates on August 10, 1862 on a prairie by the Nueces River. In the unequal engagement that followed, nineteen of the Germans were killed, while nine others who were captured were later executed. The brutality of the incident is characteristic of the partisan type warfare conducted in the Trans-Mississippi west.[183]

The name Nueces is Spanish and the plural of the word "nuez" which means "walnut" or "nut." Thus, "Nueces" means "Nuts"--the Nuts River. Could this be an example of that famous Mexican sense of humor? No. Actually, a Spanish expedition in 1689 that discovered the river found many nut trees along its banks. Pronunciation is available from standard references.

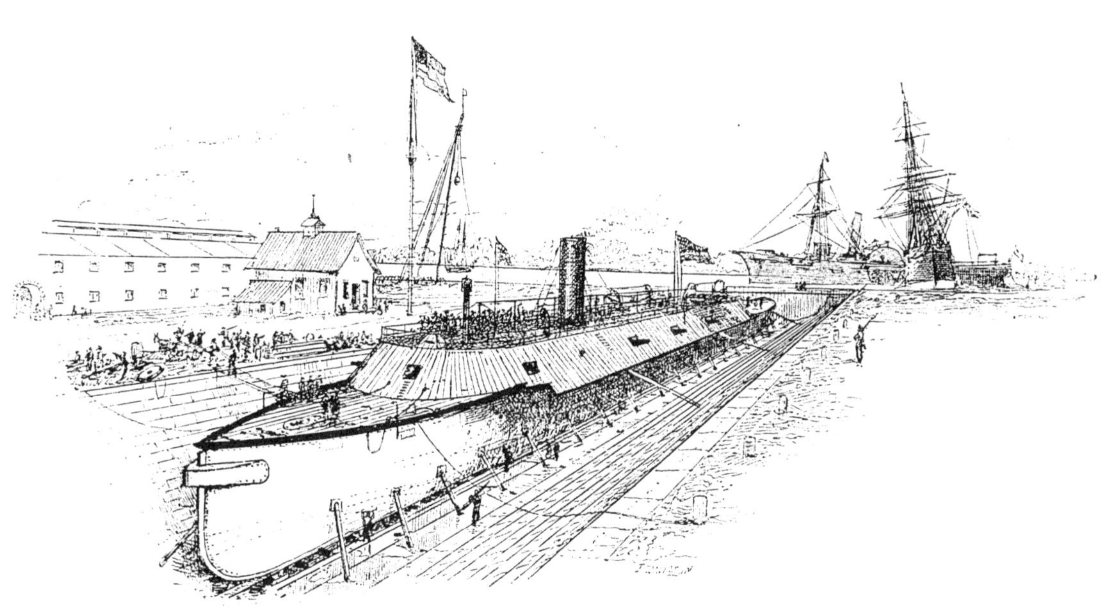

The CSS *Virginia* (*Merrimac*) at the Gosport Navy Yard, Norfolk, Virginia.

O

<u>Occoquan</u> -(OK-uh-KWAN)

as in <u>Occoquan</u> River, Virginia.

The Occoquan River branches off the Potomac River about ten miles south of Alexandria, Virginia. The Occoquan begins as an inlet on the west bank of the Potomac, then travels inland in a northwesterly direction. As a result of its location near many of the major battlefields in northern Virginia, the Occoquan is often mentioned in Civil War writings. Like most other locations in the area, the Occoquan River was the site of a number of skirmishes. In fact, on January 29, 1862 a small Federal force broke up a group of Confederates who were dancing at a party at Lee's House on the Occoquan.[184] Oh, those Reb party animals! The river's name also comes up in discussions of the "Occoquan Plan." This plan to dislodge Joe Johnston's Confederate army from its position around Manassas was proposed by Lincoln in late 1861 in an effort to get McClellan to do something with the Army of the Potomac.

The name Occoquan is derived from the Algonquian language meaning, "hooked inlet." Pronunciation guides can be found in some reference works (e.g. *Lippincott's Pronouncing Gazetteer*), but it was a lot easier to ask local Virginians and Park Service personnel in Fredericksburg.

<u>Oconee</u> -(oh-KONE-ee)

as in <u>Oconee</u> River, Georgia.

The Oconee, like the Ocmulgee, is more than 250 miles long. The river rises in northern Georgia and flows south and southeast to join the Ocmulgee and form the Altamaha River in southeast Georgia. This is another of those river names you are likely to come across while studying Sherman's March to the Sea.

Oconee is derived from an Indian name that might refer to the Cherokee snake dragon of myth and legend. It may also mean "the water eyes of the hills" (one of those translations that sounds pretty, but doesn't make a bit of sense). The correct pronunciation was obtained and verified by a number of sources.[185]

<u>Olustee</u> -(oh-LUS-tee)

as in the Battle of <u>Olustee</u>, Florida.

Florida had a population of around 140,000 at the outbreak of the Civil War. About half this number was made up of slaves. This sparsely populated state was nevertheless one of the stars on the Confederate flag. During the war, Florida sent the South fifteen thousand men to fight for the Confederate cause.[186] Most of these men fought in battles a long way from the Sunshine State. Florida was remote from the main theaters of the war, but there <u>was</u> fighting in Florida. The Battle of Olustee, or Ocean Pond, was the only major engagement that was fought on Florida soil.

A Federal military expedition under the command of Major General Quincy Gillmore was launched in February 1864. The reason for this undertaking had political roots, as well as military motives. A group of Florida Unionists, who were political supporters of Treasury Secretary Salmon P. Chase, wanted to bring Florida back into the Union under a Reconstruction government so they could send delegates to the 1864 Republican Convention who would support Chase's nomination.[187] Quincy Gillmore, who commanded the Department of the South, was persuaded to urge the War Department to mount an expedition into Florida, presumably to cut Confederate supply routes, free slaves and recruit black soldiers. It was during the implementation of this Byzantine plan that the Battle of Olustee took place.

On February 7, 1864 Truman Seymour's Division of the 10th Corps landed at Jacksonville and marched twenty miles inland toward a strategic railroad junction near the Suwannee River. Along the way, Seymour occupied small towns, freed slaves, and burned Confederate supplies. He didn't run into any substantial Confederate opposition until February 20th when he ran into about five thousand troops under Brigadier General Joseph Finegan at Olustee, a station on the Florida, Atlantic & Gulf Railroad. The battle that followed took place on land near a large lake called Ocean Pond. After hours of bloody fighting, Seymour retreated. He sustained more than 1800 casualties, against Finegan's less than 950. One of the Union regiments that took part in the battle was the 54th Massachusetts (subject of the recent motion picture *Glory*) and there has been some controversy over the years as to whether or not the black regiment was unnecessarily sacrificed to save retreating white regiments.[188]

Most people have pronunciation problems with Olustee because they don't know which syllable gets emphasized. As you can see from the pronouncer above, it is the middle one. Since I had always had a lot of trouble with the correct pronunciation of this name I checked both printed sources and then made sure they were accurate by asking several people, among them historian Ed Bearss.

Onondaga -(ON-un-DAH-guh)

as in the USS *Onondaga.*

The *Onondaga* was the first two turreted monitor built. The original monitor design had been developed by John Ericsson. George W. Quintard, using the basic principles of Ericsson's design, came up with the idea of a two turreted monitor. Early in 1864 the *Onondaga* was built at the Continental Iron Works in Greenpoint, New York. She was more 220-feet in length and was armed with two 15-inch Dahlgren smooth-bores and two 150-pound Parrott Rifles. Unlike earlier monitors, the *Onondaga* was of a new class that was both powerful and reliable. The *Onondaga* was not destined to fight any great battles. She spent her entire Civil War career in the James River and saw very little action.[189]

Pronunciation of Onondaga will present no problem for those from upstate New York. Onondaga is the name of a county in west central New York State and is also the name of a five-mile long lake in that part of the Empire State. Onondaga is an Iroquoian Indian name meaning "on the hill." The most common mispronunciation of this word is ON-un-DAY-guh. There are a few others, but the only proper way is as indicated above.

Opequon-(oh-PEK-un)

as in Opequon Creek, Virginia.

The Third Battle of Winchester on September 19, 1864 is also called the Battle of Opequon Creek. The creek heads southwest of Winchester and flows into the Potomac River near Falling Waters, West Virginia. Since the creek runs just east of Winchester it figured prominently in actions around the town. The name Opequon also crops up in the Battles of Kernstown, the first fought in March 1862 and the second in July 1864.

Mispronunciation of this name is very common. The spelling of the name offers a number of possibilities; OH-puh-KWAN is one of the more frequent mistakes, another is oh-PEEK-kwan. Opequon is the sort of name that must be heard in order to be learned.[190]

P

<u>Pamunkey</u> -(puh-MUNG-kee)

as in <u>Pamunkey</u> River, Virginia.

Formed by the confluence of the North and South Anna rivers in northeastern Hanover County, the Pamunkey flows eighty miles in a southeasterly direction and joins the Mattaponi River at West Point, Virginia to form the York River. Even a cursory study of the campaigns of the Army of Northern Virginia and its rival, the Army of the Potomac, cannot overlook this important river with the peculiar name. The name Pamunkey comes up in the Peninsula Campaign of 1862, and again in 1864 during Grant's Overland Campaign.

Pronunciation of Pamunkey doesn't seem to be a major problem among Civil War buffs. I've included it in this dictionary for those who may be relatively new to the study of the war, or those who are old campaigners but feel unsure of their pronunciation of Pamunkey.

<u>Pegram</u> -(PEE-grum)

as in John <u>Pegram</u> or William Johnson <u>Pegram</u>, C.S.A.

The Pegram brothers didn't live to make old bones, as the saying goes. John Pegram, who reached the rank of brigadier general, was a West Point graduate, fought with Bragg in the western theater of operations, transferred to the Army of Northern Virginia and fought gallantly until Hatcher's Run in February 1865 when he was killed. His younger brother, Willie, was an artillerist with the Army of Northern Virginia, reached the rank of colonel and got killed at the Battle of Five Forks in April 1865.

For years, I was saying the last name of these two gallant fighters as, **PEG-rim** and found out I was wrong. Numerous historians, both with the National Park Service and other reputable organizations corrected me and I have to assume they know what they are talking about. Further research confirmed this pronunciation.

<u>Pfanz</u> -(fontz)

as in Harry <u>Pfanz</u>, Civil War historian, author.

When it comes to the Battle of Gettysburg there are few who could match Harry Pfanz for comprehensive knowledge. Pfanz, who retired in 1981 as Chief Historian of the National Park Service, also worked for many years as a historian at the Gettysburg National Military Park. His 1987 book, *Gettysburg, The Second Day*, is recognized as the definitive work on that aspect of the great battle. No small feat when you consider the number of fine books written about Gettysburg.

Pronunciation of the Pfanz name presents a challenge for some buffs. Many, including myself, were calling him Harry **FANZ**. The only mistake we didn't make was pronouncing the 'P' at the beginning of this German name. The **'P,'** of course, is silent and **'z'** at the end is pronounced with a **'tz'** sound, as it always is in German.

<u>Philippi</u> -(FIL-uh-pee)

as in the Battle of <u>Philippi</u>, West Virginia.

Considered by many the first battle of the Civil War this small engagement which took place on June 3, 1861 in what is now West Virginia, would hardly rate a footnote, let alone be called a battle, if it weren't part of the well publicized and overinflated early Civil War career of George McClellan. A Federal contingent of five regiments attacked a camp full of raw Confederate recruits under the command Colonel George A. Porterfield, who immediately retreated. A total of fifteen casualties resulted with no one killed. Though not in immediate command at the "battle," McClellan was given credit for the easy victory. It was still very early in the war and within a week another small battle at Big Bethel, on the Virginia Peninsula, would eclipse the engagement at Philippi. Since men actually got killed at Big Bethel on June 10, 1861, it is considered the first real battle of the war.

Philippi is one of those names that gets mispronounced quite often. The town is named for an ancient city in Macedonia near the Aegean Sea. That city, now a ruin, is generally pronounced **fuh-LIP-i** or **FIL-uh-pie**. It is this ancient city pronunciation a lot of people go for. That's OK in Macedonia, but it just don't wash in West Virginia. The pronounce I have given is based on the way locals say the name and is also the pronunciation given in a number of reference works.

<u>Philippoteaux</u> -(fee-lee-pah-TOH *or* fil-luh-pah-TOE)

as in Paul <u>Philippoteaux</u>, painter of the Gettysburg Cyclorama.

The Cyclorama painting is titled, *The Battle of Gettysburg.* When Philippoteaux began work on the painting in 1881 he had already established himself as a painter of historical scenes, especially the cyclorama type painting. He collaborated with his father, military artist Felix Philippoteaux, on his first cyclorama in 1871. It was titled, "The Defense of Fort d'Issy," a panoramic scene from the Franco-Prussian War. In the decade that followed, he painted six more cycloramas, all of them depicting battle scenes in Europe and North Africa. After completing his Gettysburg cyclorama in Paris in 1884, he took it to Boston, where it was a great commercial success. In order to capitalize on the popularity of the work he made three exact copies of it so that he could exhibit it in several cities at once. In 1913 the Boston cyclorama was permanently relocated to Gettysburg.

Before he commenced painting the cyclorama, with the help of several assistants, Philippoteaux came to Gettysburg to sketch and photograph the battlefield. The painting was done on individual panels, each twenty-seven feet high.[191] The cyclorama measures 360 feet in circumference and is viewed in the round. It is an impressive and stunning piece of work. For years and years I avoided that round cyclorama building at Gettysburg, assuming it was strictly for the tourists. When I was finally persuaded to go inside, I was pleasantly surprised.

I have used two pronouncers for the name Philippoteaux. The first is the more Frenchified of the two. The second pronounce is the Americanized version of the name. You can use either one and still be understood.

<u>Pocotaligo</u> -(POH-kuh-TAL-li-goh)

as in <u>Pocotaligo</u>, South Carolina.

The town of Pocotaligo is south of the Combahee River in Jasper County, South Carolina. It is one of those names you will encounter when you study Sherman's Carolinas Campaign in early 1865. The name is derived from the Yamasee Indian language and means, "gathering place."[192] Pronunciation of Pocotaligo is a case of knowing which syllables to stress.[193]

point d'appui -(pwan-da-PWEE)

as in, "The Sunken Road was the point d'appui of Lee's line at Fredericksburg."

Here's another one of those French military terms that seem to take up so much space in this dictionary. I always thought French was the language of love (though, my limited use of it never yielded any results for me in that field of endeavor). It appears that it is also the language of war. Point d'appui means, point of support, or base. An army's position might be anchored to, or fortified by this point of support.

Pronunciation is in the manner of the French language, or as close as we Americans can come to it. Actually, it is much easier just to say, "strong point."

Polignac -(poh-leen-YAK)

as in Camille Armand Jules Marie, Prince de Polignac, Major General C.S.A.

Scion of one of France's most illustrious families, Prince de Polignac had an outstanding war record from the Crimea before coming to America. He resigned his commission in the French army in 1859 and went to Central America to explore and study the flora and fauna.[194] When the Civil War broke out, he offered his services to the Confederacy and garnered a position as chief of staff to General P. G. T. Beauregard. Polignac fought at Shiloh and Corinth. He was appointed brigadier general in January 1863, by which time he was serving under the command of General Richard Taylor in Louisiana. It was in this theater of operations that Polignac shined. During Nathaniel Banks' Red River Campaign of 1864, Polignac performed gallantly at Mansfield. In June of 1864 he was promoted to major general and given command of a division. Polignac was the only foreigner to achieve such a high rank in the Confederacy.

After the war he retired to his estate in France and wrote prolifically about the Civil War. He died in 1913, the last surviving Confederate major general.[195]

Pronunciation of the name is in the French manner. One thing that helps illustrate the American approach to foreign sounding names in the mid-19th century is the nickname that General Polignac was given by his men, "Polecat." Pronouncers for Polignac's name are surprisingly easy to find. The family figures quite prominently in French history and the name shows up in numerous reference works that also give pronunciations.[196]

Porcher -(por-SHAY)

as in William Porcher Miles, politician C.S.A.

William Porcher Miles was one of the most powerful politicians in the Confederate government. Born in South Carolina in 1822, Miles was first a mathematics professor at the College of Charleston before becoming mayor of the city in 1855. He was elected to Congress in 1857 and resigned in December 1860 to support South Carolina's secession from the Union. When the war came, Miles served as a representative of the Charleston district in the Confederate House of Representatives. His position as chairman of the Committee on Military Affairs gave him considerable political clout.

After the war he lived the life of a wealthy retired gentlemen in Virginia (his wife's family had lots of money) and in 1880 became president of the University of South Carolina. He lived until 1899.

Porcher is a French Huguenot name which over the years has retained its French spelling and pronunciation. The most common mispronunciation of the name is **POR-chur**, which sounds like the name of someone who spends enormous amounts of time sipping mint juleps on the veranda.[197] Alas, the name is not pronounced as it is spelled.

Portici -(POR-TEE-see)

as in Portici, General Joseph Johnston's headquarters at the Battle of First Manassas.

The name "Portici" comes up in two major battles of the Civil War. The first is Bull Run or First Manassas, and the second is Second Manassas. "Portici" is the name of the Francis Lewis farm which is located on the rolling pastures southwest of Bull Run. During the first battle Johnston decided that Portici house provided him with the best overall view of the action. A year and a month later, during the last stages of the Battle of Second Manassas, there was a cavalry fight on the Lewis farm. John Buford's brigade of Union cavalry, which had been posted on the Federal left flank during the battle, fought a very intense rear guard action with Beverly Robertson's brigade of Virginia cavalry. Though Buford was ultimately forced to retreat, it was the first time in Virginia that Federal cavalry had initiated a cavalry battle. The fight also prevented Confederate cavalry from crossing Bull Run at Lewis Ford and interdicting the Union line of retreat along Warrenton Turnpike.[198]

Calling your farm, or your house a name like "Portici" was not unusual for well read, well traveled Virginians who had the money to buy books and travel. The Lewis family, connected by blood to the Washingtons, had a good size farm at Manassas and a nice looking two story frame house. The house no longer stands. According to historian Douglas Southall Freeman, descendants of the Lewis family who still lived in the area when he was researching *Lee's Lieutenants* claimed that the Italian name, "Portici," was given to the place because the house burned down so many times that it reminded its owner of the frequently destroyed city beneath Mount Vesuvius.[199]

Portici is one of those names that invites mispronunciation. For years I was pronouncing this name **POR-TEE-see.** I recently became convinced I was wrong and adopted Italianesque ways of say it, using **POR-tee-chee** and **POR-TEE-chee**. When I finally got around to checking with Park Service people at the Manassas battlefield I discovered I had been right in the first place.

Powhatan -(POW-uh-TAN)

as in Powhatan County, Virginia.

Powhatan was an American Indian chief in Virginia who lived from 1550 to 1618. Powhatan founded a network of Algonquian-speaking Indian settlements called the Powhatan Confederacy; he was also father of Pocahontas. Several Confederate military organizations used the name Powhatan: the Powhatan Artillery, the Powhatan Rifles, the Powahatan Cavalry and the Powhatan Reserves.[200] All of these units were comprised of men from Powhatan County.

For many years I was pronouncing the late, great chief's name, **POW-HAT-un,** which is used in many parts of the country as the standard pronunciation. The pronunciation I have given is the one used in Virginia.

Powhite -(POW-HITE)

as in Powhite Creek, Virginia.

Powhite Creek is a very important landmark if you are studying the Battle of Gaines's Mill. Powhite Creek discharges into the Chickahominy River after meandering southward some five miles from its headwaters. The creek ran through the plantation of one Dr. William Gaines, who purchased the land in 1840 and named it "Powhite" for the creek. The plantation contained more than eleven hundred acres, and about a mile from Dr. Gaines's house was a gristmill on Powhite Creek; thus, Gaines's Mill. The fighting at the Battle of Gaines's Mill took place along yet another creek that ran just east of Powhite Creek called Boatswain's Swamp. It wasn't a swamp, just a marshy creek. On an oval shaped plateau south of Boatswain's Swamp, Fitz John Porter had his Fifth Corps set up in a defensive position; they faced north.

Gaines's Mill was the third of the Seven Days' Battles during the Peninsula Campaign. Porter's isolated corps had successfully defended itself at Beaver Dam Creek, or Mechanicsville the day before, then retreated to the Boatswain's Swamp location. The Battle of Gaines's Mill was the bloodiest of the Peninsula Campaign.

Pronunciation of Powhite has been a sort of recurring controversy over the years. Many locals in the Richmond area pronounce the name **PO-WHITE**, as in "poor white." One of the possible reasons for all this confusion is the fact that there is yet another Powhite Creek, this one branches off the James River and runs into Chesterfield County, south of Richmond. This other Powhite Creek is paralleled for part of the way by a toll road called Powhite Parkway. Most people I talked to in Richmond call this parkway the **PO-WHITE.** I have no idea how they pronounce the name of the nearby creek, but would be willing to wager it is the same. I would imagine that many people living in South Richmond (the old city of Manchester) aren't even aware that there is another Powhite Creek across the James River, northeast of Richmond in Hanover County, site of the Battle of Gaines's Mill. Well, for our purposes this is the only Powhite Creek that counts, and the way it is pronounced is **POW-HITE.**[201] Aren't you happy we got this all sorted out?

Pottawatamie -(POT-uh-WOT-uh-mee)

as in Pottawatamie Massacre.

The Pottawatamie Massacre took place on Pottawatamie Creek in Kansas on May 21, 1856. John Brown, a fanatical abolitionist, led six followers on a bloody spree along the creek to avenge the burning and pillaging of the town of Lawrence by slave staters. Visiting the homes of pro-slavery men in the middle of the night, Brown and his band dragged five of them outside and hacked them to death with long edged swords. This act of "political" violence gained Brown national recognition. He was feared and hated by the pro-slavery crowd, and championed by wealthy abolitionists from New England, who were far enough away from Kansas not to get splashed with the frequent bloodshed that resulted from their vision of America's future.

Pottawatamie is just a very long word that falls into the "divide and conquer" category of pronunciation challenges. There are no hidden sounds, extra letters, or bizarre phonetic anomalies in the name. Several reference books will give you a reliable pronounce and tell you which of the many syllables gets stressed.[202]

<u>Prioleau</u> -(**PRAY**-LOH)

as in Hamilton <u>Prioleau</u> Bee, Brigadier General C.S.A.

Charleston-born Hamilton Bee was the older brother of General Bernard Bee, who made history at the Battle of First Manassas by giving Stonewall Jackson his *nom de guerre*. Hamilton Bee lived a lot longer than his younger brother and put together a creditable war record.

Bee's family moved to Texas when he was a boy. He was secretary of the Texas senate in 1846 and joined the Texas Rangers during the Mexican War. Until the beginning of the Civil War he was a politician in Texas, even serving as speaker of the house in the state legislature. After a brief period in 1861 as a brigadier general in the Texas militia, he was commissioned a brigadier in the Confederate Army in March 1862. For most of the next two years he was in command at Brownsville, Texas where he supervised the importation of munitions from Europe, by way of Mexico. He finally got a field command during the Red River Campaign of 1864 when he headed a division of cavalry and, later on, a brigade of infantry. Not an exceptional field commander, he was an excellent administrator. After the war, he returned to Texas and lived there till he died in 1897.

Prioleau is a French Huguenot name which in South Carolina retains only a semi-French pronunciation. There is even a family in the upcountry part of the state which spells the name Praylow, thus dropping all pretense of the name's French origin.[203]

Brigadier General John <u>Pegram</u>

Q

Quinsigamond -(kwin-SIG-uh-mund)

as in USS *Quinsigamond*.

The *Quinsigamond* was one of four sea going double turreted monitors on which construction began in 1863. These gigantic ironclads (*Quinsigamond* class) were designed not only to eliminate Confederate raiders on the high seas, but also to harass British shipping should the need arise. It never did and none of the four monitors was ever launched.[204]

The *Quinsigamond* was named for Quinsigamond Lake near Worcester, Massachusetts. The chances of coming across the name in your Civil War studies are pretty remote. I included it in this dictionary because it was one of the very few words that I could find to put under the letter "Q." It is fortunate that the *Quinsigamond* was never launched because it simplifies determination of how the name is pronounced. A quick check with folks who live in Worcester (WOOS-tur) gave me my pronounce. Had the monitor actually gone to sea it's anybody's guess what pronunciation the crew might have come up with.

R

<u>Ramseur</u> -(ram-SOOR)

as in Stephen Dodson <u>Ramseur</u>, Major General C.S.A.

Stephen Ramseur graduated from West Point in 1860 and resigned from the army to join the Confederacy in April 1861. The North Carolina-born soldier was a natural leader and brave to the point of impetuosity at times. Ramseur rose quickly in the ranks, starting as colonel of the 49th North Carolina at the Seven Days battles and reached the rank of major general the day after his 27th birthday in 1864. At the Battle of Cedar Creek on October 19th of that year he was shot through both lungs and died at Belle Grove plantation the following day.

Though the family name looks French, in reality the Ramseurs came to North Carolina from Pennsylvania and were German. Originally the name was **Ramsour** and sometime during the early 19th century got changed to Ramseur.[205] Why this was done is not explained. Perhaps Stephen Dodson's ancestors thought that Ramseur looked a lot classier than Ramsour. I asked several Civil War historians for a pronounce on this name since none of the biographical dictionaries and cyclopedias (ancient or modern) made mention of Ramseur. The consensus of those I asked led to the pronounce given above.[206]

<u>Rapidan</u> -(RAP-uh-DAN)

as in <u>Rapidan</u> River, Virginia.

The Rapidan is one of the more important rivers in the Virginia Campaigns. It rises in the Blue Ridge Mountains, is seventy miles long and flows into the Rappahannock on the boundary of Culpeper and Spotsylvania Counties. The Rapidan is a prominent geographic feature of the Chancellorsville and Wilderness battles. The name is probably a contraction of "Rappahannock," not a contraction of "Rapid Ann" as some think.

Rappahannock -(RAP-uh-HAN-uk)

as in Rappahannock River, Virginia.

Lord knows, there may be somebody out there who is new at the Civil War business and doesn't know how to pronounce this one, or somebody who should know, but doesn't. Just for the record, the Rappahannock River rises in the Blue Ridge Mountains and flows southeast for 212 miles before emptying into Chesapeake Bay. It is navigable from the Chesapeake up to Fredericksburg.

Resaca -(rih-SOK-uh)

as in Resaca, Georgia.

The town of Resaca is located in Gordon County, northwest Georgia. It gets its place in Civil War history because of the Atlanta Campaign of 1864. Resaca was a stop in the vast cat and mouse game that Joe Johnston was playing with William T. Sherman. After the fighting at Rocky Face Ridge on May 8-11, 1864, Confederate forces withdrew from Dalton and established a new position north and west of Resaca. Fighting got underway on May 13th and continued into the 15th. Losses were heavy on both sides. Though tactically it could be called a Confederate victory, the fact that Johnston withdrew farther south gave the Federals the strategic advantage.

Resaca, Georgia was originally named Dublin, but returning Mexican War veterans renamed it for the Battle of Resaca de la Palma which they had fought in on May 9, 1846.[207] Pronunciation is very close to the original Spanish.[208]

Rives -(reevz)

as in Rives' Salient, Petersburg, Virginia.

Rives' Salient was an angle in the Confederate line around Petersburg. The Confederate line of earthworks ran south from the Appomattox River, then turned abruptly west at a point near where the Jerusalem Plank Road, coming out of Petersburg, passed through the line. Rives' Salient was the name of the angle and was situated on a bluff.[209] In your reading about the Petersburg Campaign you will probably encounter Rives' Salient.

Of special interest to students of the life of General Joshua Lawrence Chamberlain, of Little Round Top fame, is that Rives' Salient was where J. L. got severely wounded on June 18, 1864. Chamberlain, who was leading a brigade in the First Division of the 5th

Corps, was hit in the right thigh just below the hip, the soft lead bullet then went through his body diagonally and stopped near the surface of his left hip. The bullet not only severed blood vessels and crushed bone, but also nicked the urethra and bladder. Chamberlain recovered well enough to resume his duties, but spent the rest of his life with chronic pain and other medical complications.

Pronunciation of the name Rives could cause some problems. The mispronunciation I have most frequently heard is **rievz**, rhymes with "drives." NPS officials at the Petersburg National Military Park confirmed the pronounce I used at the top of this entry.[210]

<u>Roberdeau</u> -(RAH-bur-doh)

as in Chatham <u>Roberdeau</u> Wheat, Major C.S.A.

For an individual who died early in the war, Rob Wheat managed to make a reputation for himself that lasts until this day. Wheat was a giant of a man, standing six foot four and solidly built. He looked like the bouncer at a waterfront bar. This physically intimidating specimen of manhood was well suited to command the troops under him, the 1st Louisiana Special Battalion, which Wheat raised and commanded.

Wheat had had some unusual military experience prior to the Civil War: Though well educated, and a lawyer by occupation, Wheat very early on exhibited an interest in military matters. During the Mexican War he earned a captain's commission and saw combat. After returning to civilian life he practiced law and entered politics, being elected to the Louisiana legislature. Wheat gave up all this, however, when he became involved in the scheme of revolutionary Narcisco Lopez to liberate Cuba from Spanish rule. Wheat raised a regiment and went off to fight in Cuba. The whole affair turned into an embarrassing debacle. In 1851 Rob Wheat became involved with another revolutionary, this one wanted to establish a republic in northern Mexico. This proved a failure as well, and Wheat returned to Louisiana. After a two year stint of practicing the law in Louisiana, Wheat was bitten by the filibuster bug again. In 1854 he headed out to California to join William Walker's revolution in Baja. After that fell apart, he headed for Mexico once again, this time to assist Juan Alvarez in his successful revolution. In 1857 Wheat was with William Walker once again, who was fighting to keep control of Nicaragua. Walker had engineered the takeover of that country, had himself appointed its president, and was being plagued by an alliance of other Central American countries who were trying to kick him out. Wheat and several hundred other filibusters failed to prevent Walker's ouster. By 1860 Rob Wheat was reportedly fighting for Garibaldi in Italy. When he arrived back in the United States in 1861 he joined the newly formed Confederacy.[211]

"Wheat's Tigers," as his battalion was called, saw action at the Battle of First Manassas in July of 1861. It was during this first big battle of the war that Wheat was wounded; shot through both lungs. His wound was pronounced mortal by the examining doctor, but Wheat did not agree with the diagnosis. He told the surgeon, "I don't feel like dying yet" and then recovered. That one incident made him a living legend. Unfortunately, the fortunes of war overwhelmed his willpower at the Battle of Gaines's Mill the following year. He was killed on June 27, 1862.

Chatham Roberdeau Wheat's middle name was given him in honor of his maternal grandmother. As with many other Southerners of the time his middle name was used in identifying him. Pronunciation of Roberdeau isn't really a matter of great importance since most of Wheat's contemporaries called him "Rob." However, it is knowledge of these minute historical facts that true Civil War buffs live and thrive on. Emphasis is placed on the first syllable of Wheat's middle name.[212]

Rolla -(RAHL-uh)

as in Rolla, Missouri.

The name Rolla pops up from time to time in Civil War studies of the Western theater of operations. For example, Rolla, Missouri was one of the places Union forces retreated to after the Battle of Wilson's Creek on August 10, 1863.

Rolla is an unusual name and there are various explanations as to how the town got its name. One story has it that the name came from a popular melodrama during the early 1800s, Richard B. Sheridan's translation of Kotzebue's play, *Pizarro*, which had the subtitle, *The Death of Rolla*. Another story, less glamorous, says that the town was named for a mangy dog called "Rollo." Yet another claims the town was named for railway attorney Arthur Noyes' brother, Rolla. The most popular story is that the town's name is a crude phonetic spelling of Raleigh, North Carolina from which many of the first settlers came.[213] Given the pronunciation of the name, this story seems almost plausible. But this certainly doesn't say much for the literacy level of Rolla's founding fathers. Another version of this story appears in *The United States Dictionary of Places* which says that one "George Coppedge, nostalgic for his North Carolina home asked that it be named Raleigh. This last proposal was accepted and the name spelled as Coppedge pronounced it, 'Rolla'."[214] Thus, we have a choice of a theatrical play, an old dog, an attorney, a bunch of functional illiterates or a group of really clever town fathers who decided to spell the town's name in such a unique way that suckers like me would spend time writing about it over a hundred years later.

Rosecrans -(ROHZ-kranz)

as in William Starke Rosecrans, Major General U.S.V.

When it came to the art of maneuver, the delicate business conducting a campaign as though it were a chess game, few were the match of William Rosecrans. This much underrated Federal general, who is best remembered by most for his disastrous defeat at Chickamauga, had a superior strategic sense. Unfortunately, he was also somewhat emotionally unstable. Rosecrans had a terrible temper and was subject to mood swings. These characteristics often came into play at critical moments in his career.

After graduating from West Point in 1842 Rosecrans remained in the army for twelve years. He resigned in 1854 to pursue a more lucrative career as a civil engineer and architect. When the war came, he volunteered as an aide and engineer on General George McClellan's staff in the Department of Ohio. In June 1861 he became colonel of the 23rd Ohio and was promoted brigadier general to rank from May 16th. Rosecrans then took command of a brigade in western Virginia. He played a significant role in the Battle of Rich Mountain (he actually won the battle, but George McClellan got the credit).

Rosecrans transferred to the West in 1862 and took command of a division of John Pope's Army of the Mississippi during the Siege of Corinth. He succeeded Pope in command of the army in June 1862, fought at Iuka on September 19th and whipped the Confederates at Corinth on October 3-4. He was promoted to major general in September 1862, and a month later took command of the Army the Ohio which was concurrently redesignated the Army of the Cumberland. He led this army at the Battle of Stones River, the Tullahoma Campaign and at Chickamauga, where a terrible defeat pretty much ended his career. After October 1863, he faded into professional obscurity. During the postwar years, he did some ranching in California, got elected to Congress and worked for the Treasury. He died in 1898.

One of the things worth noting about Rosecrans were his many eccentricities. He was a hard working, compulsive sort of individual, and liked his staff to be just like him. He preferred "sandy fellows," blonds, for his staff officers, because he felt they were more industrious than brunettes. A convert to Catholicism, he was deeply religious and liked to keep his staff of "sandy fellows" up till all hours of the night, for days on end, discussing spiritual matters. At the same time, he drank heavily and swore like a stevedore, though he claimed his swearing was O. K. because he never used the name of God.[215]

Rosecrans is derived from the name, Rosenkrantz.[216] It is pretty much pronounced as it is spelled. The most common mispronunciation is **ROH-zen-kranz**. People seem to want to add an extra syllable to the name, thus rendering it much like it once was. A more careful reading of the name seems called for in these cases.[217] Some sources (Webster's New Biographical Dictionary, for example) give two pronouncers for the Rosecrans. One of them, the most commonly used, is **ROHZ-kranz**, the other is

ROH-zuh-kranz. I have used the first one because it is the one I have heard used most frequently by Civil War historians over the years. The second pronouncer gives the name a more German sound, which I believe the Rosecrans family was attempting to avoid when they changed the spelling of the name to make it look more English.

Rowanty -(roh-WAN-tee)

as in Rowanty Creek, Virginia.

If you do any reading on the Petersburg Campaign you will undoubtedly run across a lot of place names that aren't exactly household words. One of these is Rowanty Creek. You will encounter it if you read about the Battle of Hatcher's Run, which took place on February 5-7, 1865. Hatcher's Run was one of those engagements that resulted from another attempt by General Grant to extend the Federal line south and west of Petersburg to weaken the Confederate defensive position. The Byzantine complexity of the Petersburg Campaign is such that almost every engagement that took place over the nine month siege has two or three different names. In the case of Hatcher's Run, it is also called the Battle of Dabney's Mill and is sometimes identified as Armstrong's Mill, Vaughan Road and Rowanty Creek. To confuse matters even further, there were three separate engagements during the Siege of Petersburg called Hatcher's Run: Hatcher's Run of October 28, 1864, usually called Boydton Plank Road, and occasionally referred to as Vaughan Road and Burgess Mill; Hatcher's Run of December 8-9, 1864, apparently just called by that name; and finally, Hatcher's Run of February 5-7, 1865.

I will spare you the details of Hatcher's Run/Dabney's Mill/Boydton Road/Armstrong's Mill/Rowanty Creek. Suffice it to say, the Federals were successful in extending their line, casualties were heavy on both sides, considering the objective, and included Confederate General John Pegram.

I always thought it would be neat to become a real expert on the Petersburg Campaign. It would be a feat of mental gymnastics equivalent to memorizing the entire Federal Tax Code. But when I realized that such an undertaking would require monk-like isolation, and involve the constant risk of slipping into an irreversible coma, I decided against it.

Pronunciation of Rowanty is one of those cases of knowing which syllable to stress. I checked with the National Park Service folks at Petersburg and the result is the pronouncer I used above.

Ruffin -(RUF-un)

as in Edmund Ruffin, secessionist.

There is a famous photograph of Edmund Ruffin, evidently taken around the time of the firing on Fort Sumter, which shows him as an older man with flowing, shoulder length, white hair. He is wearing the uniform of the Palmetto Guard, and in his right hand he holds a rifle-musket. His mouth is firmly set and there is fire in his eyes. This guy means business.

Edmund Ruffin is generally credited with firing the first shot of the Civil War. Ruffin was with other members of the Palmetto Guard at the Iron Clad Battery at Morris Island in Charleston Harbor. Though he is credited with pulling the lanyard on an eight-inch Columbiad that launched the first hostile shot at Fort Sumter's parapet, the first round fired came from Fort Johnson on James Island. This shot was fired at 4:30 a.m. on April 12, 1861 and it was to give the signal for the other forty-seven guns around the harbor to open up. The lanyard that fired this shot was probably pulled by Lieutenant Henry Farley at the order of Captain George S. James.[218] The shell itself burst directly above Fort Sumter. The shot that Ruffin fired reportedly was the first one to hit Fort Sumter.

Edmund Ruffin was sixty-seven years old the morning Fort Sumter was fired on. He was already famous in the South as an agronomist. His discovery of the restorative effects of calcareous manure on worn out soil was considered a work of genius. Ruffin owned a plantation on the Pamunkey River in Virginia worked by more than two hundred slaves. Aside from calcareous manure, Ruffin's main interest was secession politics. He was absolutely fanatical in his hatred of the North. This hatred is best illustrated by the fact that Ruffin, a voracious reader, "shunned Webster's dictionary as Yankee trash."[219] The fire eating old man committed suicide in June 1865 because he was unable to live under the hated Yankees.

Pronunciation of Ruffin's last name usually doesn't present any difficulty. However, over the years I have heard a few people say it as, **ROOF-un**. Thus, its inclusion in this dictionary. Mark Boatner in his *Civil War Dictionary* gives a pronouncer for Ruffin (essentially the same one I use) and other reference works concur.

Major General Stephen Dodson Ramseur

S

Sabine -(suh-BEEN)

as in Sabine Pass, Texas.

The Texas coast operations of General Nathaniel Banks in the late summer of 1863 led to a naval engagement at Sabine Pass on the 8th of September. Four thousand men under General William Franklin, along with a naval escort, set out from New Orleans on September 5, 1863 to capture Sabine Pass, Texas. Sabine Pass is a five mile long tidal inlet on the Gulf of Mexico that provides a deep water channel into Sabine Lake. The lake is at the confluence of three rivers, the Sabine, Neches and Angelina. Sabine Lake and the Sabine River are part of the common boundary between the states of Louisiana and Texas. The object of this operation was to raise the Federal flag over Texas to discourage possible French support of the Confederates with troops from Mexico. The Federal force of twenty-six ships, led by four gunboats was routed by Confederate artillery at Fort Griffin. Two of the gunboats and 350 men were captured. The Battle of Sabine Pass preserved Texas for the time being from successful invasion by the Union.

The name Sabine is derived from the Spanish, "Sabinas." It was named by the Spaniards for the red cedars growing along the river. Speakers of the French language shifted the word to its present form. Pronunciation of the Sabine can cause real problems. In some parts of the country the same name, same spelling is pronounced SAY-bine[220]and in other parts SAB-been.

Salm-Salm -(zahm-zahm)

as in Felix Constantin Alexander Johann Nepomuk, Prince zu Salm-Salm, Colonel U. S. V.

Salm-Salm was a veteran of the Prussian cavalry during the Schleswig-Holstein War of 1848. He arrived in the United States in 1861, and offered his services to the Union cause. He didn't make much progress in getting an appointment until he had an interview with Abraham Lincoln, who apparently took a liking to him. He spoke no English and there were rumors that he left Europe under a cloud of suspicion regarding certain pecuniary matters.[221] This soldier of fortune finally landed a spot as chief of staff to the equally suspicious, General Louis Blenker, a division commander in the Army of the Potomac. In October 1862 he became colonel of the 8th New York (the 1st German

Rifles, a regiment Blenker had raised). The 8th N. Y. saw little action and was disbanded in April 1863. In June of the following year Salm-Salm was placed in command of the 68th New York and transferred to the West, where he fought at the Battle of Nashville.

After the war, Salm-Salm headed for Mexico and went to work for the Emperor Maximilian. When Maximilian was overthrown by Juarez, the Prince was captured and nearly got himself shot by a firing squad. He managed to get out of that jam, made it back to Germany and joined the Grenadier Guards. He was killed at the Battle of Gravelotte in 1870 during the Franco-Prussian War.

Even more fascinating than Prince Felix was his wife. He met Agnes Leclerq while camped with his regiment in Washington. Agnes Leclerq's background is obscure. According to one story, she was a French-Canadian who became an actress with a traveling show. Another story had her as a circus rider, and yet another rumor hinted that she was an Indian princess, stolen and sold to a circus manager who took her to South America. She escaped, the story goes, while the circus was in Havana and made her way to Boston, and eventually to Washington, D. C. Whatever the case may have been, Prince Felix fell in love with her and they got married. Agnes turned out to be a very capable political wire puller, and any progress that Prince Felix made he owed to his wife's machinations.[222] Her personal appeals to Juarez even saved Salm-Salm from the firing squad.

Pronunciation of Salm Salm is affected by the rules of the German language, in which the letter **'S'** at the beginning of a word or syllable is pronounced like the English **'Z.'** The only time this varies is when **'S'** as the first letter is followed by **'t'** or **'p,'** in which case it takes the **'sch'** sound. Obviously, names like Schaeffer and Schwinn already have the **'sch'** sound spelled out.

<u>Scharf</u> -(skarf)

as in John Thomas <u>Scharf</u>, Confederate naval officer, Confederate naval historian.

J. T. Scharf is most famous for his book, *The History of the Confederate States Navy.* If you do any studying or research into the naval area of the Civil War you will undoubtedly run into Scharf's name.

Maryland-born John Scharf was a midshipman in the Confederate Navy who had done a brief stint in the army prior to becoming a swabbie.[223] He was involved in the February 1864 raid that destroyed USS *Underwriter* and also the unsuccessful attempt to eliminate two Union blockade boats guarding the Appalachicola River in Florida. Scharf also served aboard CSS *Sampson* on the Savannah River. He was captured in 1865 while undertaking a government mission to Canada.[224]

Pronunciation of this German name has obviously been Americanized. Had I not come across an old article by Bell I. Wiley on Civil War name pronunciations I never would have questioned the pronunciation of John Scharf's name.[225]

Schimmelfennig -(SHIM-uhl-fenig)

as in Alexander Schimmelfennig, Brigadier General U.S.V.

General Schimmelfennig may just have the most famous long name of any Civil War general. Yet, despite its vast length, the name is pronounced exactly as it is spelled. I have included it in this dictionary for two reasons: the name is so long it scares the wits out of anyone who is attempting to say it for the first time, and it is a name that is attached to one of the better bizarre stories to come out of the war.

Prussian-born Alexander Schimmelfennig was one of the "Forty-Eighters," political refugees who supported the unsuccessful revolutions that took place in 1848 in Germany, and the rest of Europe for that matter. He had been an engineer in the Prussian army and fought in the Schleswig-Holstein War of 1848 before joining the revolutionary army in the Palatinate. Among the revolutionaries he fought with were Louis Blenker, Carl Schurz and Franz Sigel. He followed these men and other revolutionaries into exile, first to Switzerland, then England, and finally, America. He arrived in the United States in 1851 and took up residence in Philadelphia. He worked as an engineer and by the time the war came was working in Washington for the War Department as a draftsman.

When the war broke out Schimmelfennig got off to a bad start because of a bout with small pox. He had gotten a commission as colonel of a regiment he was helping to raise when he was stricken. After he recovered, he received command of the 74th Pennsylvania, a regiment raised by prominent German-Americans in Pittsburgh. Schimmelfennig did not see any active field service until the Second Manassas Campaign. By that time he was part of Sigel's Corps and a brigade commander in Carl Schurz's division. He was promoted to brigadier general in November 1862 and fought as a brigade and division commander in the luckless Eleventh Corps at Chancellorsville and Gettysburg.

It was at Gettysburg that Schimmelfennig became one of those comical footnotes to history: In the confusion of the Eleventh Corps retreat through the town of Gettysburg on the afternoon of July 1, 1863 the general was apparently hit over the head by someone's rifle-musket, and when he came to found himself within Confederate lines (the Rebels were right on the heels of the fleeing Eleventh Corps). In order to avoid capture he headed down an alleyway along Baltimore Street and hid in the pigsty behind the Garlach residence. Mrs. Garlach took pity on the poor general so she snuck food and water out to him. Schimmelfennig remained hidden for three days, and reportedly did not come out of his porcine abode until he was certain the Confederates had evacuated the town.[226] Though what he had done was sensible, he gained some unwanted notoriety. He continued on in the army and finally died of tuberculosis in 1865.

As I have indicated above, pronunciation of Schimmelfennig's name is relatively easy. The only possible problem may be in knowing which syllable or syllables gets stressed. The pronounce I have given is based on years and years of hearing the name intoned by Gettysburg historians and battlefield guides.

Schoepf -(shepf)

as in Albin Francisco Schoepf, Brigadier General U.S.V.

Ezra Warner, in his *Generals in Blue,* says that Albin Schoepf was working as a porter in a Washington hotel sometime in the 1850s when he was noticed by Commissioner of Patents Joseph Holt, and given a clerkship at the Patent Office. The job title of porter can be interpreted in a number of ways, depending on the size and status of the hotel involved. One must assume that the type of hotel an important bureaucrat like Holt would frequent was one of the better ones, therefore, it can be assumed that Schoepf was a bit more than just a bellhop. In any case, it is remarkable that this recent immigrant to the United States (he arrived here in 1851) should have risen from hotel employee to brigadier general in less than a decade. He obviously had something on the ball.

Albin Francisco Schoepf was born in an area of Poland that had become part of the Hapsburg Monarchy as a result of the 18th century partitioning of that country. Thus, his father was Austrian and his mother Polish. By 1848 he had risen to the rank of captain in the Austrian army. The year 1848 was a fateful one in Europe, a time of revolution and rising nationalism. One of the countries where revolution was taking place was Hungary, then a part of the Austro-Hungarian Empire. Like many other young men of his time, Schoepf got involved. He left the Austrian army and joined the Hungarian revolutionaries under Kossuth. When the rebellion was suppressed, Schoepf escaped to Syria and eventually made his way to the United States. His position at the Patent Office under the patronage of Joseph Holt led to his following Holt to the War Department in 1861 during the final weeks of the Buchanan Administration. When the war came, a combination of Schoepf's past military experience and Holt's favorable reputation with the Lincoln Administration led to Schoepf getting an appointment as brigadier general of volunteers. This was in September of 1861.

The newly minted general was then sent to Holt's home state of Kentucky, where he was to spend most of his active military career. He fought as a brigade commander at the Battle of Mill Springs and at Perryville commanded a division in General Charles C. Gilbert's Third Corps of Buell's Army of the Ohio. Apparently, Schoepf was purged from active field command after Perryville because of his association with Gilbert's Corps. A military commission formed to investigate General Don Carlos Buell's handling of operations in Tennessee and Kentucky found fault with Gilbert's performance, among others, at Perryville. This is probably the reason why Schoepf ended up spending the rest of the war as commandant of the Federal prison at Fort Delaware. After the war, Schoepf returned to the patent office, and in time rose to the position of chief examiner. He died in 1886.

Pronunciation of Schoepf's name is pretty much a case of adhering to the rules of pronunciation associated with the German language. The **'oe'** in the middle of the name is pronounced as if it were just an **'e,'** and the **'pf'** at the end of the name is pronounced as **'p'** with an **'f'** sound attached (I realize that this can be difficult, and if you must choose to pronounce only one of those last letters, choose **'f'**). German spelling and pronunciation has its peculiarities. Undoubtedly, the Germans feel the same way about English. In checking around with different Civil War historians I could get no one to commit to saying "this is the definitive pronunciation of General Schoepf's name." Since Schoepf was a relatively recent immigrant to this country at the time of the Civil War one must assume he hadn't yet invented some bizarre Americanized pronunciation of his name.

<u>Schurz</u> -(shurts *or* shoorts)

as in Carl <u>Schurz,</u> Major General U.S.V.

Carl Schurz did everything: he was born in Prussia, became a revolutionary in 1848, fled to America after exile, became a crusader in the anti-slavery cause, charter member of the Republican Party, was an editor, a social reformer, and a leading voice in the German immigrant community. Because he helped elect Abraham Lincoln he was appointed brigadier general early in the war. Though lacking military experience he did a creditable job. He also encouraged thousands of German-Americans to join the Union cause. Much of his military service was spent as part of the unlucky Eleventh Corps of the Army of the Potomac. Routed at Chancellorsville, and again at Gettysburg, the Eleventh Corps and its German-American commanders were widely ridiculed. Schurz got his share of obloquy, much of it undeserved.

After the war Shurz went on to a distinguished career in the U.S. Senate and was Secretary of the Interior during the Hayes administration. He was also a widely read journalist and a statesman until after the turn of the century.

Pronunciation of Shurz's last name is somewhat difficult for people who are not familiar with German names. The letter **'z'** in the German language is always pronounced like it has a **'t'** in front of it. Thus, the **'z'** at end of the name Shurz is pronounced as though it were **'TSS.'** If you wish, you can put a German inflection on the **'u'** as well. This would make the **'u'** rhyme with the **'oo'** in "ooh!" (the sound the audience makes on Wheel of Fortune when they show a new Winnebago). I have given two pronounce options, **SHURTS** and **SHOORTS**, and it is entirely up to you just how esoteric you want to sound when you discuss this general.

<u>Schuylkill</u> -(SKOOL-kil or SKOO-kul)

as in <u>Schuylkill</u> County, Pennsylvania or the <u>Schuylkill</u> River.

Schuylkill County is located in the mountainous northeast corner of Pennsylvania and is famous for its coal mines. Many of the men in the 48th Pennsylvania were coal miners from this county and played an important part in one of the most spectacular incidents of the Civil War, the Battle of the Crater.

By late June 1864 Grant's plan to take Petersburg and move on Richmond from south of the James River had bogged down and become a siege operation. Lieutenant Colonel Henry Pleasants of the 48th Pennsylvania, a mining engineer before the war, proposed to Ninth Corps commander Ambrose Burnside the idea of digging a mine shaft under Confederate lines, filling it with explosives and blowing a large gap through which an assault column could attack. Burnside approved of the scheme and ultimately Grant did as well, though with some reservations. Work on the shaft got underway on June 25, 1864 and was completed by July 23rd. The shaft was over five hundred feet long and terminated at a point twenty feet beneath Confederate lines at Elliott's Salient. Four additional days were required to place 320 kegs of black powder (some 8,000 pounds) in the shaft and seal it. The explosives were detonated at 4:42 on the morning of July 30, 1864. and created a crater 170 feet long, between sixty and eighty feet wide, and about thirty feet deep.[227] The Federal assault that followed turned into a disaster. Confusion caused by the immense explosion, little or no direction from commanding officers (Generals Ledlie and Ferraro were getting drunk in a bombproof behind the lines at the time) and a successful Confederate counterattack rendered the whole Union effort naught. General Grant described the assault as a "stupendous failure."[228]

Pronunciation of the name Schuylkill is a mystery to many who do not live in Pennsylvania. Schuylkill is a Dutch name meaning "hidden stream."[229] It is also the name of a river that originates in Schuylkill County and flows southeast into the Delaware River at Philadelphia. I have given two pronouncers for the name; the first is the proper way, while the second is much more commonly used (a sort of abbreviated version of the first).

Scioto -(sie-OH-tuh)

as in USS *Scioto*.

The *Scioto* was one of twenty-three gunboats launched in 1861 that were referred to as "ninety day gunboats." This appellation was given to them because that is how long they took to build and launch. The *Scioto* was one of the unlucky ones; she was sunk by a torpedo in Mobile Bay in April 1865.[230]

The *Scioto* was named for a river in Ohio and the pronunciation is available in a number of reference books. Ohioans reading this entry may be wondering what on earth prompted me to include the name of this well known river in my dictionary. Consider the fact that when I first spotted the name Scioto on a map (I was a callow youth from New York at the time) a little voice in my brain that pronounces all new words for me said, "skee-OT-toh." It was years before I got to Ohio to get the straight dope.

Semmes -(semz)

as in Raphael Semmes, Captain CSS *Alabama*.

After a career in the U. S. Navy that began in 1826, during which he rose to the rank of commander, Raphael Semmes join the Confederate States Navy when his home state of Alabama seceded in 1861. After a brief stint as head of the Confederate Lighthouse Service, Semmes, who believed that the South's small navy could best be served by employing commerce raiders, was given command of the cruiser the *Sumter*. For six months in late 1861 Semmes stalked the seas and captured seventeen U. S. merchant ships. By now the South had begun a program of acquiring more and better cruisers for commerce raiding.

In 1862 the CSS *Alabama* was built in England and Raphael Semmes was assigned the command. For the next twenty-two months, from August 1862 to June 1864 the *Alabama* captured or sunk fifty-five prizes. As a commerce raider the CSS *Alabama* became legendary. Equally legendary was the final battle fought by the *Alabama*. In June 1864 the *Alabama* put into Cherbourg, France for repairs and while there was challenged by the USS *Kearsarge*. In the battle that followed, the *Alabama* was sunk. Semmes managed to escape capture by being picked out of the sea by an English yacht. He returned to the Confederacy and was promoted to rear admiral. In 1865 Semmes commanded the James River Squadron. After the war he practiced law in Mobile.

Pronunciation of the Semmes' name presents a difficulty for many people because of the double **'m'** in the middle and the **'e'** just before the final letter. It is the sort of spelling that suggests several pronunciations. The most glaring mispronunciation I have heard occurred recently: I was at a Civil War conference at which the person giving a talk on naval warfare referred to the good captain as **SEE-miss**. That particular way of saying it makes it sound like the name of some virulent form of skin disease, or possibly a very painful bladder infection. Be advised, it is pronounced as indicated in my pronounce above, in all cases. Please note that Raphael Semmes had a brother named Paul Jones Semmes who served as a brigadier general in the Lee's Army of Northern Virginia. Paul Semmes was mortally wounded on the Rose Farm at Gettysburg on July 2, 1863. Raphael Semmes died in 1877.

Sorrel -(sor-RELL)

as in Gilbert Moxley Sorrel, Brigadier General C.S.A.

Gilbert Moxley Sorrel was chief of staff for Army of Northern Virginia corps commander, James Longstreet. To most of his contemporaries he was known simply as Moxley Sorrel; he dropped the Gilbert (Why on earth did he do that?). His grandfather had been a French army engineer who emigrated to America by way of Santo Domingo. Moxley was born in Savannah, Georgia. He started out at First Manassas as a volunteer ADC to Longstreet, eventually became an invaluable member of Old Pete's staff and in the final stages of the war was a leader of troops as a brigade commander. His postwar memoir, *Recollections of a Confederate Staff Officer,* is good reading and a great source of material on Longstreet.

Discovering the proper pronunciation of Sorrel's last name was not difficult. It is a French-English name and there is a specific way of pronouncing it. However, the fact that Stonewall Jackson's famous horse was named "Little Sorrel" has caused some confusion. The name of Jackson's horse is pronounced differently, as the reader will find out in the next entry.

Pronouncing Sorrel's last name the same as that of Jackson's horse conjures up the bizarre vision of General Jackson using Longstreet's Chief of Staff as a form of transportation. Since Jackson weighed about 175 pounds, and stood six feet in height, the sight of the diminutive Sorrel being forced to gallop around the battlefield with Jackson on his back would have inspired some memorable equestrian statues of the Mighty Stonewall.[231]

Sorrel -(SOR-ul)

as in Little Sorrel or Old Sorrel

Stonewall Jackson's favorite mount was called "Little Sorrel," though in actuality the horse's was named "Fancy." He was acquired by Jackson in April of 1861, and was already eleven years old at that time. According to Jackson staff member Henry Kyd Douglas, he was a "plebeian looking little beast, not a chestnut: he was stocky and well made, round barreled, close coupled, good shoulder, excellent legs and feet, not fourteen hands high, good but heavy head and neck, a natural pacer with little action and no style."[232] Little Sorrel survived his owner by more than twenty years. Jackson had two other mounts, one called "Gaunt Sorrel," possibly named "Superior," and another gray horse given to him in Maryland, sometimes referred to as "Trojan Horse."

Sockdolager -(SOK-DOL-uh-jur)

as in "Well, I guess I know enough to turn you inside out, old gal...you sockdolagizing old man-trap!"

The word sockdolager is old-time slang. It means something unusually large or heavy, like a hard finishing blow; *His right jab was a real sockdolager.* "Sockdolagizing," used as a verb in the above quote would then mean hard hitting, very forceful. Thus a "Sockdolagizing old man-trap" would be a very aggressive woman who dominated men with force, who charmed them and tamed them with a heavy hand, or its feminine equivalent, a sharp tongue. That, at any rate, is the best interpretation I can come up with for this line from a very forgettable 19th century stage comedy called *Our American Cousin.* What makes it unforgettable, of course, is that it was the play Abraham Lincoln was watching at Ford's Theater when he was shot by John Wiles Booth. The line quoted was the line being said by actor Harry Hawks on stage when the fatal shot rang out.

Sockdolager is a word rarely heard these days. One look at it and many people would not venture pronouncing it. It looks like a word from a foreign language, or a nonsense word of some sort (which indeed it is). Its derivation is obscure. According to I. Moyer Hunsberger, author of *The Quintessential Dictionary*, the word is based on **sock** (a blow) plus **doxology** (in the slang sense of **finish**).

Sooy -(SOO-ee)

as in William Sooy Smith, Brigadier General U.S.V.

William Sooy Smith was one of eleven Union generals named Smith. There is a certain degree of anonymity that goes with being named Smith. One must feel anonymous with such a last name (I speak as an outside observer of various Smiths I have known over the years.) Perhaps, it is for that reason that so many people with such a last name are liable to have some clever first or middle name, to lend some distinction, or memorability. In the case of William Sooy Smith, it is obviously his middle name that makes him unique. In fact, he wasn't called Bill or William by his friends and acquaintances, but "Sooy," his middle name.

Smith was born in Ohio, worked his way through college, graduated, then got an appointment to West Point and graduated there in 1853. Since Sooy Smith was sixth in his class at the Point, he went into engineering. Engineering outside the army was much more lucrative than inside and it is probably for that reason he resigned his commission a year after graduation and got a job with the Illinois Central Railroad.

When the war came, Smith, having had a West Point education was commissioned colonel of the 13th Ohio. He fought at Shiloh, after which he was appointed brigadier general and at Perryville was a division commander in the Army of the Ohio. He commanded a division in the Vicksburg Campaign and afterward made chief of all cavalry operations in West under General Sherman. During the Meridian Campaign, February to March 1864, "The Sooy Smith Expedition," a cavalry raid from Memphis to West Point, Mississippi, resulted in a humiliating defeat for Smith. He was badly whipped and forced to retreat by Nathan Bedford Forrest whose force was half the size of his own seven-thousand-man column. Sooy Smith resigned from the army in July 1864 because of ill health.

Following the war, his career in engineering was spectacular: his contributions and innovations in the field of bridge building were monumental. He constructed the first all-steel bridge in the world over the Missouri River.[233] He was also an early pioneer in skyscraper construction. Smith's specialty in these constructions was the foundation.

Sooy is one those names that seem to beg mispronunciation. The word quite simply looks strange. William Sooy Smith got his middle name from his father, Sooy Smith. The first time I saw the name I thought it might be some really potent form of soy sauce or the name of a Dr. Seuss character. The name Sooy is odd, but not unknown: while researching the general's middle name I came upon one Joseph Leander Sooy, a fairly well known late 19th-century Methodist clergyman from New Jersey.[234]

Soulé -(SOO-LAY)

as in Pierre Soulé, Confederate Extraordinaire.

Pierre Soulé was one of the more exotic characters in the pantheon of Confederate notables. Soulé was exiled from his native France at the age of fifteen for conspiring against the ruling Bourbons. He spent a year in the Pyrenees as a shepherd and then returned to France becoming a journalist. He was jailed in 1825 for anti-government writings, escaped to England, and made his way to Haiti. He finally ended up in U. S., learned English while working as a gardener; studied the law all by himself and was admitted to the bar in the state of Louisiana. Soulé was elected to the state legislature in 1846, the U. S. Senate the same year, and was appointed Minister to Spain in 1853. While in Spain, Soulé denounced the monarchy there, wounded the French minister in a duel, conspired with Spanish revolutionaries and supported filibusters to Cuba to liberate that island from Spanish control and bring it into the Union as a new slave state.[235]He was also primary author of the Ostend Manifesto, which proposed the purchase of Cuba.

Pierre Soulé is of interest to us because of his role in the events that led directly to the Civil War. After the death of John C. Calhoun in 1850 Soulé, who was then a Democratic senator from Louisiana, became a leader of the states rights wing of the Southern Democracy.[236]His strong support of slavery and expansionism though, was at odds with his opposition to secession. When Louisiana did secede in 1861 he abided by the state's decision and supported the new Southern Confederacy. After the Federal capture of New Orleans in 1862, he was arrested and sent to Fort Lafayette, New York, held for five months and paroled. He fled to the Bahamas, ran the blockade to New Orleans and then offered his services to the Confederacy.[237] No one in Richmond really trusted this radical, highly temperamental firebrand, and as a result, he was never given any important assignments. He faded into obscurity after the war and died in 1870.

Soulé is a French name. The acute accent over the final **'e'** gives it a long **'a'** sound.

Stahel -(shtahl)

as in Julius Stahel, Major General U.S.V.

Bet you didn't know that Julius Stahel won the Medal of Honor. General Stahel, born in Hungary, fought with Kossuth in the 1848 revolution for Hungarian independence and came to America in 1859. Stahel joined Louis Blenker's 8th New York Regiment (the 1st German Rifles) at the beginning of the war and succeeded Blenker as colonel of the regiment. He was with Franz Sigel's Corps at Second Manassas. After a stint commanding the cavalry in the defenses of Washington, D.C., Stahel became commander of a cavalry division in the Shenandoah Valley in 1864. At the Battle of Piedmont in June of 1864 he fought with distinction, was wounded and was awarded the Medal of Honor for his exploits in the battle. Stahel spent most of his postwar career in the diplomatic service, posted mostly in Japan and China.

I have opted for the German pronunciation of Stahel's last name. It is reasonable to assume that the name was Germanic. Hungary at the time of his birth and for many years thereafter was part of the Austro-Hungarian Empire. The ethnic mix in this part of Europe was very diverse. General Stahel was probably a diverse mixture himself ethnically, but his name nevertheless appears German. Stahel's Hungarian surname was actually Számvald.[238] One assumes he adopted the German name while still in the Austrian Army, or that his name was a hyphenated one. I ran this name by a lot of historians and Park Service people and, though no one would commit to saying I was correct in my pronunciation, no one would flatly disagree with me either. Research on this one continues. For the present, **shtahl** should suffice.

Staunton -(STAN-tn)

as in Staunton, Virginia.

Staunton is a town in the Shenandoah Valley. It lies south of Harrisonburg, north of Lexington and is west of Charlottesville, which is on the other side of the Blue Ridge Mountains. The rival armies of the South and the North, beginning with General David Hunter's on June 6, 1864, were constantly passing through Staunton during the fighting in the Valley, though no major engagement ever took place there. If you tour the battlefields of the Shenandoah Valley you are bound, at one time or another, to stop or pass through Staunton just as the armies did. Unless you are from Virginia you're going to be pronouncing the town name, **STAWN-tn**. And why not? What's that **'u'** doing there if you're not going to pronounce it? Nearby locals will quickly correct you.

I have to assume that the pronunciation is one of those examples of towns named by English settlers during the 18th century in various parts of colonial America. Massachusetts is full of these kinds of place names: Leominster is pronounced **LEM-minster**, Concord is pronounced **KONG-kurd** and on and on. But just to confuse all of us, Taunton, Massachusetts is pronounced **TAWN-tn**. This type of weird pronunciation still prevails in England: Liecester is pronounced, **LES-tur**, Salisbury is pronounced **SAULZ-bree**.

Stoughton -(STOH-tun)

as in Edwin Henry Stoughton, Brigadier General U.S.V.

Vermont-born Edwin Stoughton, a graduate of West Point in 1859, had a promising career going in the military until one night in 1863. Stoughton took part in George McClellan's Peninsula Campaign in 1862 as colonel of the 4th Vermont, then after a leave of absence, was promoted to brigadier general and assigned to command a brigade in the Washington defenses. His headquarters was in Fairfax Court House, Virginia.

It was there on the night of March 8, 1863 that John S. Mosby, with twenty-nine men, stole into the Union encampment and captured thirty-nine men, including Stoughton. A story, never verified, made the rounds that Mosby had penetrated the Union picket lines with the aid of one Antonia Ford, a pretty young woman who lived in Fairfax. After telling Mosby and his men how to sneak into the Federal camp, Miss Ford allegedly plied young Stoughton with enough champagne to render him insensible. Supposedly, when Mosby found him, Stoughton was passed out amidst numerous empty champagne bottles. Mosby uncovered the sleeping general and slapped him on the rear end to wake him up. Many of these details were later denied by Mosby, who claimed he had gotten information on weak spots in the Union picket line from a deserter.

Mosby was telling the truth. The Union deserter was Sergeant J. F. Ames, a native of Maine, who had served with the 5th New York Cavalry prior to deserting. Ames knew the location of the Union pickets and the general layout of Fairfax Court House. He led Mosby's men into Stoughton's headquarters camp. Nonetheless, nine people, including the seductive Antonia Ford (who apparently made a habit of befriending Union officers for whatever reason), were arrested and sent to the Old Capitol Prison in Washington. All nine were eventually released since no evidence of conspiracy could be found.[239]

Whatever the truth was, Stoughton's career was a shambles. After spending time in Libby Prison in Richmond, he was exchanged in May 1863, his brigadier commission expired. He was not reassigned or reappointed. Just another hapless victim of "Antonia-Gate." No longer wanted by the army, he moved to New York City and set up a law practice. He died there in 1868.

Pronunciation of Stoughton is no great phonetic puzzle. Several standard reference works contain accurate pronouncers. I have included it in the dictionary for those who find words with 'o-u-g-h' spellings phonetically ambiguous and thoroughly rough going.

<u>Strasburg</u> -(STRAWS-burg)

as in <u>Strasburg</u>, Virginia.

Strasburg is in the northern, or lower end of the Shenandoah Valley. It is a town south of Winchester and just west of Front Royal. Strasburg is quite near the Cedar Creek Battlefield of October 1864. No major battles took place in Strasburg, but it is still an important location, and one which should be properly pronounced.

Like most Yankees I look at the spelling and blurt out **STRASS-burg**. After all, there is a town in Lancaster County, Pennsylvania with this very name. I have tried to come up with some elaborate theory as to how the Virginia pronunciation came about. I even considered the fact that many Germans settled in the Shenandoah Valley and possibly some sort of corruption of the original German pronunciation occurred over the years. However, it all seemed too contrived, too complicated and I settled for a simpler explanation. It is just STRASS-burg said with a southern drawl while yawning. It is possible that the town meeting held to decide on a name dragged on so long that people were just tuckered out when a name was finally chosen.[240]

<u>Streight</u> -(strate)

as in Abel D. <u>Streight</u>, Colonel U.S.V.

The colonel was famous as the leader of "Streight's Raid," a mounted foray through the hills of northern Alabama that commenced at Nashville on April 11, 1863 with a boat ride and lasted seventeen days. The purpose of the raid was to destroy southern railroads. Streight's force of mounted infantry was unique in that mules were used instead of horses by many of the men. This caused serious problems, especially when Streight ran into Nathan Bedford Forrest's cavalry. Bluffed into surrendering at Straight-Neck Precinct, Alabama by General Forrest, who had one-third the men the Federals had, Streight ended up in Libby Prison in Richmond. Following his daring escape, along with more than one hundred other prisoners, in February 1864, he returned to duty and served until the end of the war. He was breveted brigadier general, U.S. Volunteers for his gallantry and meritorious service.

Pronunciation of Colonel Streight's last name is made confusing by that 'e' in the middle. An old article in a 1970 copy of *Civil War Times Illustrated* written by Bell Wiley was the source of the correct pronunciation. Wiley's article, titled *Get it Right*, coincidentally is about proper pronunciation. He says that he got the straight dope on Streight's name from one Howard Bales, who as a boy delivered newspapers to Streight's widow. I'm certainly glad we got all that straightened out.

Pierre Soulé, Confederate Extraordinaire

T

Taliaferro -(TAHL-i-vur)

as in William Booth Taliaferro, Major General C.S.A.

This Virginia-born lawyer and politician was a veteran of the Mexican War and also led the Virginia militia during John Brown's Harpers Ferry Raid in 1859. He was the first non-professional soldier to gain command of a division in Lee's army.

Serving first under General Richard Garnett in western Virginia, he eventually fell under the command of Stonewall Jackson and took part in the Valley Campaign of 1862. Taliaferro was badly wounded in at the opening of the Second Manassas Campaign at Brawner's Farm and after the Battle of Fredericksburg was transferred to Charleston. He spent the rest of the war in South Carolina, Florida and Georgia. After the war he returned to Virginia state politics.

The pronunciation of Taliaferro's last name seems to bear absolutely no connection to its spelling. In doing some research into the derivation of this unusual name I came across some interesting information. In the Italian language the name "Tagliaferro" means, "iron cutter." In Old French "taille fer" means "iron cutter," as well. It is from this French term that the English word "telfer," which also means "iron cutter," is derived.[241] Whether the name is French or Italian is a difficult to decide. It is possible that the Taliaferros who came to Virginia in the 17th century were descended from a Norman knight named Taillefer, who came to England with the Norman Invasion of 1066. It is also possible that they are connected with a Venetian musician named Taliaferro who settled in England during Elizabethan times.[242] Whatever the case may be, the Taliaferros who settled in Virginia were from England and pronunciation of the name as **TAHL-i-vur** apparently started in England, long before the family got to America.

Taney -(TAH-nee)

as in Justice Roger Taney or Taneytown Road, Gettysburg.

Maryland-born Roger Taney served as Andrew Jackson's Attorney General and Secretary of the Treasury before he was nominated as Chief Justice of the Supreme

Court in 1835. Taney was Chief Justice from then until his death in 1864. He is remembered principally because of the Dred Scott Decision in 1857. Taney delivered the majority opinion of the court which challenged the Missouri Compromise and edged the country ever closer to civil war. Taney also had the distinction of having sworn in Abraham Lincoln for his first term in office.

The "Taney" in Taneytown Road is pronounced just as the Judge's last name is.[243] The Taneytown Road, an important roadway during the Battle of Gettysburg, connects Gettysburg with Taneytown, Maryland, just below the border. Taneytown is named for Frederick Taney, who founded the town in 1740.[244]

Teche -(tesh)

as in Bayou Teche, Louisiana.

Bayou Teche is an important name you will come across in reading about Nathanial Banks' Red River Campaign of 1863. As part of an overall plan to open up the Mississippi River in conjunction with Grant's efforts at Vicksburg, Banks was to attack Port Hudson on the east bank of big river. Banks however, didn't want to go ahead with this until he had cleared the west bank of the Mississippi of Confederates. His plan was to send a force up the Atchafalaya River and Bayou Teche to Alexandria, Louisiana which would clear the Rebels off the west bank of the Mississippi and flank their defenses at Port Hudson.

It was a very complex and overly ambitious plan. The Atchafalaya River and Bayou Teche run roughly parallel to the Mississippi, draining south through the delta, and ultimately into the Gulf of Mexico. Confederate general Richard Taylor had a force of just under three thousand at Fort Bisland on the southern end of Bayou Teche. Banks figured he could bypass Taylor by sending troops around the Confederate right flank and up Grand Lake, a large lake that was, in fact, an extension of the Atchafalaya River.

Meanwhile, Federals under Generals William H. Emory and Godfrey Weitzel would attack Fort Bisland head on, to keep Taylor in place while he was being flanked. Once this was done, the flanking Federals could swing west from Grand Lake, head inland to Bayou Teche, and cut off Taylor's line of retreat at Irish Bend. Nothing went according to plan and Taylor ultimately escaped the trap set by Banks. If all this confuses you, think of how badly muddled a dolt like Nathaniel Banks must have been. A quick look at a detail map of this area of operations would make a modern general, with helicopters and swamp buggies at his disposal, hesitate to deploy.

The word "Teche" is probably a French rendering of the word "Deutsch." German colonists in the area of the bayou called it "Deutsch," the French however dominated the area eventually and corrupted the name.[245] Pronouncers for this name are readily available in a number of reference works.

<u>Tecumseh</u> -(ti-KUM-suh)

as in William <u>Tecumseh</u> Sherman, Major General U.S.V.

There is no point in a book of this size to go into a biography of General Sherman. If you are a Civil War buff (and why else would you be reading this book?) you know all about Uncle Billy. However, I have included his middle name in this pronouncing dictionary because it is so often mispronounced by people. I can't count the number of times I've heard people who should know better call the general, William **ti-KUM-see** Sherman. There is no **'ey'** or **'e'** sound at the end of that word.

When Sherman was born in 1820 his father named him Tecumseh after a great Shawnee chief he much admired. That's right, Sherman's given name was Tecumseh. The "William" was added ten years later when Sherman, by then living with the Ewing family, was baptized a Catholic. Catholicism requires a saint's name for baptism.

Throughout his life Sherman's nickname was "Cump," short for Tecumseh. One of more amusing typos I have come across in years of Civil War reading occurred in 1986 when I bought the first edition of the *Historical Times Encyclopedia of the Civil War.* On page 681 under the entry for General Sherman it says about halfway through the first paragraph, "After receiving an early education in Ohio, Sherman, called 'Chump' by his friends..."

<u>Theophilus</u> -(*th*ee-AH-fuh-lus)

as in <u>Theophilus</u> Hunter Holmes, Lieutenant General C.S.A.

Theophilus Holmes was nearly sixty years old when the Civil War started. He graduated from West Point in 1829, the same class as Robert E. Lee. He was also a West Point classmate of Jefferson Davis (though Davis graduated in 1828), which helped him considerably with rapid promotion when he joined the Confederacy. Holmes fought in the Second Seminole War and the Mexican War.

When he resigned from the U. S. Army in April 1861 Theophilus Holmes was a major. Almost immediately after joining the Confederacy he was appointed brigadier general. He commanded a brigade at First Manassas, but saw no action and was promoted to major general in October 1861. Holmes fought at Malvern Hill during the Seven Days Battles in 1862, where his performance left much to be desired. He was sent to command the vast Trans-Mississippi Department in July 1862. By October of 1862 he was promoted to lieutenant general. He was replaced in the Trans-Mississippi Department by Kirby-Smith in 1863 and put in charge of the District of Arkansas, where he blundered at the assault of Helena in July of that year. By 1864 he returned to his native North Carolina, where he commanded the state's reserves.

The name Theophilus is not often heard these days. In fact, I would be stunned to run into anyone who possessed such a first name. Back in the 19th century, however, the name Theophilus was not at all stunning. Guidance on the proper pronunciation of this old fashioned name is easily obtained in standard reference books. Further checking disclosed no unusual variations in the pronunciation of Theophilus by General Holmes or his contemporaries.

<u>Tilghman</u> -(TIL-mun)

as in Lloyd <u>Tilghman</u>, Brigadier General C.S.A.

Though he graduated from West Point in 1836, Maryland-born Lloyd Tilghman spent most of the years prior to the Civil War working as a civilian construction engineer for a number of railroads. He entered Confederate service in Kentucky, his longtime residence, in 1861. Tilghman eventually ended up commanding Fort Henry on the Tennessee River. After a gallant defense in February 1862, he surrendered to General Ulysses Grant. After he was exchanged, in September 1862, he took command of a brigade in Earl Van Dorn's Army of the West but he and his command missed the Battle of Corinth, Mississippi. The following year, during the Vicksburg Campaign, he was killed at Champion Hill.

The name Tilghman becomes a pronunciation problem for some because of that somewhat gratuitous **'gh'** right smack in the middle of it. I find myself wanting to say **TILG-mun**, or **TIL-guh-mun**. The Tilghman family of Maryland, whose history includes two distinguished jurists as well as a Confederate general, pronounces the family name as though the **'gh'** were not there.[246]

<u>Totopotomoy</u> -(tot-tuh-POT-uh-mee)

as in <u>Totopotomoy</u> Creek, Virginia.

Totopotomoy Creek is a small meandering stream that branches off the Pamunkey River. The reason it got into the history books is that a series of small engagements took place there at the end of May 1864 as part of Grant's Overland Campaign.

Having leap-frogged from The Wilderness to Spotsylvania and then to the North Anna River, the Army of the Potomac and the Army of Northern Virginia, faced each other briefly along the Totopotomoy. The Totopotomoy was just one more temporary line of defense Lee established to keep Grant away from Richmond. Whatever happened along that creek was eclipsed by the bloodbath that followed a few days later at Cold Harbor.

I've always thought it was fortunate that a major battle never took place along the banks of Totopotomoy Creek. Imagine the difficulty of having to say "Totopotomoy" every time the battle was discussed. The name of the creek is taken from that of an Indian chief who was an ally of English colonists in Virginia in the 17th century.

It would require psychic powers to correctly guess how Totopotomoy is pronounced from the way it spelled. Fortunately, the National Park Service has rangers and historians who know the correct way.[247]

Tourgee -(toor-*ZH*AY)

as in Albion Winegar Tourgee, Lieutenant, 105th Ohio, postwar Carpetbagger, novelist.

Albion Tourgee's military career isn't what got him into the history books. It was what he did after the war that puts him in this dictionary. He had a creditable service record to be sure, but his literary efforts during the Reconstruction period are what he is mainly noted for.

Tourgee was born in Ohio, the descendent of Huguenots from France who had made their way from New England to the Hudson Valley in New York, then to Ohio's Western Reserve. He was well educated and was a student at the University of Rochester when the war broke out. Tourgee enlisted in a New York regiment and took part in the Battle of First Manassas. It was at this first big battle of the war that Tourgee's bad luck began. He was hit in the back by a speeding gun carriage during the Union rout and was in a coma for three days. It took Tourgee a year to recover (he had been paralyzed from the waist down) and during his convalescence he managed to complete his studies and get his degree. Once he could walk again, he returned to Ohio to study law and to do some recruiting for the army. He was back in active service again, this time as a lieutenant, and on October 8, 1862 took part in the Battle of Perryville, where he caught some shrapnel in the hip. Later in 1862 he was fighting at Stones River, where he got captured and spent four months as a prisoner. He was exchanged, fought at Chickamauga, and injured his back again at Chattanooga. He finally quit the army at the end of 1863. Let it never be said that Albion Tourgee didn't do his part.[248]

By the time the war ended in 1865 Tourgee, who was suffering with weak lungs in addition to a having a bad back, decided that he needed to live in a milder climate. He chose Greensboro, North Carolina, where he set up a law practice and a nursery business. Tourgee had also received a letter encouraging him to settle in the Old North State from the provisional governor, who was actively soliciting Northern capital and talent to his war devastated state.[249] By 1868 Tourgee was a judge in the superior court and had become heavily involved in Reconstruction politics. He became a well known advocate of African-American rights. Aside from his legal and political career in the postwar years, his greatest contribution was his writing. His first novel, *A Royal Gentleman*, was about miscegenation. However, the novel that made him famous came out in 1879, and was titled *A Fool's Errand*. It was basically a fictionalized narrative of his own experience as a carpetbagger, but also an exposé of the history and activities of the Ku Klux Klan. *A Fool's Errand* eventually sold some two-hundred thousand copies and was compared to *Uncle Tom's Cabin*.[250]

Pronunciation of Tourgee's name is as I have indicated above. During his lifetime Tourgee evidently had run into problems with people mispronouncing his name. He had always been proud of his Huguenot heritage and pronounced his name in the French manner. His friends, and especially his enemies in North Carolina, quite often pronounced the name **TOR-ghee** or **tor-JEE**. This sort of thing was probably what motivated him in the early 1880s to restore the accent to second to the last **'e'** in the name. Thus, after 1882 the name was no longer spelled "Tourgee," but became "Tourgée."[251] Whether this inspired his fellow Americans to pronounce the name correctly is not known.

<u>Tredegar</u> -(TRED-de-gar)

as in <u>Tredegar</u> Iron Works, Richmond, Virginia.

The only major rolling mill in the Confederacy was the Tredegar Iron Works. Located on the James and Kanawha Canal along the James River in Richmond, Virginia, its foundries and machine shops made it the principle armorer of the south. During the war it was run by Joseph Reid Anderson, who had run it before the war and after a brief stint at field command during the Seven Days battles returned to his old job. With limited resources, and a scarcity of skilled mechanics, Anderson managed to keep Tredegar in operation until nearly the end of the war.

The Tredegar Iron Works was named after a town in England famous for its iron-works. The name of the company that operated the mill was Joseph R. Anderson & Company. Anderson had gotten control of the company in the 1840s, greatly expanded it and, in fact, ran it after the Civil War until his death in 1893. Anderson was one of Richmond's top businessmen and a pioneer in race relations.[252]

Pronunciation of Tredegar is often difficult for those not familiar with the history of Richmond. Though pronouncers can be found in a number of reference books, hearing it said by someone at the Museum of the Confederacy or the Richmond National Battlefield Park is a much better way to learn.

Trenholm -(Tren-um)

as in George Alfred Trenholm, Confederate Treasury Secretary.

George Trenholm was considered to be one of the wealthiest men in the Confederacy. The Charleston-born banker left school at the age of sixteen and went to work for the city's largest cotton shipper, John Fraser & Company. He eventually got rich and became head of the firm as well as its majority owner. Trenholm also dabbled in railroads, steamships, banks, hotels and plantations. He was sort of the Donald Trump of his day. Somehow, in the midst of all this money making he even found time to serve in the South Carolina legislature.

When the Civil War came, Trenholm put his financial acumen at the disposal of the Confederacy. He opened a foreign branch of his company, now called Fraser, Trenholm & Co., in Liverpool, England to act as the Confederacy's agent in selling cotton and tobacco (gotten through the blockade on Trenholm's ships) and buying everything from rifle-muskets to coal. He did the job well, and made a lot of money doing it. In July 1864 he succeeded Christopher Memminger as the Confederacy's treasury secretary, but even George Trenholm couldn't help the financially failing Confederacy in this post.

When the war ended, Trenholm, like the rest of the South, was bankrupt. However, he reorganized his firm and was started putting together another fortune. Some people just have the knack. George Trenholm died in Charleston in 1876.

Trenholm is pronounced in the English manner.[253] It is a nice change from the French Huguenot names one generally associates with South Carolina.

Trostle -(TROH-sul)

as in the Trostle Farm, Gettysburg, Pennsylvania.

The farm of Abraham Trostle is an important landmark on the Gettysburg Battlefield. The farm, which is located a mile and a half south of town, comprised about 135 acres in 1863. The house and barn are in the rear of Sickel's Third Corps salient at the famous Peach Orchard along Emmitsburg Road.[254] During the battle Bigelow's 9th Massachusetts Battery fought a gallant holding action at the farm, and near the Trostle barn was where General Daniel Sickels was hit by the artillery round that cost him his leg.

The most common mispronunciation of the name Trostle is **TRAH-sul** or **TRAHS-tul.** The family still lives in the Gettysburg area and pronounces their name as they always have, **TROH-sul** with the long **'o'** sound in the first syllable.

U

Unadilla -(yoo-nuh-DILLA)

as in the USS *Unadilla.*

The *Unadilla* was a "ninety-day gunboat" completed in 1861. Among the ships built during that first year of war were twenty-three so-called, "ninety day gunboats." These were light-draft, wooden gunboats armed with one big gun (an 11-inch Dahlgren) and a pair of howitzers. Each of the gunboats displaced 630 tons, was steam driven and double masted. The *Unadilla* was part of the Federal fleet that attacked Beaufort, South Carolina in November 1861. For most of the rest of the war she was on blockade duty along that part of the Atlantic coast.[255]

Unadilla is a peculiar looking word. When I first encountered it I immediately conjured up an image of one those hideous looking, swift moving crawly things you find darting around your basement, or perhaps some weird variety of meat eating plant life that grows in the jungles of South America. Common sense, of course, told me that most naval vessels are named for people or places. There is a Unadilla River in New York state that connects into the upper reaches of the Susquehanna. There's even a small town there called Unadilla.

Pronunciation of this fascinating name could be difficult. There are a few place names beginning with the letters **'Una'** that take the **'uhn'** sound, like Unalaska Island in the Aleutian chain, and others that take the **'oo'** sound, like Mount Una in New Zealand or the Una River in former Yugoslavia.

Urquhart -(UHR-kut)

as in David Urquhart, Colonel C.S.A. or Charles Fox Urquhart, Major, 3rd Virginia.

David Urquhart was chief aide to General Braxton Bragg for most of Bragg's tenure as commander of the Army of Tennessee. Urquhart is cited in some of the history written about Bragg's campaigns in Kentucky and Tennessee. After the war, he wrote a long article for the Century Magazine's *Battle and Leaders* series. The article, entitled *Bragg's Advance and Retreat* covers the Kentucky Campaign of 1862 and the Battle of Stones River in December of that year.

Charles Fox Urquhart was an 1860 graduate of VMI and a resident of Southampton County, Virginia when the war began. Urquhart enlisted as a private on May 3, 1861 as part of a company called the Southampton Greys and he had been promoted a lieutenant by July 1.[256] Urquhart and the Greys saw their first combat at Williamsburg on May 5, 1862. The regiment fought at Seven Pines and in the Seven Days Battles. During this period Charles Urquhart was promoted to captain. After fighting on the Peninsula ended, the 3rd Virginia, as part of Pryor's Brigade, fought at Second Manassas. Right around this time, Urquhart was promoted to major. He was killed at Antietam on September 17, 1862.[257]

The name Urquhart is a Scottish one. The Urquharts are descendants of Galleroch de Urchart, according to Mark Antony Lower in his book, *A Dictionary of Surnames.* Lower, who was writing in 1860, complains in the entry on Urquhart that Sir Thomas Urquhart, who lived in the mid 17th century, drew up his pedigree, "which is one of the finest pieces of fictitious genealogy in existence, commencing with Adam, for whom he makes himself the hundred-and-forty-third in descent." Lower continues, "Another of his ancestors was Nimrod, the mighty hunter; another married that daughter of Pharaoh who found Moses in the bulrushes; while another espoused a daughter of Bacchus!"[258]

There is a woodcut portrait of Mark Antony Lower facing the title page of his book. He looks like the quintessence of Victorian respectability. He also looks vexed, undoubtedly the result of dyspepsia after reading Sir Thomas Urquhart's genealogy.[259]

Utoy -(**YOO-toy**)

as in the Battle of Utoy Creek, Georgia.

The engagement at Utoy Creek was one of the many actions that took place during the Atlanta Campaign which began on May 7, 1864 and ended with the fall of Atlanta on September 2nd. Utoy Creek took place on August 5-6, 1864. The battle resulted from yet another attempt by Sherman envelop the Confederate right flank and cut their rail lines to the south of Atlanta. He had failed at Ezra Church on July 28th, and the same thing happened again at Utoy Creek. It wasn't until the Battle of Jonesboro more than three weeks later that the end finally came.

Utoy is such a strange looking word, yet not a difficult word to pronounce. I suspect the principal problem people might have with this one is in expecting a strange looking word to have an even stranger pronunciation. I checked my pronunciation of Utoy with specialists on the War in the West, including Dr. Richard McMurry, author of *John Bell Hood and the War for Southern Independence* and *The Road Past Kennesaw: The Atlanta Campaign of 1864.*

V

Vallandigham -(vuh-LAN-di-gum)

as in Clement Laird Vallandigham, Copperhead.

According to Mark Boatner, in his *Civil War Dictionary*, Clement Vallandigham may have been the model for Edward Everett Hale's *Man Without a Country*. Compared to some of thc characters who have flitted, bat-like, across the American scene since the Civil War, Vallandigham looks pretty harmless, but in the 1860s this was not the case. Clement Vallandigham was a pariah.

Before the Civil War, Vallandigham was a lawyer-politician from Ohio. He began his legal career in New Lisbon, Ohio in 1842 and three years later was elected to the state legislature. In 1847 he moved to Dayton and became a part owner of the a newspaper there. He became a congressman in 1858. Vallandigham was a Democrat who advocated states rights and was totally opposed to the abolitionist movement. By 1860 he had established a national reputation as a conservative Democrat.

When the war came, Vallandigham publicly stated his opposition to it. He believed that it was wrong to coerce the South into returning to the Union. Blaming the war on Lincoln and the Republican Party, he refused to support any war measures in Congress. It did not take long for the leadership of the Democratic Party, which had largely taken a stance supporting the war, to ostracize Vallandigham. He was not reelected in 1862. In addition, it was believed by many that he was a member of the Knights of the Golden Circle, a pro-Confederate subversive organization that constituted the most radical element among the Copperheads. Vallandigham was not a member, but it didn't much matter to his enemies.

Determined to remain in politics, Vallandigham ran for governor of Ohio in 1863. He did not get the nomination of his party. Meanwhile, his anti-war, anti-administration statements in public speeches finally got him arrested in May 1863. He was tried for expressing sympathy for the enemy (prohibited by General Order Number 38 issued by General Burnside's Department of Ohio), convicted and sentenced to two years in prison. His sentence was commuted by Lincoln to banishment to the Confederacy. Previously unsympathetic Democrats were so angered by this that they promptly nominated him for governor at their June convention. None of this helped Old Clement however, as he was taken to Wilmington, North Carolina and from there shipped out to the island of Bermuda. From there he made it to Canada, where he conducted his campaign for the governorship of Ohio. He lost the election, but for a while the situation had the Lincoln Administration worried.

Vallandigham secretly returned to the United States in June 1864. He lived in Ohio (the Feds knew, but didn't take any action) and even attended the 1864 Democratic Convention that nominated George McClellan.

After the war, Vallandigham may not have been a man without a country, but he was certainly a man without a party. The Democrats, famous for their fickleness to this day, wanted nothing to do with him. He resumed his law practice and died of a gunshot wound, accidently self inflicted in June 1871.

Vallandigham is simply a long name, and not an impossible one to pronounce. If you simply look at it as a collection of syllables you will have no problem. Just remember, the **'h'** in the last syllable, **'ham'** is silent. Many people mispronounce the name **vuh-LAN-ding-ham**, not only pronouncing that **'h,'** but adding an extra **'n.'**

Valverde -(val-VURD-ee)

as in the Battle of Valverde, New Mexico.

Early in the war the Confederacy formulated a plan to seize New Mexico Territory and invade Colorado Territory. This vast area contained valuable mineral resources and cattle the South could use.[260] Confederate Brigadier General Henry Sibley arrived on the scene in December 1861 to assist the self proclaimed Confederate government already set up in the territory under John R. Baylor. Sibley had an army of about 3,700 men. In February 1862 he marched northward, up the west bank of the Rio Grande, then crossed to the east side of the river and sought to bypass Fort Craig. Sibley planned to cut off the Federal garrison at Fort Craig from its headquarters in Santa Fe. Meanwhile, Colonel E. R. S. Canby and a force of some 3,000 Federals left Fort Craig, five miles to the south, headed up the west bank of the river, crossed the river at Valverde Ford and attacked the Confederates. The engagement that followed is called the Battle of Valverde.

During the battle the Federals initially gained the upper hand, but a vigorous Confederate counterattack won the day for the South. One of the more famous participants in this engagement was Kit Carson, who commanded part of the Union forces.

Pronunciation of Valverde might present a problem for some people because of its Spanish origin. Many, including myself at times, are not sure what to do with that extra **'e'** at the end of such a word. Sometimes it is a silent **'e'** and sometimes it is not. Pronouncers are available in a number of reference books.[261]

<u>Van Vliet</u> -(van-VLEET)

as in Stewart <u>Van Vliet</u>, Brigadier General U.S.V.

Van Vliet was a Mexican War veteran, a West Point graduate, and when the war broke out, a captain in the U.S. Army. He became Chief Quartermaster of the Army of the Potomac under George McClellan and was appointed a brigadier general in August 1861. Just after the Peninsula Campaign his commission expired; it was not confirmed by Congress (probably because of virulent anti-McClellan feeling at the time). He spent the remainder of the war in New York City coordinating supplies and transportation.

Van Vliet is a Dutch name and presents no real pronunciation problem for those familiar with the Dutch names that are found sprinkled up and down the Hudson River Valley in New York, or in the vicinity of Grand Rapids, Michigan. However, for those who find a name beginning with 'Vl' unusual, a pronouncer might be helpful.

<u>Van Wyck</u> -(van-WIKE)

as in Charles Henry <u>Van Wyck</u>, Brigadier General U.S.V.

Descendant of an old Dutch family from Long Island, Van Wyck was a lawyer and politician before the war. At the outbreak of war he raised a regiment, the 56th New York, and was commissioned its colonel. It doesn't appear that Van Wyck saw much combat. The record of his regiment's participation in McClellan's Peninsula Campaign is vague and Van Wyck's presence during the various engagements in doubt. Ezra Warner's *Generals in Blue* indicates that there is "a curious contradiction" between the *Official Records* and accounts printed in the series, *Battle and Leaders,* about Van Wyck's presence at the Peninsula battles. Be that as it may, Van Wyck was a typical political general during the war. His service was probably motivated by postwar political ambitions. In fact, after the war Van Wyck pursued a new political career in Nebraska espousing the cause of Populism.

Van Wyck is a Dutch name. The picture of Van Wyck that appears in Warner's book shows that the general bears a remarkable resemblance to modern day screen actor Kirk Douglas.

<u>Varina</u> -(vuh-REE-nuh)

as in <u>Varina</u> Howell Davis, wife of Jefferson Davis.

Varina Howell was Jefferson Davis' second wife. When he married Varina in 1845 he was twice her age, she being eighteen, Davis thirty-seven. Varina Davis was a good match for Jefferson possessing a strong character and a lively intellect. In addition, she was emotionally stronger than Davis.

Both were strong willed and ambitious, and this occasionally led to trouble in the marriage. In fact, two years into the relationship Jefferson and Varina nearly called it quits. He had just returned from the Mexican War and gotten elected to the U. S. Senate. In the first twenty-seven months of the marriage Davis had already been absent for a total of fourteen months, away fighting the war or campaigning. Now, he wanted Varina to drop everything and go to Washington. In addition, there was growing resentment between Varina and Joseph Davis, Jefferson's influential older brother.[262] This soap opera eventually resolved itself, but it revealed the character of the two individuals involved. Both very stubborn, both wanting to hold the upper hand in any relationship.

They were similar in many ways, but different too. Whereas Jefferson Davis was hypersensitive to criticism and subject to a number of physical ailments, Varina was of a hardier nature. She bore six children during their long marriage and endured the hardships of wartime Richmond (and its class conscious society) with great aplomb. Her political astuteness and ability to judge the character of others was of great help to Jefferson Davis in his difficult job as President of the Confederacy.

Pronunciation of Varina Davis' name is keyed on the 'i' sound in the second syllable.[263] Many people say **vuh-RIE-nuh**, an understandable error for those not familiar with the name.

<u>Vasa</u> -(VAH-sah)

as in Gustavus <u>Vasa</u> Fox, Assistant Secretary of the Navy 1861-66.

Gustavus V. Fox's biggest contribution to the Civil War was in modernizing the U.S. Navy. At the outbreak of the war the Navy was in pretty sad shape. Less than half of the ninety ships commissioned were fit for service, and its nine thousand officers and men were scattered across the globe. To add to this deplorable condition, the Gosport Navy Yard at Norfolk, Virginia was abandoned in April 1861 leading to the loss of eleven more ships and more than 1,200 cannon. By the end of the Civil War, the Navy had over 600 ships in service, including a fleet of ironclads that had revolutionized naval technology. Gustavus Fox shares the credit for this accomplishment with Secretary of the Navy Gideon Welles. He was a great administrator and extremely capable planner.

The name "Gustavus Vasa" is derived from that of Gustavus I of Sweden, also known as Gustavus Vasa. Gustavus I was the first of four Swedish kings from the House of Vasa. The Vasa Dynasty derived its name from the family estate in Uppland, Sweden.[264]

Viele -(VEE-lay)

as in Egbert Ludovicus Viele, Brigadier General U.S.V.

An 1847 graduate of West Point, Viele served in the Mexican War and on the frontier before resigning in 1853 to become a civil engineer. Viele was chief engineer of Central Park in New York City and Prospect Park in Brooklyn in the years before the war. When the war came he served as a captain of engineers with the 7th New York Militia in the Washington defenses. He then commanded a brigade in an expeditionary force that undertook the reduction of Fort Pulaski on the Savannah River, and then commanded his own brigade in the march on Norfolk, Virginia in May and June of 1862. After a brief stint as military governor of Norfolk, he went to Ohio to superintend the draft. He resigned and returned to civilian life in October 1863.

Viele's name is a well known one in the history of New York City. He was Commissioner of Parks for a time in the 1880s and also a Democratic congressman. Viele's engineering monographs on the topography of Manhattan Island were so thorough that they proved to be of great value to builders of skyscrapers in later years. General Viele died in 1902 and is buried at West Point.

Pronunciation of Viele's name presents a number of problems. Both his sons, the poet Francis Viélé-Griffin (an assumed name: he was actually named after his father), and Herman Knickerbacker Vielé, a painter and author, put an acute accent over the final 'e' in the family name.[265] Viélé-Griffin put an additional acute accent over the first 'e' in the name to further complicate matters. All this would seem to indicate that the name was pronounced as though it were a French or Spanish name, putting a long **'a'** sound on that final **'e.'** Yet, I have heard the name pronounced **vee-ALE-lee, veel, VEE-el-ee** and a few other variations. Further research into this curious name led to the discovery that it was probably Huguenot, though General Viele's ancestors came to New York in the 17th century from the Netherlands. Whatever the origin of the name was, Francis Viélé-Griffin, the general's son, was brought up in France, wrote in French and established himself as a writer associated with the French symbolist movement in literature. He apparently pronounced his name **vyay-LAY gree-FAHN.**[266] According to Chase Viele, a direct descendent of General Viele's brother, there are still various pronunciations of the family name. He said that in Buffalo, New York, where he lives, it is pronounced **VEEL-ee**, but his Manhattan relatives most often pronounced the name **VEE-lay** and other Vieles in Newport, Rhode Island use **vee-LAY**. This is because, he continues, they all use an accent on the final **'e'** of the name. Since General Viele apparently used an accent on the final **'e'** occasionally we can assume he pronounced it **VEE-lay** as well.[267]

<u>Villepigue</u> -(VIL-ih-PIG)

as in John Bordenave <u>Villepigue</u>, Brigadier General C.S.A.

John Villepigue was from Camden, South Carolina and graduated from West Point in 1854. Prior to the Civil War he was a professional soldier. He resigned his commission as a lieutenant in the U. S. Army in March 1861 to accept an appointment as captain in the Confederate artillery. He was assigned to the defenses of Pensacola Harbor in Florida, and after a short time was appointed colonel of the 1st Georgia Battalion. Villepigue was badly wounded in November 1861 in a two-day artillery battle between Federal ships and his own batteries at Fort McRee in Pensacola Harbor. After recuperating from his wound he was transferred to Mobile, Alabama, and in March 1862 was promoted to brigadier general. Villepigue was then ordered to join General Braxton Bragg at Corinth, Mississippi. Once there, he was assigned to command Fort Pillow on the bluffs overlooking the Mississippi River 80-river miles north of Memphis, Tennessee. He did a commendable job in defending the fort against superior Federal forces, but was forced to withdraw in June of 1862. Villepigue was then assigned command of a brigade under General Earl Van Dorn at Corinth. By November of that year Villepigue had contracted a "fever," and died at Port Hudson, Louisiana.

The name Villepigue is often mispronounced **VIL-uh-PEEK**. This is because, like I used to do, they mentally substitute a **'q'** where there is a **'g.'** Villepigue is obviously a French name, and everybody knows that those French names end with **'que,'** not **''gue.'** Well, it is certainly an easy mistake to make. My source on the proper pronunciation is the oft cited Neuffer book on South Carolina names. By the way, General Villepigue was from Kershaw County in South Carolina, which furnished six generals to the Confederacy.[268]

<u>Vivandière</u> -(vee-vahn-DYAIR)

The vivandière was a tradition borrowed from the French army by some of the ethnic regiments formed at the beginning of the Civil War. The vivandière was a female attendant, quite often the wife of one of the soldiers in the regiment, who acted as a sutler and nurse to the men.

One of the first regiments arriving in Washington in the early days of the war accompanied by vivandières was the 39th New York, the polyglot Garibaldi Guard. Provincial Washingtonians were disturbed by the sight of young women, all uniformed in the same bizarre chasseur costume as the men, marching along with each company of the regiment. Washington newspapers reported that the vivandières were the wives of men in the ranks. However, it turned out that two of the young women were runaways from Jersey City[269] (one could hardly blame them for fleeing to a more interesting place).

Vivandières were pretty much confined to regiments made up of foreign-born soldiers, especially Frenchmen. According to Mark Boatner in the Civil War Dictionary, there were only about a dozen of these women on both sides during the war.[270] The word "vivandière" has French and Latin roots. During the 15th century the word meant, "hospitality giver." Later on in military history it meant, "one who sells food and drink to the troops." Among the more famous vivandières in Civil War armies were; Marie Tebe (French Mary) of the 114th Pennsylvania Volunteers, Anna Etheridge (Michigan Anna) of the 2nd Michigan, and Bridget Divers (Irish Biddy) of the 1st Michigan Cavalry.[271]

Vogdes -(VAH-JIS)

as in Israel Vogdes, Brigadier General U.S.V.

Pennsylvania-born Israel Vogdes graduated from West Point in 1837. He was a captain in the 1st Artillery at Fort Pickens in Pensacola Harbor when the war broke out. He took part in the defense of the fort and was taken prisoner in October 1861. Vogdes was exchanged the following year and had a major role in designing and building artillery emplacements in the vicinity of Charleston, South Carolina. He was commissioned brigadier general of volunteers in November 1862. He continued to serve in the army after the war and retired in 1881.

Finding out the proper pronunciation of the name Vogdes became one of the great searches of my life. Most Civil War historians I consulted would not even attempt to pronounce the name. None of the usual printed sources yielded anything. While on a visit to Gettysburg I checked with several people and finally got what I feel is a definitive pronouncer. According to Louise Arnold-Friend, a licensed battlefield guide at Gettysburg and lifelong resident of the area, the name Vogdes is pronounced VAH-jis, just as though it were spelled with the 'g' and the 'd' reversed, V-o-d-g-e-s.[272] Since General Vogdes comes from Pennsylvania and Louise comes from Pennsylvania, where is name is not unknown, I decided to go with the pronouncer I have above.

Voltigeur -(vol-ti-*ZH*ER)

Voltigeur is one of those French names borrowed by the American military during the 19th century. Originally, voltigeur companies were units made up of conscripted men who were shorter than normal height (trust me, you can't make stuff like this up) who were assigned to infantry battalions in the French army to act as skirmishers. They were trained as fast moving units used to spearhead an attack. After a time, these units became famous for their courage and fighting ability, and also the fact that they were all short guys. I imagine a modern day military unit of this type would be called something like, "The Vertically Challenged Special Forces."

During the Mexican War the U. S. Army established a regiment of voltigeurs. This unit comprised half mounted and half foot soldiers. Mounted men were paired with men on foot, and the two would ride double when speed was of the essence. As with the French army, these men were used as skirmishers, but they were not necessarily less than average height. By the time of the Civil War, the term "voltigeur" had merely become a fancy name adopted by some units.

Brigadier General Egbert Ludovicus Viele

Wager -(WAY-jur)

as in Henry Wager Halleck, Major General U.S.A.

New York-born Henry Halleck could easily be the subject of a book, and indeed has. Anyone who studies the Civil War is bound to encounter this man. It is not within the scope of this slender volume to even adequately capsulize the biography of this controversial general. Suffice it to say, that Henry Halleck was a much better administrator than he was a field general. He was also a competent military theorist and scholar. His nickname was "Old Brains."

For many years I found myself pronouncing Halleck's middle name, **WAG-ur**, as though it had a double **'g'** in its spelling. I suspect this is because the word **wager**, as in "to bet," simply could not be a name as far as my brain was concerned. Therefore, I decided it must be another word altogether (even though it was spelled the same) and as such, must have a different pronunciation. I was wrong and I would wager there are others who make the same mistake.[273]

Watie -(WAYT-ee)

as in Stand Watie, Brigadier General C.S.A.

Stand Watie was the last Confederate general to surrender his command (June 1865), which is one of many unique distinctions Watie possesses. Born in Georgia in 1806, he was one of the signatories to the 1835 treaty by which the Cherokees gave up their lands in Georgia and moved to the Indian Territory (today's Oklahoma). This treaty divided the Cherokees politically and Watie became leader of the minority faction, which supported the treaty.

Stand Watie prospered as a planter in the years prior to the Civil War. When war came, he was persuaded by his followers to ally himself with the Confederacy. He raised a company from his tribe in 1861 and was later appointed colonel of the 2nd Cherokee Mounted Rifles by the Confederate government. Watie led troops at Elkhorn Tavern (Pea Ridge). Watie gained a reputation as a superb hit-and-run cavalry raider. He was promoted to brigadier general in May 1864, the only Indian to attain such rank in the Confederate Army.

Pronunciation of Stand Watie's name is often a mystery to people. The name itself is a anglicized version of his real name: "Degataga" which translates to Stand in English, and "Oowatie" or "Uweti," his father's name which was later contracted to Watie.[274] The most common mispronunciation for Watie is **WAHD-ee**. I suppose this pronunciation results from the fact that Stand **WAYT-ee** sounds too much like one of those demeaning character names given to Chinese servants in old movies or television westerns. How many people remember the Cartwright's irrepressible Chinese cook, "Hop Sing," on the long running television series *Bonanza*? Also, we can't forget "Hey Boy," the faithful oriental retainer of Paladin in *Have Gun Will Travel*.[275]

Watervliet -(WAW-tur-vleet)

as in Watervliet Arsenal, New York.

The United States Arsenal at Watervliet, New York was established in 1813 and has produced cannon for all our wars since that time. Though you may come across this name in your studies of Civil War artillery, you are more likely to encounter the more easily pronounced name of the Cold Spring Foundry, which was located much farther down the Hudson River Valley just across from West Point. During the Civil War, it manufactured some 1,700 guns and 3,000,000 projectiles.[276]

In any case, knowing how to pronounce Watervliet may come in handy. Watervliet is a Dutch name, as so many of the place names in New York's Hudson River region are and means, "flat lands."

Waud -(wode)

as in Alfred Waud, Civil War artist.

In the era before it was possible to reproduce photographs for publication, newspapers and magazines depended on the sketch artist to illustrate a story. Alfred R. Waud was such an artist. He emigrated to America from England in 1850 and worked as an illustrator for periodicals and books. When the war came he worked for the *New York Illustrated News*. His fame as an artist came, however, when he joined the staff of *Harper's Weekly*. In *Harper's* Waud illustrated the trials and tribulations of the Army of Potomac and was the paper's most popular illustrator. His sketches were sent from the battlefield to the publisher in New York, were copied onto wooden blocks, then printed from electrotype metal impressions of the woodcut.[277]

Pronunciation of Waud's last name is a source of some confusion. Many people see that **'u'** in the middle and want to say the name as "wahd." According to Bell I. Wiley, the name was pronounced "wood." Researching the matter more thoroughly I came across an article in the *Civil War Times Illustrated* from a few years ago (April 1982) by Frederick Ray about Civil War artists. Ray states that Waud pronounced his name "Wode." Since Frederick Ray had written a biography of Waud and also numerous magazine articles on the man I thought he qualified as an authoritative source. In asking various historians and Park Service people about Waud's name I never got the same answer twice on pronunciation.

Winder -(WINE-der)

as in Charles Sydney Winder or John Henry Winder C.S.A.

Taking our two Winders in alphabetical order: Charles S. Winder, born in Maryland to a distinguished family, was educated at West Point. He became a professional soldier and is most remembered as a brigadier general in Stonewall Jackson's command. His moment in the limelight came at the Battle of Cedar Mountain on August 9, 1862. Up until that time, Winder had been commander first of the famed Stonewall Brigade and then the Stonewall Division. At Cedar Mountain he commanded Jackson's old division, Jackson having assumed what was effectively a "corps" command during the Valley Campaign of April-June 1862. During the course of the action Winder was assisting a battery involved in an artillery duel with the Federals and was horribly mangled by an incoming shell. He died a few hours later. Winder was not the sort of commander the enlisted men invented an affectionate nickname for, like Old Charlie or Chuck. He was a merciless disciplinarian, and though his troops respected him, they also despised him. Winder was often hissed when he rode by the men in ranks.

Charlie's older uncle was John Henry Winder. This Winder was also a Marylander, a West Point graduate and professional soldier. The Winder family seemed to have an affinity for discipline. General Henry Winder was provost marshal and prison commandant in Richmond from 1861 to 1864. This meant he was responsible for Libby Prison and Belle Isle. By 1864 Winder was in charge all prison facilities in Alabama and Georgia, including Andersonville. He eventually became commissary general of all Confederate prisons east of the Mississippi. Winder was called a brute and a monster by some who were in his charge, while others said he was very humane. His strict adherence to rules and regulations and harsh discipline were definite factors in making him unpopular, even hated. Unfortunately, Winder was the victim of wartime shortages of food and provisions. His treatment of prisoners was much influenced by the dwindling resources of the Confederacy.

Pronunciation of the Winder name is fairly obvious. Many people with this last name, if not all, choose **WINE** for the first syllable pronunciation. After all, the alternative is saying the name as **WIN-der** which in parts of the South could refer to those glassed openings in the walls of a house that let in daylight. The inclusion of the name in this dictionary comes about because a surprising number of people mispronounce the name;

so many, in fact, that several standard reference books on the Civil War, like Mark Boatner's *Civil War Dictionary*, give a pronouncer for it.

Wirz -(wertz)

as in Heinrich Hartmann Wirz, Commandant of Andersonville.

Heinrich or Henry Wirz may have been the first person in the history of modern war to be tried as a war criminal. He may also have been the first alleged war criminal to claim that he was only following orders. There seems little doubt that the unfortunate Wirz was a scapegoat and the victim of the hysteria that gripped the nation in the wake of the Lincoln Assassination. Henry Wirz was commandant of one of the most infamous prisoner of war camps in history, Andersonville.

Wirz was born in Switzerland in 1823 and from childhood had wanted to be a doctor. Unfortunately, this was not to be. Circumstances led him to take up a career in business. Details of Wirz's early life in Europe are sketchy, but we do know that his business career was a failure because he got into serious money trouble, spent some time in prison because of it, ended up divorced, and was probably asked to leave the country by Swiss authorities. He arrived in America in 1849 and settled in the South. When the war came Wirz joined the 4th Louisiana Infantry, became a sergeant and was wounded at the Battle of Seven Pines. The wound rendered him unfit for further field service (he had gotten shot in the right forearm) and he was assigned as an adjutant to General Henry Winder, who was in charge of Richmond prisons. In December 1862 Wirz was sent on a diplomatic mission to Europe and did not return to America until February 1864. Upon his return, he was assigned to the new prison set up at Andersonville, Georgia. Wirz was in charge of the interior of the stockade, and after the departure of the prison's commandant in June 1864 he was in full charge of the operation. He held the position of commandant until the end of the war, and was ultimately tried for murdering prisoners and conspiracy to deliberately cause the death of countless other prisoners. He was convicted and hanged in November 1865.[278]

Despite the charges made against him, it seems unlikely that Henry Wirz ever murdered anyone. As far as conspiracy is concerned, Wirz was the victim of circumstance. Andersonville (officially called "Camp Sumter") was established three years into the war because it was felt that the large number of Union prisoners concentrated in Richmond, Virginia was burdening the local food supply and represented a military hazard to the populace. The sixteen-and-a-half acre site selected in Sumter County, Georgia was thought adequate for a few thousand prisoners and the first 500 transfers began to arrive in February 1864. By July there were 32,000 Union enlisted men crowded into the crudely built stockade that had been expanded to enclose 26 acres. The death rate soared, food was in short supply and the situation was quickly out of control. More than 12,000 died at Andersonville, the kind of staggering figure the world would not see again until World War II. To blame Wirz for all this was preposterous.

Wirz is a German name. The letter **'z'** in the German language is pronounced as though it were **'tz.'**

Wofford -(WAH-furd)

as in William Tatum Wofford, Brigadier General C.S.A.

A Georgia-born lawyer and politician, Wofford started as colonel of the 18th Georgia at the beginning of the war. He became part of Hood's Texas Brigade during the Peninsula Campaign, was at Second Manassas, South Mountain and Sharpsburg (Antietam). Wofford succeeded to brigade command before Antietam and four months later, January 1863, was promoted to brigadier general. He fought continuously as part of Longstreet's Corps of the Army of Northern Virginia, participating in all the army's major campaigns.

General Wofford apparently did his job adequately during the war. He is not the sort of general who inspires Civil War round tables to name themselves after him and he is probably completely unknown outside of Civil War history circles. However, his name pops up often enough in the books so that knowing how to pronounce it assumes some importance.[279]

Brigadier General Charles Syney Winder

Y

Ypres -(EE-pruh *or* eep)

as in the Battle of Ypres.

The first Battle of Ypres took place between October 30 and November 24, 1914. The Second Battle of Ypres went from late April to late May 1915. Both these battles were bloodbaths, and very typical of World War I. Thus, you can readily appreciate the fact that this particular entry has absolutely nothing to do with the American Civil War. However, if you read extensively on the subject of the Civil War, you may eventually turn to other wars in military history. In fact, comparisons are often made between the Civil War and World War I in military histories. This especially true when it comes to Grant's campaign from The Wilderness to Petersburg.[280] In addition to all this, I had absolutely nothing worthwhile from the Civil War to include in this dictionary under the letter "Y."

Ypres is a town in Belgium, Flanders to be exact, that has been the scene of many battles. The name means "leper" in Flemish. During the First World War the name was completely beyond the linguistic ability of English speaking troops and as a result, it was called "Wipers" by many of the British soldiers.

Z

<u>Zoan</u> -(ZOH-an)

as in <u>Zoan</u> Church, Chancellorsville, Virginia.

Zoan Church is a battlefield landmark at Chancellorsville. Located at the intersection of Mine Road and Old Orange Turnpike (modern day Route 3) the original building has been replaced. During the early stages of the battle, Zoan Church, which is three-and-a-half miles east of Chancellorsville, was the location of three brigades of Richard Anderson's Division of Lee's Army. Anderson had been sent by Lee on April 29, 1863 to block Federals who were descending on Chancellorsville. By digging in on a line between Zoan and Tabernacle Churches, Anderson could block any Federal move to the east towards Fredericksburg.

Zoan is a biblical name for Tanis, an ancient city in lower Egypt. Old maps often mislabel the church "Zoar" or "Zion." Standard reference works are a source of pronouncers for this name. I also checked with the staff at the Fredericksburg and Spotsylvania National Battlefield, whose domain comprises the Chancellorsville battlefield.

<u>Zouave</u> -(ZWAHV *or* zoo-AHV)

as in Ellsworth's Fire <u>Zouaves.</u>

Prior to the Civil War many American militia units adopted the fancy drill and gaudy uniform of the Algerian light infantry, a colorful component of the French colonial armies. It seems ridiculous now that any serious military unit would go into a combat situation dressed up like a band of escaped genies. Yet this was very much the case in 1861 when outfits like the New York Fire Zouaves marched off to war under the leadership of "silly colonels" like Elmer Ellsworth. Wearing baggy, bright red trousers, white gaiters and short, bright blue embroidered jackets, all topped off with a fez or a turban, these companies of weekend warriors marched naively into the first modern war.

I had always thought that most of these units replaced their costumes with regular uniforms as the impractical garments wore out. I also thought that many discovered to their misfortune that the gaily colored Zouave uniforms made excellent targets. As it turns out, there were more Zouave units by the end the Civil War than there were at the beginning!

Many people look at the word "Zouave" and find themselves saying, **ZOO-ahv** or **ZOH-ahv**, pronouncing it as a two syllable word, putting the stress on the first syllable. We are dealing with the French language here where the logic of English phonetics does not apply. There are some options in pronunciation, however. Some English language dictionaries, *Random House Unabridged* for example, do give the options of pronouncing it **zoo-AHV** or **ZWAHV**. You will notice that no matter which of these options you use, they both sound pretty much the same. They both rhyme with "suave." Just remember not to put the emphasis on the first syllable. Should you mistakenly do this, some professional historian you run into at a conference or a battlefield tour will take great delight in swiftly correcting you. Remember, many of these people have doctorates in this stuff we call a hobby. They have spent so much time and money getting these advanced degrees they are bound to get picayune and almost can't help the occasional arrogant display of superior knowledge. Nonetheless, when among close friends and relatives feel free to emphasize whatever syllable you like with promiscuous abandon. My only caveat would be that you are much better served by saying it correctly all the time; you can never be sure there isn't a closet lexicographer within earshot.

Hawkins' Zouaves

Baxter's Zouaves

Duryea's Zouaves

NOTES

1. Ezra J. Warner, *Generals in Blue,* p. 6.
2. Ibid., p. 6.
3. Source of the West Point nickname was Mary Elizabeth Sergent's book, *They Lie Forgotten*, p. 114. The Civil War historian cited was Robert V. Bruce, a Pulitzer Prize winning author and longtime resident of northern New England.
4. William N. Still, Jr., *Historical Times Illustrated Encyclopedia of the Civil War*, p. 5.
5. Harry Roach, *Gettysburg, Hour by Hour,* p. 43.
6. *The Century Dictionary and Cyclopedia,* Vol. IX, p. 32.
7. Warner, *Generals in Blue*, p. 560.
8. Bergen Evans, *Dictionary of Mythology,* p. 28.
9. Though pronouncers for the name Aquia were available in several reference books, I nevertheless checked with the NPS at Fredericksburg.
10. Apparently Cathole Road went through an area where there were many small caves in which wildcats lived.
11. Many thanks to Robert K. Krick, Chief Historian at the Fredericksburg and Spotsylvania National Military Park for making the Green book known to me.
12. Fletcher Pratt, *The Navy: A History,* p. 248.
13. Ibid., p. 424.
14. *Lippincott's Pronouncing Biographical Dictionary*, p. 198.
15. *Century,* p. 233.
16. Margaret Leech, *Reveille In Washington*, p. 362.
17. Michael Kauffman, *John Wilkes Booth and the Murder of Abraham Lincoln,* Blue & Gray Magazine, p. 19.
18. *Lippincott's,* p. 218.
19. I pleasantly surprised to find a pronouncer for this name so easily. I first checked the *Century Dictionary and Cyclopedia* and found one, then verified in *Lippincott's Pronouncing Biographical* and *Webster's New Biographical.*
20. Stephen Z. Starr, *The Union Cavalry in the Civil War,* Vol. 1, p. 350.
21. William McFeeley, *Grant, A Biography,* pp. 497-498.
22. Wayne Motts, *McPherson's Memorial,* Blue & Gray Magazine, April 1990, p. 32.
23. Stephen Sears, *To the Gates of Richmond,* p. 214.
24. Claude and Irene Neuffer, *Correct Mispronunciations of Some South Carolina Names*, p. 18.
25. Historians Robert K. Krick (Fredericksburg-Spotsylvania NMP) and Dennis Frye (Harpers Ferry NHP) verified the pronouncer on Bolivar.
26. Historians Ted Alexander at Antietam National Battlefield Park and Dennis Frye of Harpers Ferry National Historic Park concurred on these two pronouncers.
27. This information came from Robert K. Krick, Chief Historian, at the Fredericksburg & Spotsylvania National Military Park.
28. I discussed this Boteler riddle with National Park Service Historian Dennis Frye, who grew up in the area of Boteler's Ford, and works at Harpers Ferry National Historical Park. He said that the two pronouncers I was using in the dictionary were the ones most

commonly understood by locals.

29. Imagine, driving nearly six-hundred miles to date a girl who didn't really like me all that well! At least I got the benefit of seeing Botetourt County.

30. Many thanks to Marion Brown Hagerstand of Oklahoma, who told me that among her people, the Cherokee, taking someone's name is a way of honoring them.

31. *Webster's New Biographical Dictionary,* p. 131.

32. Robert K. Krick, *Lee's Colonels*, p. 68.

33. Robert K. Krick and Dennis Frye.

34. Robert E. L. Krick, *40th Virginia Regiment,* pp 32-34. According to Krick, Brockenbrough was popular with the officers and men of the brigade. Though not a spectacular leader, he was competent and well liked. There were no complaints from members of the brigade over Brockenbrough's actions at Falling Waters. Some fifty officers in the brigade signed a letter protesting Brockenbrough's being passed over for command.

35. Bloomfield is a town of about three-thousand in Davis County, Iowa. I called the town hall and was referred to a local realtor name Julian Campbell. Mr. Campbell is apparently the town's unofficial historian. Though he wasn't especially familiar with General Bussey, he knew the family name and told me that the town had even had a mayor by that name some twenty years ago. In addition, just a couple of counties away there was even a town called Bussey. It became abundantly clear to me that I had finally stumbled upon the most likely pronunciation of Cyrus Bussey's name.

36. Herman Hattaway and Archer Jones, *How the North Won,* p. 197.

37. R. Ernest Dupuy and Trevor N. Dupuy, *The Encyclopedia of Military History,* pp. 65-66.

38. Robert D. Huffstot, *The Carondolet* ,Civil War Times Illustrated, August 1967, pp. 6-7.

39. *Random House Dictionary of the English Language, Second Edition Unabridged,* p. 328.

40. Douglas Southall Freemen, *Lee's Lieutenants*, Volume 3, p. 346.

41. Leech, p. 113.

42. Anthony Battillo, *Red-Legged Devil's from Brooklyn,* Civil War Times Illustrated, February 1972, p. 11.

43. *Webster's New Geographical Dictionary*, p. 252.

44. James I. Robertson, Jr., *Soldiers Blue and Gray,* p. 167.

45. Ibid., p. 166.

46. Sears, p. 216.

47. Judith Anthis and Richard McMurry, *Rebels in the Sky, The Confederate Balloon Corps,* Blue & Gray Magazine, August 1991, pp. 20-24.

48. David Eggenberger, *An Encyclopedia of Battles*, p. 104.

49. Dupuy, R. Ernest & Trevor N., *The Encyclopedia of Military History,* pp. 741-742.

50. Hattaway and Jones, p. 47.

51. It doesn't help matters when reference works like *Webster's New Biographical Dictionary* give the pronunciation of the name as KLEE-burn. A few others make the same mistake. There are numerous differing opinions on the correct pronunciation of the Cleburne name. I expect I'll get much mail on this one.

52. One of my sources for the correct pronunciation of General Cleburne's name was Jerry Russell, Arkansas native and avid student of Cleburne's life. Jerry says he will not gladly

suffer fools who mispronounce Cleburne's name. He is also president of the Conference of Civil War Round Tables and National Chairman of HERITAGEPAC, a Civil War preservation lobbying group. Russell pointed out to me that there is a Cleburne County in Arkansas which is pronounced KLEE-burn, and also a town in Texas called Cleburne which is pronounced the same way. The late general's name, however, which Russell says is originally a Norman-English name (thus making Cleburne an Orange Irishman), is pronounced Clay-burn.

53. Jerry Russell is, again, the source on this information.

54. Hunt & Brown, *Brevet Brigadier Generals in Blue,* p. 117.

55. Warner, *Generals in Blue,* p. 86.

56. Neuffer, p. 38.

57. Ibid., p. 39.

58. Information on Governor Cony's name provided by the Maine State Museum.

59. I contacted Ken Burns and asked what his source of the "Kooch" pronunciation was. His letter of reply indicated that, to the best of his knowledge, Shelby Foote was the source.

60. According to Dr. Jerry Carron, a member of MOLLUS and a Civil War lecturer well known in Connecticut, three of his American history professors at three different colleges pronounced the name as "kooch": Henry Steele Commager, at Columbia University; William B. Hesseltine at University of Wisconsin; and Frank L. Klement at Marquette.

61. Mark M. Boatner, III, *The Civil War Dictionary,* p. 205.

62. *Funk & Wagnalls Standard Dictionary*, p. 298.

63. Information on the correct pronunciation of Governor Crapo's name was provided by the Michigan Historical Museum in Lansing.

64. Stewart Safakis, *Who Was Who in the Civil War,* p. 156.

65. *Random House Dictionary,* p. 490.

66. William A. DeGregoria, *The Complete Book of U. S. Presidents*, p. 358. Actually, Bill McKinley put together a very creditable war record: He started out as a private in the 23rd Ohio and rose to the rank of brevet major by the end of his service. At Antietam he was a commissary sergeant and managed to get coffee and food to the men at the front. His monument is near the Burnside Bridge at Antietam National Battlefield Park.

67. It might be of interest to you presidential assassination buffs that Czolgosz used an Iver Johnson .32 caliber pistol to shoot McKinley. He fired two shots into the chief executive at 4:07 P.M. on September 6, 1901. The location was the Temple of Music at the Pan American Exposition in Buffalo, New York. The shots were fired at point blank range, the first one hit a button near the president's breastbone and did not penetrate the skin, the second shot entered between the naval and the left nipple, passed through the stomach, nicked the top of the left kidney, and lodged in the pancreas. McKinley died of the wounds on September 14, 1901 at 2:15 A.M. in Buffalo. Another good source of information on this incident is Margaret Leech's book, *In the Days of McKinley.*

68. Boatner, p. 218.

69. Pronouncers for the name "Darius" are available in numerous reference books. In addition, Civil War historians, Ed Bearss among them, pronounce the general's first name this way.

70. Lawrence L. Hewitt, *The Confederate General,* Vol. II, p. 60.

71. Neuffer, p. 47.

72. William Burton, *Melting Pot Soldiers*, pp. 166, 210.

73. Pronunciation guidance for the name Des Arc is available in a number of standard references, like *Webster's New Geographical Dictionary,* for example. However, I did verify with a genuine Razorback, Jerry Russell, President of the Civil War Round Table Associates in Little Rock.

74. Harry W. Pfanz, *Gettysburg, The Second Day*, p. 522.

75. Neuffer, p. 49.

76. Eric Campbell, *Baptism of Fire, The 9th Massachusetts at Gettysburg,* Gettysburg Magazine, July 1991, p. 47.

77. L. Van Loan Naisawald, *Grape and Canister,* p. 152.

78. These were non-regulation doeskin britches, which Dilger probably started wearing when he transferred to the Western Theater of the Civil War.

79. Stephen Z. Starr, *The Union Cavalry in the Civil War,* Volume I, p. 96.

80. The riot took place during a time when Know-nothing, anti-foreign sentiment was running high in the country. According to New York historian Gerald Wolfe, the immediate cause of the outbreak of mob violence was a bitter rivalry that had developed between English tragedian, William McCready and Edwin Forrest, America's best know actor. McCready was playing Macbeth at the Astor Place Opera House and as soon as the performance got underway a huge mob gathered outside the theater. Meanwhile, the audience inside began throwing rotten eggs and other assorted vegetables at the stage to express their disapproval of McCready and all Englishmen. Eventually, a riot ensued, the militia was called from the nearby Tomkins Street Armory, and the riot escalated. When it was all over, 31 people were dead and 150 wounded. Who says New York has only gotten violent in the last few years? This and other information is available in a delightful little book called, *New York, A Guide to the Metropolis* by Gerald R. Wolfe.

81. Burton, p. 170.

82. Ibid. p. 59.

83. Leech, p. 85.

84. My thanks to Mike Aikey of the Capital District Civil War Round Table in Albany, New York. Mike has done extensive research on Colonel D'Utassy and plans to have his work published at some date in the near future.

85. Pratt, p. 282.

86. Hunt and Brown, p. 637.

87. *Lippincott's,* p. 899. The entry I found in this venerable tome was for Karl August Egloffstein, 1771-1834, a German general who served in the French army. He was related to our man.

88. According to Marshall Krolick, Civil War writer and member of the Chicago Civil War Round Table, EE-lon is the definitive pronunciation. Marshall has done a lot of research on the cavalry at Gettysburg and conducts one of the best tours of the often overlooked East Cavalry Field.

89. *Nelson's Bible Dictionary,* p. 265. My thanks to Ruth Turney, a fellow round table member, for this valuable information.

90. *The Random House Dictionary,* p. 644.

91. Ibid., p. 660.
92. George W. Adams, *Caring for the Men, The Image of War,* Vol. IV, p. 238.
93. Warner, *Generals in Blue*, p. 153.
94. William C. Davis, *Jefferson Davis, The Man and His Hour,* p. 6.
95. After hearing a speech at the New England Civil War Conference given by William C. Davis recently I asked him if the FIE-nis pronunciation was correct; after all, he had used it himself. He told me he had always heard it pronounced that way and the best of his knowledge it was the way the name was traditionally pronounced by Jefferson Davis's family.
96. Allen Nevins, *Frémont, Pathmarker of the West,* pp. 1-10.
97. Bernard DeVoto, *The Year of Decision, 1846,* p. 38. For those of you who don't instantly recognize this elitist literary reference, Childe Harold's Pilgrimage is a long narrative poem by Lord Byron. Childe Harold is a disillusioned romantic whose life is totally devoted to the pursuit of pleasure (sounds like a modern day college student). Anyway, Harold decides to go on a pilgrimage throughout Europe. The poem is combination travelogue and one of those "Hey man, like I'm trying to find myself, in my own space, in my own time" type narratives.
98. Sears, p. 94.
99. William N. Still, *The New Ironclads, The Image of War,* Vol. II, p. 54.
100. Elsdon C. Smith, *New Dictionary of American Family Names,* p. 171.
101. Smith, p. 392.
102. George F. Jones, *German-American Names,* p. 213.
103. Charles M. Spearman, *The Battle of Stones River,* Blue & Gray Magazine, Feb. 1989. pp. 54-56.
104. Robert K. Krick, *Jackson vs. Garnett,* Blue & Gray Magazine, July 1986, pp. 30-32.
105. The details of just how Garnett's sword turned up appear in an excellent article in Gettysburg Magazine (published by Morningside Bookshop) Issue Number 5, July 1991. The article is titled, *The Death and Burials of General Richard Brooke Garnett* by Stephen Davis. Davis says that many years after the war former Confederate general George H. Steuart came across the sword and scabbard of General Garnett in a second-hand shop in Baltimore. The blade was inscribed "R. B. Garnett, U.S.A." and was a model 1840 Mounted Artillery officer's sword, probably given to Garnett when he graduated from West Point in 1841. Davis also gives the reader all the details and speculation surrounding the death of Richard Garnett.
106. I found that standard sources, like the *New Century Cyclopedia of Names,* were of little help on this one. Other notables named Garnett were listed with pronouncers, but, alas, no General Richard or Robert Garnett. I finally checked with historian Robert K. Krick, well versed on anything to do with the Army of Northern Virginia, and got a definitive answer.
107. This information was given to me by Louise Arnold-Friend of the U.S. Army Historical Institute at Carlisle Barracks. Louise is also a licensed battlefield guide and native of Gettysburg. She says the GET-is pronunciation of the founder's name is a long standing tradition in Gettysburg.
108. Nueffer, p. 71.
109. Boatner, p. 891.
110. John L. Thomas, *The Liberator, William Lloyd Garrison, A Biography,* pp. 236-237.

111. Neuffer, p. 75.

112. Frederick Stackpole, *Chancellorsville, Lee's Greatest Battle,* p. 64.

113. My thanks to Don Pfanz and Frank O'Neill of Fredericksburg and Spotsylvania National Battlefield for their help with this information.

114. Wayne Craven, *The Sculptures at Gettysburg,* p. 86.

115. Craven, p. 89.

116. Lee A. Wallace, Jr., *A Guide to Virginia Military Organizations 1861-1865,* p. 83.

117. Nathaniel Cheairs Hughes, Jr., *General William J. Hardee, Old Reliable,* pp. 4-5.

118. I checked with Al Gambone, who has recently written a soon to be published biography of Hartranft, and he confirmed my pronouncer. He also mentioned that some of old time residents of the Norristown area used the pronunciation "HART-ran-nift," some sort of throwback to Pennsylvania Dutch pronunciation.

119. Terry Jones and William C. Davis, ed., *The Confederate General Vol. III,* p. 355.

120. Faust, p. 355.

121. Ezra Warner, *Generals in Gray,* p. 378.

122. Hindman with a long 'i' in the first syllable is given a s a pronouncer in standard reference works like *Lippincott's Pronouncing Biographical Dictionary.* This same pronunciation is also used by several Civil War historians specializing in the Western Theater of the war like Dr. Richard McMurry.

123. Burton J. Hendrick, *Statesmen of the Lost Cause,* pp. 390-398.

124. Charles L. Dufour, *Nine Men in Gray,* p. 297.

125. W.A. Swanberg, *First Blood,* p. 328.

126. Sefakis, p. 319.

127. Hunt & Brown,, p. 295.

128. Sears, p. 123.

129. Sears, p. 123.

130. Edwin C. Bearss.

131. Jeffry D. Wert, *The Confederate General, Vol. III,* p. 141.

132. Many thanks to Jerry Russell, President of the Civil War Round Table Associates. Jerry knows Mr. Imboden of Kansas City.

133. Neuffer, p. 93.

134. Sears, p. 107.

135. Sifakis, p. 362.

136. Sears, p. 159.

137. *Lippincott's,* p. 1434; *Century,* p. 568, Boatner, p. 458; and others. In addition, the name is not unknown in New England in modern times and when it is said, it is pronounced "Keeze."

138. Warner, *Generals in Blue,* p. 272.

139. Edwin B. Coddington, *The Gettysburg Campaign, A Study in Command,* p. 163.

140. Many thanks to Louise Arnold-Friend, a licensed battlefield guide at Gettysburg and a researcher at the Carlisle Barracks, for giving me the proper pronunciation of General Knipe's name.

141. Allan Nevins, *Ordeal of the Union: Fruits of Manifest Destiny 1847-1852,* p. 548.

142. H. L. Mencken, *The American Language, Supplement II,* p. 425.

143. James S. Pula, *For Liberty and Justice, The Life and Times of Wladimir Kryzanowski,* pp. 6-21.

144. I talked with several people in the National Park Service about the Krzyznowski name and the dazzling variety of pronunciations I heard led me to question people in my local area who speak Polish. As a result of this inquiry and Iwo Cyprian Pogonowski's *Hippocrene Practical Dictionary of Polish-English, English-Polish* I was able to come up with what I considered the most understandable, reasonably authentic version of pronouncing the name. However, I still expect that I will hear from Polish-American Civil War buffs on this matter once they've read this book.

145. My thanks to Sophie Zembruski, who has hosted the Polish-American program on radio station WATR in Waterbury, Connecticut every Sunday morning for years beyond count. Sophie gave me the most sensible Americanized pronunciation of General Kryzanowski's name I have yet heard and I decided to use it.

146. This was told to me by Ted Alexander, Historian at the Antietam National Battlefield Park.

147. Warner, *Generals in Gray,* p. 204.

148. Jim Ogden, Historian Chickamauga-Chattanooga National Battlefield Park verified the town name, Maxine Turner of Georgia Tech., among others from the Peachtree State, provided verification on McLaws name.

149. Stephen B. Oates, *With Malice Toward None,* p. 112.

150. Marshall Krolick, Chicago Civil War Round Table.

151. Edmund Wilson, *Patriotic Gore,* p. 458.

152. Max J. Herzberg, *The Reader's Encyclopedia of American Literature,* p. 1139.

153. Emory M. Thomas, *Bold Dragoon, The Life of Jeb Stuart,* pp. 116-117.

154. Sears, p. 173.

155. William A. Frassanito, *Gettysburg, A Journey in Time,* p. 145.

156. Pfanz, p. 486.

157. Gregory A. Coco, *A Vast Sea of Misery,* p. 62.

158. Park Service people at Gettysburg verified "LIE-stur" as correct.

159. Among the historians I heard use "lee-uh-NIE-dis" were Dr. Richard McMurry, Dr. Richard Sommers and William C. Davis.

160. Terry L. Jones, *The Confederate General,* Vol. IV, p. 74.

161. Jones, p. 75.

162. Jones, p. 75.

163. *Lippincott's,* p. 1587; *Century,* p. 625.

164. Arthur Bergeron of the Louisiana State Park Department, a Civil War historian who has done considerable study on General Lovell, confirmed this pronunciation.

165. Thanks to the folks at the Luray Town Hall for saying the name over and over several times for me.

166. Boatner, p. 496.

167. Wiley wrote an article about pronunciation of Civil War names in the "Civil War Times" titled *Get it Right.*

168. *Lippincott's Gazetteer,* p. 1561; *Webster's Geographical,* p. 837.

169. William N. Still, *The New Ironclads, The Image of War,* Vol. II, p. 56.
170. Lawrence L. Hewitt, *The Confederate General,* Vol. IV, p. 151.
171. I talked with a number of historians and Park Service people who said they always pronounced it MAY-nee, but began to have doubts after I asked my question. Rather than spread paranoia I decided to go with MAY-nee. My thanks to Tammy Calvin, a park ranger at Stones River National Military Park, who was willing to state without hesitation or disclaimer that MAY-nee was the way it was pronounced in that part of Tennessee. Also, thanks to Mary Bray Wheeler, author-historian, who lives in that part of Tennessee as well.
172. Neuffer, p. 119.
173. Many thanks to Orvis Fitts of the Kansas City Civil War Round Table for giving me the local pronunciation of Marais des Cignes.
174. Proper pronunciation of Marye's Heights is yours for the asking from any Park Ranger or historian at Fredericksburg and Spotsylvania National Military Park.
175. Burton, p. 10.
176. Warner, *Generals in Blue,* p. 318.
177. Jean Arbeiter and Linda D. Cirino, *Permanent Addresses,* p. 240.
178. Swanberg, p. 2.
179. Nueffer, p. 126.
180. Coddington, p. 287.
181. Boatner, p. 685.
182. Faust, p. 535.
183. Phillip Rutherford, *Defying the State of Texas,* Civil War Times Illustrated, April 1979, pp. 16-19.
184. E. B. Long, *The Civil War Day by Day,* p. 164.
185. Nueffer, p. 130; *Webster's Geographic,* p. 880;
186. Faust, p. 264.
187. Faust, p. 545.
188. William Marvel, *Stampede At Olustee,* Blue & Gray Magazine, March 1986, p. 49.
189. William N. Still, *The New Ironclads, The Image of War,* Vol. II, p. 55.
190. Actually, one quick look at *Webster's New Geographical Dictionary.*
191. Faust, p. 581.
192. Neuffer, p. 140.
193. The Neuffers give the pronounce POKE-uh-TAL-li-goe, but after hearing it I decided on the pronounce I used at the top of the entry.
194. Faust, p. 590.
195. Boatner, p. 657.
196. *Webster's New Biographical dictionary* is the most readily available modern work with Polignac in it. Several older books like *Lippincott's* and the *Century Dictionary and Cyclopedia* also contain references.
197. Neuffer, p. 142.
198. John Hennessy, *Return to Bull Run,* pp. 430-434.
199. Douglas Southall Freeman, *Lee's Lieutenants, Vol. I.* p. 66.
200. Wallace, p. 324.
201. *Richmond Times dispatch, 1970,* a column by Charles Houston. Houston's column

discusses what he calls "that little ever recurring controversy about the origin and pronunciation of Powhite." In the column he quotes at length from a letter he has received from a Mrs. John T. Wightman from Ashland, an elderly widow. Mrs. Wightman writes to Houston that she is the great granddaughter of Dr. William Gaines who owned a plantation on Powhite Creek in Hanover County, the site of the Battle of Gaines' Mill, and the creek's name is not pronounced POE-white, but POW-HITE. Mrs. Wightman says the name is of Indian origin. to quote Mrs. Wightman, "it might be Po-white in Chesterfield, but in Hanover it is Pow-hite."

202. *Webster's New Geographical,* p. 977; *Lippincott's Gazetteer,* p. 1797; and others.

203. Neuffer, p. 143.

204. Pratt. pp. 340, 433.

205. Gary W. Gallagher, *Stephen Dodson Ramseur, Lee's Gallant General,* p. 5.

206. Historians Robert K. Krick, Dennis Frye and Ed Bearss.

207. *Webster's Geographical,* p. 1010.

208. Civil War historian and author Dr. Richard McMurry confirmed this pronunciation for me. McMurry is also a Georgian.

209. Alice Rains Trulock, *In the Hands of Providence, Joshua L. Chamberlain and the American Civil War,* pp. 198-199.

210. Thanks to Chris Caulkins and Jim Blankenship.

211. Michael D. Jones, *Chatham Roberdeau Wheat and His Louisiana Tiger,* Blue & Gray Magazine, Nov. 1985, pp. 24-25.

212. Charles L. Dufour, *The Gallant Life of Roberdeau Wheat,* p. 202.

213. Kelsie B. Harder, *The Illustrated Dictionary of Place Names,* p. 465.

214. *United States Dictionary of Places,* p. 288.

215. T. Harry Williams, *Lincoln and His Generals,* pp. 186-187.

216. Mencken, p. 412.

217. According to Rosecrans' biographer, William M. Lamers, the descendants of Harmon Henrick Rosenkrantz, who arrived in America in 1651, used twenty-three variations in spelling the family name over the years. General Rosecrans' grandfather changed the name to "Rosecrans" because he didn't want to be mistaken for a Hessian. A more complete discussion of the Rosecrans family name can be found in Lamers' book, *The Edge of Glory, A Biography of William S. Rosecrans.*

218. Time-Life, *The Civil War, Brother Against Brother, Vol. I,* p. 141.

219. W.A. Swanberg, *First Blood,* p. 16.

220. *Lippincott's Pronouncing Gazetteer* lists a small town in Indiana six miles west of Indianapolis using this pronunciation. Of course, this was back in 1882, but it does help illustrate that pronunciation of Sabine is, and has been, a problem.

221. *Century,* p. 889.

222. Burton, pp. 89-90.

223. Sifakis, p. 571.

224. Ibid., p. 571.

225. Bell I. Wiley, *Get It Right,* Civil War Times Illustrated, p. 30.

226. There are numerous accounts of General Schimmelfennig's Strange Predicament. Since I know the story (one version of it anyway) by heart I have not cited any source or

sources. You can still look down the alleyway next to 323 Baltimore Street in Gettysburg that Schimmelfennig took to get the Garlach pig sty.

227. Boatner, p. 648.

228. Faust, 190.

229. Harder, p. 498.

230. Pratt, p. 424.

231. Aside from having hard Moxley Sorrel's name pronounced numerous times over the years by various historians and NPS personnel, I also found that Mark Boatner gives a pronouncer for the name in his *Civil War Dictionary.* In addition, Bell Wiley, who edited the third edition of Sorrel's reminiscences, *Recollections of a Confederate Staff Officer,* indicates on the first page of editor's introduction that the name is "pronounced Sor-rel'.."

232 Henry Kyd Douglas, *I Rode With Stonewall,* p. 206.

233. Warner, *Generals in Blue,* p. 465.

234. *Lippincott's,* p. 2220. A pronounce, "soy," is also given in this entry. I chose to go with the pronunciation used in the Chicago area where General Smith found much of his postwar fame. Sources in Chicago included the Chicago Historical Society and the Newberry Library.

235. James M. McPherson, *Battle Cry of Freedom,* p. 108.

236. *Dictionary of American Biography*, p 406.

237. Ibid., p. 407.

238. In the midst of the usual hubbub which accompanies that event packed week at Gettysburg College every summer called "The Civil War Institute" I asked Gabor Borritt, the only Civil War historian I know who is Hungarian, what his thoughts were on the Stahel name. It was my understanding that he found the pronounce I have used acceptable. However, if Gabor wishes to dispute this I feel certain he will let me know at the next Institute.

239. Blake Magner, *How to Steal a General,* Civil War Times Illustrated, Nov-Dec. 1991, pp. 22, 73-75.

240. Historian Dennis Frye of the Harpers Ferry National Historic Park confirmed this pronunciation. Frye is recognized as an authority on the Civil War history of the Shenandoah Valley; he is also a lifelong resident.

241. Elsdon C. Smith, *American Surnames,* p. 128.

242. Mencken, pp. 454-455.

243. Any number of sources can be cited for the proper pronunciation of the Taney name; Park Service personnel at Gettysburg, Ed Bearss, etc. However, for those who require printed confirmation I will cite page 2280 of the 1915 edition of *Lippincott's Pronouncing Biographical Dictionary.* Contained therein is the pronouncer "taw'ne."

244. Stewart, p. 473.

245. Ibid., p.473.

246. *Webster's Biographical,* p. 989; *Lippincott's,* p. 2320.

247. My thanks to Don Pfanz of the Fredericksburg and Spotsylvania National Military Park.

248. Richard Nelson Current, *Those Terrible Carpetbaggers,* p. 47.

249. Ibid. p. 46.

250. Edmund Wilson, *Patriotic Gore,* pp. 533-536.
251. Current, pp. 401-402.
252. Maurice Duke and Daniel P. Jordan, *A Richmond Reader, 1733-1983,* p. 304.
253. Neuffer, p. 165.
254. Coco, p. 60.
255. Frank J. Merli, *Squadron of the South, The Image of War, Vol. V,* p. 102.
256. Krick, *Lee's Colonels,* p. 378.
257. Lee A. Wallace, *3rd Virginia Infantry,* pp. 14, 26, 27-31.
258. Mark Antony Lower, *A Dictionary of Surnames,* p. 362.
259. Pronunciation of Urquhart varies from place to place. Quite often it can be heard pronounced UK-hart, or UK-kart. I have gone with UHR-kut (used also by the Neuffers as a South Carolinian pronunciation) since it closely approximates the way I have heard the name said in Virginia.
260. Faust, p. 776.
261. Historian Ed Bearss confirmed my pronouncer on Valverde.
262. Davis, pp. 168-170.
263. According to William C. Davis, vuh-REE-nuh is the traditional, correct pronunciation of Varina Davis' name.
264. *Webster's Biographical,* p. 1018.
265. *New Century,* p. 4018.
266. *Twentieth Century Authors - First Supplement,* p. 1032.
267. Egbert Viele has one of the most spectacular and bizarre mausoleums in the West Point Post Cemetery. It is a pyramid inside of which are the sarcophaguses of Viele and his wife. Peering through the open grilled iron door you can see recumbent statues of the couple on their sarcophagus lids. On the frieze over the door of the mausoleum are words written in the Etruscan language. Viele's pyramid has got to be one of the real hot spots in the West Point area on Halloween night!
268. Neuffer, p. 171.
269. Burton, p. 171.
270. Boatner, p. 880.
271. H. Sinclair Mills, Jr., *The Vivandiére,* pp. 1, 8, 10, 14.
272. I had originally checked on the Vogdes name with historian Ed Bearss and was HAH-chis as a pronouncer. When I heard Louise Arnold-Friend's version of the name, VAH-jis, I decided to go with the local native's pronouncer. Ed Bearss' was very close, close enough to convince me that Louise was correct.
273. I confirmed the pronunciation of Wager with Judy Hallock, who is related to the late general. Hallock is the author of a biography of another Civil War who, like her ancestor, would never win a personality contest. I refer to the late, extremely unpleasant Braxton Bragg.
274. *Webster's American Military Biographies,* p. 468.
275. It occurs to me that the Stand WAYT-ee pronunciation sounds like it might have evolved from some stereotypical Hollywood Indian brave saying to young Degataga, "I go get help from rest of tribe, you stand waitie."
276. Boatner, p. 165.

277. Frederick Ray, *Artists of the Civil War,* Civil War Times Illustrated, April 1982, pp. 19-20.

278. *Andersonville Facts & Figures,* Editors, Blue & Gray Magazine, Dec.-Jan.'85-'86, pp. 9-10.

279. Historian Robert K. Krick said that WAH-furd was correct as far as he knew. The Neuffers agreed (more or less) in their book on South Carolinian pronunciations, using "WAW-fud" as their pronouncer.

280. Hattaway & Jones, p. 692.

BIBLIOGRAPHY

Many of the books and periodicals listed below were cited, and have been footnoted where applicable. Other books on this list were used for reference, background material, and verification of a lifetime's accumulation of facts floating around this Civil War buff's memory.

Books:

Appleton's Cyclopedia of American Biography, 7 vols. New York: 1887.

Appleton's: The New Century Cyclopedia of Names, 3 vols. New York: 1954.

Arbeiter, Jean and Linda D. Cirino. *Permanent Addresses, A Guide to Resting Places of Famous Americans.* New York: 1983.

Bearss, Edwin Cole. *Hardluck Ironclad, The Sinking and Salvage of the Cairo.* Baton Rouge: 1980.

Boatner, Mark M. *The Civil War Dictionary, Revised Edition.* New York: 1987.

Burton, William L. *Melting Pot Soldiers, The Union's Ethnic Regiments.* Ames: 1988.

Coco, Gregory A. *A Vast Sea of Misery.* Gettysburg: 1988.

Coddington, Edwin B. *The Gettysburg Campaign, A Study in Command.* New York: 1984.

Current, Richard Nelson. *Those Terrible Carpetbaggers, A Reinterpretation.* New York: 1988.

Davis, William C. and Julie Hoffman, editors. *The Confederate General,* 6 vols. Harrisburg: 1991.

Davis, William C. and Bell I. Wiley, editors. *The Image of War: 1861-1865*, 6 vols. New York: 1981.

Davis, William C. *Jefferson Davis, The Man and His Hour.* New York: 1991.

Davis, William C. *The Civil War, Brother Against Brother,* Vol 1. New York: 1983.

DeGregorio, William A. *The Complete Book of U. S. Presidents.* New York: 1984.

DeVoto, Bernard. *The Year of Decision 1846.* Boston: 1943.

Dictionary of American Biography, 20 vols. New York: 1930.

Douglas, Henry Kyd. *I Rode With Stonewall.* Chapel Hill: 1940.

Dunkling, Leslie. *The Guinness Book of Names, 5th Edition.* London: 1991.

Dufour, Charles L. *The Gallant Life of Roberdeau Wheat.* Baton Rouge: 1957.

Dufour, Charles L. *Nine Men in Gray.* Lincoln: 1993.

Dupuy, R. Ernest and Trevor N. Dupuy. *The Encyclopedia of Military History, Second Revised Edition.* New York: 1986.

Eggenberger, David. *An Encyclopedia of Battles.* New York: 1985.

Ehrlich, Eugene and Raymond Hand, Jr. *NBC Handbook of Pronunciation,* 4th Edition. New York: 1991.

Eisenhower, John S. D. *So Far From God, the U. S. War With Mexico 1846-1848.* New York: 1989.

Evans, Bergen. *Dictionary of Mythology.* New York: 1970.

Faust, Patricia L., ed. *Historical Times Illustrated Encyclopedia of the Civil War.* New York: 1986.
Flexner, Stuart Berg, ed. *The Random House Dictionary of the English Language, Second Edition, Unabridged.* New York: 1987.
Frassanito, William A. *Gettysburg, A Journey in Time.* New York: 1975.
Frassanito, William A. *Grant and Lee, The Virginia Campaigns 1864-1865.* New York: 1983.
Freeman, Douglas Southall. *Lee's Lieutenants,* 3 vols. New York: 1942-1944.
Furgurson, Ernest B. *Chancellorsville 1863, The Souls of the Brave.* New York: 1992.
Gallagher, Gary W. *Stephen Dodson Ramseur, Lee's Gallant General.* Chapel Hill: 1985.
Green, Bennett Wood. *Word Book of Virginia Folk Speech.* Richmond: 1899.
Hanks, Patrick and Flavia Hodges. *A Dictionary of Surnames.* New York: 1988.
Harder, Kelsie B. *The Illustrated Dictionary of Place Names in the U.S. and Canada.* New York: 1985.
Hattaway, Herman and Archer Jones. *How the North Won.* Urbanna: 1983.
Hendrick, Burton J. *Statesmen of the Lost Cause.* New York: 1939.
Hennessy, John J. *Return to Bull Run, The Campaign and Battle of Second Manassas.* New York: 1993.
Herzberg, Max J., ed. *The Reader's Encyclopedia of American Literature.* New York: 1962.
Hook, J. N. *The Book of Names.* New York: 1983.
Hughes, Jr., Nathaniel Cheairs Hughes. *General William J. Hardee: Old Reliable.* Wilmington: 1987.
Hunt, Roger D. and Jack R. Brown. *Brevet Brigadier Generals in Blue.* Gaithersburg, 1990.
Johnson, Robert Underwood and Clarence Clough Buel, editors. *Battles and Leaders of the Civil War,* 4 vols. New York: 1888.
Jones, George F. *German-American Names.* Baltimore: 1990.
Katzner, Kenneth. *The Languages of the World.* London: 1986.
Krick, Robert E. L. *40th Virginia Regiment.* Lynchburg: 1985.
Krick, Robert K. *Lee's Colonels,* 4th Edition, Revised. Dayton: 1992.
Krick, Robert K. *9th Virginia Infantry.* Lynchburg: 1982.
Lamers, William M. *The Edge of Glory, A Biography of William S. Rosecrans.* New York: 1961.
Leech, Margaret. *Reveille in Washington.* New York: 1941.
Lippincott's Pronouncing Gazetteer of the World. Philadelphia: 1882.
Long, E. B. *The Civil War Day by Day.* New York: 1971.
Lower, Mark Antony. *A Dictionary of Surnames.* Ware, Hertfordshire: 1988.
Mackey, Mary Stuart and Maryette Goodwin Mackey. *The Pronunciation of 10,000 Proper Names.* New York: 1922.
McFeely, William S. *Grant, A Biography.* New York: 1981.
McPherson, James M. *Battle Cry of Freedom.* New York: 1988.

Mencken, H. L. *The American Language, Supplement II.* New York: 1948.
Merriam-Webster. *Webster's New Biographical Dictionary.* Springfield: 1988.
Merriam-Webster. *Webster's New Geographical Dictionary.* Springfield: 1988.
Mills, H. Sinclair. *The Vivandiere, History, Tradition, Uniform and Service.* Collingswood, 1988.
Nelson's Bible Dictionary. Nashville: 1993.
Neuffer, Claude and Irene. *Correct Mispronunciations of Some South Carolina Names.* Columbia: 1983.
Nevins, Alan. *Frémont, Pathmarker of the West.* New York: 1939.
Nevins, Alan. *Ordeal of the Union: Fruits of Manifest Destiny 1847-1852.* New York: 1947.
Oates, Stephen B. *With Malice Toward None, The Life of Abraham Lincoln.* New York: 1977.
Pfanz, Harry W. *Gettysburg, The Second Day.* Chapel Hill: 1987.
Pogonowski, Iwo Cyprian. *Hippocrene Practical Dictionary, Polish-English, English-Polish.* New York: 1993.
Pratt, Fletcher. *The Navy, A History.* New York: 1941.
Pula, James S. *For Liberty and Justice, The Life and Times of Wladimir Kryzanowski.* Chicago: 1978.
Read, Allen Walker. *Funk & Wagnalls Standard Dictionary, International Edition.* New York: 1964.
Roach, Harry. *Gettysburg Hour by Hour.* Gettysburg: 1993.
Sears, Stephen. *To The Gates of Richmond, The Peninsula Campaign.* New York: 1992.
Sifakis, Stewart. *Who Was Who in the Civil War.* New York: 1988.
Smith, Benjamin E. *The Century Cyclopedia of Names.* New York: 1904.
Smith, Elsdon C. *American Surnames.* Philadelphia: 1969.
Smith, Elsdon C. *New Dictionary of American Family Names.* New York: 1956.
Sorrel, Gilbert Moxley and Bell I Wiley, ed. *Recollections of a Confederate Staff Officer.* Jackson: 1958.
Stackpole, Edward J. *Chancellorsville, Lee's Greatest Battle.* Harrisburg: 1958.
Starr, Stephen Z. *The Union Cavalry in the Civil War,* 3 vols. Baton Rouge: 1979.
Stewart, George. *American Place Names, A Concise and Selective Dictionary.* New York: 1970.
Swanberg, W. A. *First Blood, The Story of Fort Sumter.* New York: 1957.
Thomas, Emory M. *Bold Dragoon, The Life of Jeb Stuart.* New York: 1986.
Thomas, John L. *The Liberator, William Lloyd Garrison, A Biography.* Boston: 1963.
Thomas, Joseph. *Lippincott's Universal Pronouncing Dictionary of Biography and Mythology.* Philadelphia: 1915.
Trudeau, Noah Andre. *Bloody Roads South, The Wilderness to Cold Harbor.* New York: 1989.

Trulock, Alice Rains. *In The Hands of Providence, Joshua L. Chamberlain and the American Civil War.* Chapel Hill: 1992.
United States Dictionary of Places. New York: 1988.
Wallace, Lee A., Jr. *A Guide to Virginia Military Organizations 1861-1865.* Lynchburg, 1986.
Wallace, Lee A., Jr. *3rd Virginia Infantry.* Lynchburg: 1986.
Warner, Ezra J. *Generals in Blue, Lives of the Union Commanders.* Baton Rouge: 1964.
Warner, Ezra J. *Generals in Gray, Lives of the Confederate Commanders.* Baton Rouge: 1959.
Williams, T. Harry. *Lincoln and His Generals*. New York: 1952.
Wilson, Edmund. *Patriotic Gore, Studies in the Literature of the American Civil War.* Boston: 1984.
Wolfe, Gerald R. *New York, A Guide to the Metropolis.* New York: 1988.

Periodicals:
America's Civil War
Blue & Gray Magazine.
Civil War, The Magazine of the Civil War Society.
Civil War Times Illustrated.
Gettysburg Magazine.
The Kepi.
Military History.

Quigley's Quick Pronouncer

Abatis -(AH-buh-tee)
Adelbert -(uh-DEL-burt)
Albemarle -(AL-buh-MARL)
Alcibiades -(al-suh-BIE-ah-deez)
Alpheus -(al-FEE-iss)
Ammen -(AM-en)
Apalachicola-(AP-uh-LACH-uh-KOH-luh)
Aquia -(uh-KWI-uh)
Armistead -(ARM-sted)
Aroostook -(uh-ROOS-tuk)
Asboth -(AS-both)
Atchafalaya -(uh-CHAF-uh-LIE-uh)
Atzerodt -(ATZ-uh-rot *or* ADZ-uh-rot)
Auchmuty -(AWK-MYOOT-ee)
Averell -(AV-rul *or* AHV-rul)
Ayres -(airz)

Badeau -(buh-DOH)
bas-relief -(BAH-ri-LEEF)
Bearss -(bahrss)
Beaufort (N. C.) -(BOH-furt)
Beaufort (S. C.) -(BYOO-furt)
Berdan -(bur-DAN)
Biloxie -(buh-LUK-see)
Birdseye -(BERD-zee *or* BAIRD-zee)
Boatswain -(BOH-sun)
Beouf -(buf or boof ['oo' as in "book"])
Bonham -(BONE-um)
Bolivar -(BAHL-i-vur)
Boteler -(BOHT-lur *or* BOT-lur)
Botetourt -(BOT-uh-tot)
Boudinot -(BOO-duh-not)
Bowdoin -(BOHD-in)
Breathed -(BRETH-ud)
Brockenbrough -(BRO-ken-broh)
Buford -(BYOO-furd)
Bussey -(BUS-ee)

Cabell -(KAB-ul)
Cairo -(KAIR-roh)
Cannae -(KAN-ee)
Carondelet -(ka-RON-da-LET)
Catharpin -(kuh-*TH*ARP-un)
Catoctin -(ka-TOK-tin)
Chapultepec -(chuh-POOL-tuh-pek)
Chartres -(SHAHR-truh)
chasseur -(sha-SOOR)
chevauz de frise-(shuh-VOH-duh-FREEZ)
Chickahominy -(CHIK-uh-HOM-uh-nee)
Chickamauga -(CHIK-uh-MAW-guh)
Chimborazo -(CHIM-buh-RAH-zoh)
Cheves -(CHIV-is)
Chillicothe -(chil-uh-KAHTH-ee)
Churubusco -(choo-roo-BOOS-koh)
Clausewitz -(KLOW-zuh-vits)
Cleburne -(KLAY-burn)
Clough -(kluff)
Cluseret -(kloo-zuh-RAY)
Colquitt -(KOL-kwit)
Combahee -(KUM-BEE)
Congaree -(KON-guh-REE)
Cony -(KOH-nee)
Corps D'Afrique -(KOR-dah-FREEK)
Couch -(kowch)
coup de main -(KOO-duh-MAHN)
coup d'oeil -(KOO-DOY)
Crapo -(KRAY-poh)
Cruikshank -(KROOK-shank)
Cupola -(KYOO-puh-luh)
Czolgosz -(CHAWL-gawsh)

Daguerre -(dah-GAIR)
Dahlgren -(DAL-gren *or* DAHL-gren)
Darius -(duh-RIE-us)
Deas -(daze)

DeBow -(duh-BOH)
D'Epineuil -(DAY-pee-noy)
Des Arc -(DEZ-ARK)
DeSaussure -(DES-suh-soe)
DeTrobriand -(duh-TROH-bri-AHN)
deVecchi -(duh-VEK-kee)
Dilger -(DIL-gur)
Duffié -(DOO-fee-AY)
Dumfries -(DUM-freez)
Duryée -(dur-YAY)
D'Utassy -(doo-TASSY)

Eads -(eedz)
Edisto -(ED-is-TOE)
Egloffstein -(EG-lahf-shtien)
Ely -(EE-lee [place: EE-lie])
Elon -(EE-lon)
enfilade -(EN-fuh-LAYD)
Enroughty -(en-RUFF-tee *or* DAR-bee)
erysipelas -(ER-uh-SIP-uh-lus)
Esten -(ES-ten)
Ewell -(yool)
Evander -(i-VAN-dur)

Fascine -(fuh-SEEN)
Fauquier -(FAW-keer)
Fessenden -(FESS-en-den)
Finis -(FIE-nis)
Frémont -(fruh-MONT *or* FREE-mont)

Galena -(guh-LEE-nuh)
Galusha -(guh-LOO-sha)
Garesché -(GAR-uh-SHAY)
Garnett -(GAHR-nit)
Gettysburg -(GET-iss-burg)
Gist -(gist [with a hard 'g'])
Gouverneur -(GOO-vur-NOOR)
Govan -(GUV-en)
Grimké -(GRIM-kee)
guidon -(GUY-din)
Guinea -(GIN-ee)

Gutzon -(GUT-sun)

Hardee -(HAR-DEE)
Hagerstown -(HAY-gurz-town)
Hamtramck -(ham-TRAM-ik)
Hartranft -(HART-ranft)
Haverhill -(HAY-vrul)
Hébert -(ay-BAIR)
Henrico -(hen-RIE-koh)
Herr -(hur)
Heth -(heeth)
hors de combat -(or-duh-kohn-BAH)
Hotze -(HOT-suh *or* hots)
Hough -(huff)
Houghtaling -(hoh-TALING)
Hovey -(HUV-ee)
Huger -(YOO-JEE)

Imboden -(IM-boh-den)

Jäger -(YAY-gur)
Joinville -(*zh*wan-VEEL)
Jomini -(*ZH*JOE-mee-nee)

Kanawha -(kan-NOW-wha)
Kearny -(KAR-nee)
Keitt -(kit)
Keyes -(keez)
Knipe -(nipe)
Kossuth -(KAH-sooth)
Krzyzanowski-(kzhi-zha-NOV-ski *or* krez-uh-NOV-ski)
Kyd -(kid)

LaFayette -(luh-FAY-et)
Lamon -(luh-MON)
Lanier -(luh-NEER)
Latané -(LAT-un-AY)
Leister -(LIE-stur)
Leonidas -(lee-ON-i-dis *or* lee-uh-NIE-dis)
Liddell -(lid-DEL)

Liddell-Hart -(LID-ul - HART)
Loudoun -(LOW-din)
Lovell -(LUV-ul)
Luray -(loo-RAY)
lunette -(loo-NET)
Lysander -(lie-SAN-dur)

McIvor -(muh-KEE-vur)
Mackall -(MAKE-awl)
McPherson -(muk-FUR-sun)
Madrid -(MAD-rid)
Magrath -(muh-GRAW)
Mahan -(muh-HAHN)
Mahopac-(MAY-oh-pak *or* muh-HOH-pak)
Maney -(MAY-nee)
Manigault -(MAN-i-GOH)
Marais des Cygnes -(MAIR-duh-SEEN)
Marye's -(muh-REEZ)
Massanutten -(MAS-uh-NUT-en)
Massaponax -(MAS-uh-PON-uks)
Mattaponi -(MAT-uh-puh-NIE)
Maury -(MAW-ree)
Meagher -(mar *or* muh-HAR)
Meigs -(megz)
Metairie -(MET-uh-ree)
Monocacy -(muh-NOK-uh-see)
Moultrie -(MOOL-tree)
Mumma -(MOO-mah)
Mummasburg -(MUM-miz-burg)

Nahant -(nuh-HAHNT)
Natchitoches -(NAK-uh-TOSH)
Norfolk -(NOR-fuhk)
Nueces -(noo-AY-sis)

Occoquan -(OK-uh-KWAN)
Oconee -(oh-KONE-ee)
Olustee -(oh-LUS-tee)
Onondaga -(ON-un-DAH-guh)
Opequon -(oh-PEK-un)
Ossipee -(OS-uh-pee)
Ouachita -(WASH-i-TAW)
Ould -(old)

Pamunkey -(puh-MUNG-kee)
Pegram -(PEE-grum)
Pfanz -(FONTZ)
Philippi -(FIL-uh-pee)
Philippoteaux -(fil-luh-puh-TOE)
Pocotaligo -(POH-kuh-TAL-li-goh)
point d'appui -(pwan-da-PWEE)
Polignac -(poh-leen-YAK)
Porcher -(por-SHAY)
Portici -(por-TEE-see)
Powhatan -(POW-uh-TAN)
Powhite -(POW-HITE)
Pottawatamie -(POT-uh-WOT-uh-mee)
Prioleau -(PRAY-LOH)

Quinsigamond -(kwin-SIG-uh-mund)

Ramseur -(ram-SOOR)
Rapidan -(RAP-uh-DAN)
Rappahannock -(RAP-uh-HAN-uk)
Resaca -(ri-SOK-uh)
Rives -(reevz)
Roberdeau -(**RAH**-bur-DOH)
Rolla -(RAHL-uh)
Rosecrans -(ROHZ-kranz)
Rowanty -(roh-WAN-tee)
Ruffin -(RUF-un)

Sabine -(suh-BEEN)
Salm-Salm -(zahm-zahm)
Scharf -(skarf)
Schimmelfennig (SHIM-ul-fenig)
Schoepf -(shepf)
Shurz -(shurts or shoortz)
Scioto -(sie-OH-tuh)
Semmes -(semz)
Sorrel -(sor-RELL)

Sorrel [the horse] (SOR-ul)
sockdolager -(SOK-DOL-uh-jur)
Sooy -(SOO-ee)
Soulé -(SOO-LAY)
Stahel -(shtahl)
Staunton -(STAN-tun)
Stoughton -(STOH-tun)
Strasburg -(STAWS-burg)
Streight -(strate)

Taliaferro -(TAHL-i-vur)
Taney -(TAH-nee)
Teche -(tesh)
Tecumseh -(ti-KUM-suh)
Theophilus -(*th*ee-AH-fuh-lus)
Tilghman -(TIL-mun)
Totopotomoy -(tot-tuh-POT-uh-mee)
Tourgee -(toor-*ZH*AY)
Tredegar -(TRED-di-gar)
Trenholm -(TREN-um)
Trostle -(TROH-sul)

Unadilla -(yoo-nuh-DILLA)
Urquhart -(UHR-kut)
Utoy -(YOO-toy)

Vallandigham -(vuh-LAN-di-gum)
Valverde -(val-VURD-dee)
Van Vliet -(van-VLEET)
Van Wyck -(van-WIKE)
Varina -(vuh-REE-nuh)
Vasa -(VAH-sah)
Viele -(VEE-lay)
Villepigue -(VIL-i-PIG)
Vivandiére -(vee-vahn-DYAIR)
Vogdes -(VAH-JIS)
voligeur -(vol-ti-*ZH*ER)

Wager -(WAY-jur)
Watie -(WAYT-ee)
Watervliet -(WAW-tur-vleet)
Waud -(wode)
Winder -(WINE-dur)
Wirz -(wertz)
Wofford -(WAH-furd)

Ypres -(EE-pruh)

Zoan -(ZOH-an)
Zouave -(zwahv *or* zoh-AHV)

On Thursday, May 15, 1884, Major Stein, General Longstreet, and General Rosecrans pondered the Fredericksburg battlefield. Once again it was "Civil War Spoken Here."